When Free Exercise
and Nonestablishment
Conflict

KENT GREENAWALT

# When Free Exercise and Nonestablishment Conflict

Harvard University Press

Cambridge, Massachusetts, and London, England   2017

Second Printing

*Library of Congress Cataloging-in-Publication Data*

Names: Greenawalt, Kent, 1936– author.
Title: When free exercise and nonestablishment conflict / Kent Greenawalt.
Description: Cambridge, Massachusetts : Harvard University Press, 2017. |
  Includes bibliographical references and index.
Identifiers: LCCN 2016057559 | ISBN 9780674972209 (alk. paper)
Subjects: LCSH: Religion and state—United States. | Church and state—United
  States. | Freedom of religion—United States.
Classification: LCC KF4865 .G74 2017 | DDC 342.7308/52—dc23
LC record available at https://lccn.loc.gov/2016057559

*Dedicated to*
*Brin, Andrei, and Gibson Greenawalt,*
*a deeply loving family*

# Contents

When Free Exercise
and Nonestablishment
Conflict

# Introduction

## Basic Structure

One of the most significant provisions of our federal constitution is the beginning of the First Amendment: "Congress shall make no law respecting an establishment of religion, or prohibiting the free exercise thereof." Together these clauses preclude the government from imposing a particular religion on its citizens and protect their freedom to believe and engage in religious practices as they see fit. In these respects, the clauses together can be seen as promoting religious liberty and a separation of church and state.[1] At this core, the clauses clearly coalesce. But across a fairly wide range, one can also see their actual potential coverage, and their underlying values, as in tension.

This book seeks to explore those tensions, explaining what can be said on each side and what resolution may be wisest. Two clear illustrations of tension involve ceremonial prayers carried out by the government itself in public settings and special concessions made to religious practices that are at odds with ordinary legal duties. For those and many other matters a sharp division exists between people who strongly favor religious exercise and see the scope of nonestablishment as limited and those who tend to regard virtually any favoring of religious practice as a forbidden establishment, or as another form of unacceptable denial of equality, or both.

What the Supreme Court has developed as constitutional law in this

1

domain is much more complicated than either of these fairly simple alternatives.[2] One cause of this is that, as the Court itself has recognized, the two clauses "often exert conflicting pressures."[3] Regrettably, a good bit of the prevailing law is genuinely confusing, whether one looks at majority opinions in individual cases or tries to put together a combination of decisions. One basic reason why neither inquiry yields clear general principles is that when we think carefully, simple straightforward answers that should apply across the board are unavailable.

One value of nonestablishment is the notion that when the government gets involved with religious matters it not only favors some religions over others. Given that public officials are not especially sensitive about religious beliefs and practices, and may be largely guided by political objectives, their involvement may well actually interfere with healthy religious choices and practices. As initially understood, this concern about state "corruption" of religion was, as Andrew Koppelman has developed,[4] mainly about protecting the liberty of Protestant outlooks favoring individual faith, but has now expanded to cover freedom of choices concerning religion more generally. Just what one sees as the core concerns about not establishing religion can affect how one sees needed free exercise and vice-versa. In what follows, I assume both a broad sense of the free exercise of religion, which includes a choice not to engage in religion, and a fairly extensive range for nonestablishment. Readers who reject one or both of these premises may not see the "tensions" I identify in quite the same way.

When one reflects on actual and arguable tensions between free exercise and nonestablishment, it is important to recognize different kinds of contexts in which those can come into play. These include judicial evaluations of constitutional requirements, assessments by other officials of constitutional limits, and evaluations of what is just and wise.

The most obvious context for considering these tensions is when a court is deciding whether a government practice violates free exercise and the government's countervailing claim is that the practice is required to avoid forbidden establishment; or the court is determining if what may violate the Establishment Clause is actually required by free exercise. But the kinds of conflicting claims can often be less stark. Suppose a challenge is made to some religious practice within the government as an unacceptable establishment of religion. The answer may be that it is supported by free exercise values although not constitutionally required for that reason. One aspect of this book is to explore how the values may influence constitutional arguments even when they do not imply that the practice they support is constitutionally required.

Another important recognition is that court resolutions are not the only appropriate focus. There may be constitutional violations that courts will, for one reason or another, not address or not be able to discern. Legislators and executive officials should consider themselves subject to such constraints even if judicial invalidation of their choice is highly unlikely. Further, within the range of what is constitutionally permissible, these values can nevertheless come into play for what is a wise and just choice about what the law should be or how officials should behave. Finally, when it comes to private citizens, these competing values can bear on whether and why they should support possible political decisions.

The chapters that follow explore how the competing values may best be conceived in different contexts. It provides an account of present law, insofar as that is clear, and suggests what legal approaches would make the most sense. It also asks how far we should see the conflicting values in play for certain choices by citizens that are not directly controlled by constitutional restraints. The aim here is to explain things in a way that is easily accessible for nonlawyers and for lawyers whose basic work lies well outside this area.

Three cautions are worth adding at the outset. The first is that how these matters are best viewed can depend on the nature of particular cultures. As I mention briefly at certain points, some aspects of liberal democracy can have weight for all countries that fit within that category, but those aspects are not decisive about everything. Relevant among other things are the degree and virtuosity of religious beliefs and practices and a country's cultural traditions. Even in respect to a particular country, the best approaches can shift over time as the culture changes. Thus, although much of my analysis has broader relevance, what I recommend particularly is about our place and time, and may not be best either for all other liberal democracies or for a century from now in the United States.[5] What are now crucial features in the United States are that most of our citizens maintain religious beliefs, that these vary a great deal in content, and that a significant number of people are atheist or agnostic.

My second caution is that a person's overall outlook about human life in this universe is likely to have some effect on how she sees a balance of competing factors. Although particular considerations and arguments may be acknowledged to have force by both a fundamentalist Protestant who believes everything in the Bible is literally true and by an atheist who is convinced that all religion is foolish, such persons may well differ about the degree of force these considerations carry. My aim here is to provide an account that does not itself depend on religious convictions. But for what it is worth, I consider myself a liberal Protestant, with a less optimistic view of human nature than is sometimes connected to liberal Protestantism, and with degrees of uncertainty about many aspects of the place of our lives in a larger setting.

Finally, we must all be aware that the tensions that are the main focus of this book are not the only ones that exist in constitutional analysis and related value judgments. For example, hostile negative statements about racial minorities reveal a tension between freedom of speech and equal protection. More directly for the subjects of this book, free speech and equality concerns about race, gender, and same-sex marriage come into play regarding how claims of religious freedom should be assessed. I shall mention these at various points; my focus on free exercise and nonestablishment should not be taken to downplay the comparative relevance of these other related conflicts in values.

Beyond this introduction, the book contains five following parts. The first part focuses on religious practices in government domains, including public schools. Among the narrow practices addressed are these: legislative prayers; worship and the hiring of clerics in the military and for prisons; prayers and Bible readings in public schools; the relevance of how far "ceremonial deism" indicates that religious language on coins and in the Pledge of Allegiance does not really amount to a genuine assertion of religious truth; and the status of symbols in public places and in schools.

The book's second part addresses exemptions from legal duties and financial support for religious practices. The issue about exemptions has been, and continues to be, crucial in respect to the constitutional right of women to obtain abortions, and it is now highly controversial about how far individuals and organizations should be excused from legal duties to afford equal treatment to same-sex married couples. This question sharply raises the more general issue how far harm to others should bear on the constitutionality and wisdom of an exemption. A form of exemption that is not a subject of much public debate is the priest-penitent privilege. Is it appropriate to allow clerics not to testify about confessions made to them, and should their privilege be more absolute than that given to lawyers, doctors, and psychotherapists?

In respect to financial support, the Supreme Court doctrine has shifted over the last decades. It remains disputed both what that doctrine should be and what choices legislators should make.

One question raised by exemptions and some forms of financial aid is what actually counts as "religion," and whether it should be treated as special. These far from simple questions, addressed most fully in Chapter 8, can affect what is sensible line-drawing.

The third part addresses three special concerns about public schools. Even if they are not to engage in religious practices, how far, if at all, may they teach religion as true, teach about religion, or omit the place of religion when it is definitely relevant, as in most of history? These issues present sharp questions whether teaching moral norms or history without mentioning religion, or by failing to afford it a reasonable place, constitutes an unfair disadvantaging of the place of religion. A crucial consideration here is how far objective presentations are actually feasible and can be perceived as fair by parents.

The second concern is whether a nonreligious topic such as evolution may be omitted for religious reasons or at least supplemented by possible alternatives, such as "intelligent design," for what it may not be able to fully explain. The third problem involves what limits may, and should, exist in public schools on private communications by teachers and students about religious truth.

The fourth part explores more broadly a subject that arises across a wide range, including privileges not to comply with antidiscrimination laws. If some special treatment is to be given to religious practices or claims, should similar accordance be granted to analogous nonreligious ones? One may think similar treatment should always or sometimes be viewed as constitutionally required, although the Supreme Court has yet to say so, and two modern federal exemption laws, the Religious Freedom Restoration Act and the Religious Land Use and Institutionalized Persons Act, draw the line at religion. Whatever may be constitutionally required, is it wise for legislators to treat religious and nonreligious claims similarly? I urge that here we have no simple answer, that a great deal depends on which particular exemptions are being offered.

The final part reaches substantially beyond actual legal issues and focuses

on the appropriate place of religious convictions in the making and interpreting of law. The claim that "public reasons" should be central in liberal
democracies puts religion to one side in political life, but many believers
will think that their religious sense of what is morally right appropriately
influences their position about aid to the poor, protection of animals, and
exemptions for same-sex marriage, and perhaps even military engagement.
My broad claim is that "public reasons" do have an important and special
role, but that it is often hard for individuals to carve these out from their
more fundamental convictions, and that it is misguided to insist that they
should always strenuously attempt to do so.

In what follows in this Introduction, I shall provide a brief account concerning special features of the religion clauses and of the actual defensible
practices of constitutional interpretation. Those who are familiar with all this
can skip over these parts, but because these matters bear very importantly
on what we can expect, and hope for, from the Supreme Court, they warrant
clarification for readers who are unfamiliar with the relevant controversies.
In addition to describing various possibilities, I also provide a brief summary
of well-established positions, and what approaches seem to me seriously
misguided or wise.

## The Language of the Relevant Clauses and Their Significance

In this section, we shall delve into the language of the religious and other
crucial clauses, and their significance at the time of adoption. How much
all that matters for existing and appropriate constitutional interpretation of
modern coverage is postponed for the next part, but everyone agrees that an
original understanding is of potential relevance for how a constitutional provision should now be viewed and is an essential element for understanding
development over time.

We need to begin with the simple, but important, fact that when they
were originally adopted, the religion clauses, like most other provisions in
the Bill of Rights, applied only against the federal government. They did
not constrain what states, and localities within them, could do. In fact, the
states differed significantly in their treatments of religion, based partly on the
groups that had lived within their original settlements.

At the beginning of the colonies that became part of the United States,
both religious affiliations and attitudes toward religion varied greatly.[6] Many

of those who emigrated to America did so partly because they felt disadvantaged by the establishment of the Anglican Church in England. However, that did not necessarily mean that they rejected establishment. Whereas the Quakers in Pennsylvania were supportive of religious liberty, the conservative Protestant Christians in most of New England, although they did not allow the government to intervene with religious bodies, created a stricter form of limitations on religious practice than existed at the time in England itself. And in Virginia, which Anglicans controlled, the establishment was also stricter than in England. Maryland was a Roman Catholic colony, although one that was tolerant of other religions. Although practices and rules had altered in significant ways in the century and a half before the country's independence, six new states still had established religions in one form or another. It would be obviously misguided to assume that people generally thought that no religion should be favored by any government and that religious convictions should play no role in decisions about what the law should be.

It is true that the key framers of the Constitution, although describing themselves as religious, had liberal outlooks that basic decisions in political life should be made on grounds of independent reason, but, of course, their views would not, and should not, simply control what counts as the original understanding of the religion clauses. There are three points here, two that are obvious and one that is not. The first point is that the understandings of people subject to adopted legal rules count as well as those of the enactors. The second point is that constitutional amendments had to be approved within states. The understandings of those who ratified count as well as those of the body that proposed. Many of the necessary ratifiers were within states that retained established religions. The third possible consideration is that when the original Constitution was proposed by the constitutional convention, leaders, including James Madison, suggested that what *really* counted were the views of the ratifiers, not those of the proposers. This perspective, articulated partly to counter any political objections to the convention itself, may not have carried over to subsequent amendments proposed by Congress, but it certainly suggested that the views of ratifiers carried more than minimal significance.

Let us turn now to the language itself. Both clauses are cast in terms of Congress. One could see that as not restraining the executive branch. However, given both the early notion that Congress would dominate federal law and that the executive powers would be quite limited; and given also the great extension over time of executive power and the range of administrative regulation in law making, it would be extremely odd to say that executive officials may do things absolutely forbidden to Congress. Applications of constitutional constraints regarding religion and free speech cast in terms of Congress have been uncontroversially applied to executive action. I will simply assume in what follows that this is obviously right although it does stretch the wording itself.

That Congress shall make no law "prohibiting the free exercise" of religion could be seen as a very limited constraint. Suppose Congress passes a law that "interferes" with free exercise, but does not actually "prohibit" it. Is that permissible? Were the constitutional language applied in this way, that would make it crucial what counts as "prohibits" and "free exercise." If a law taxes a religious practice does that "prohibit" free exercise? If the law forbids a practice outside church that the religious body believes God requires, is that part of religious "exercise"? As the law has sensibly developed, the clause has been perceived as reaching significant interferences that arguably fall short of actual prohibition. What counts as religious exercise is a more troubling question, although not typically addressed in those terms. The last section of this chapter and later chapters address that issue.

Still more critical questions about language concern the Establishment Clause. Is it about avoiding establishment itself or only noninterference by the federal government? This question bears crucially for the later application of the clause to the states, which some have objected is totally misguided. In regard to the relation between the national government and states, noninterference was obviously the original sense, as indicated by "no law respecting an establishment of religion." The federal government could neither require states to establish religion nor forbid them from doing that, since either kind of law would be "respecting" establishment. But what of the District of Columbia, federal territories, and federal agencies? I believe the language did bar establishing religion in these settings (although some of what occurred in territories with large Native American populations has been argued to be at odds with that premise).[7] A religion could not be established for the District of Columbia or within an embassy abroad. Putting this together, the clause essentially was one of noninterference regarding states and one of direct limitation for territories and institutions of the national government.

This brings us to the Fourteenth Amendment and the application of the religion clauses to all governments within the United States. The Fourteenth

Amendment was adopted after the Civil War, and southern states were required to approve it if they wanted to be represented again in the central government. Clearly the main objective was to assure at least a degree of equality for African-Americans, a great proportion of whom had been slaves. According to its language, "No State shall make or enforce any law which shall abridge the privileges or immunities of citizens of the United States, nor shall any State deprive any person of life, liberty, or property without due process of law, nor deny to any person within its jurisdiction the equal protection of the laws." At the time of adoption, it was not generally conceived that the amendment made most of the Bill of Rights applicable to the states. Probably the most natural language that might implicitly be taken as doing that, at least for "citizens," is that guaranteeing "privileges and immunities," but in the late nineteenth century the Supreme Court interpreted that provision very narrowly. When it finally mandated the coverage of most of the Bill of Rights for states in the mid-twentieth century it relied on the Due Process Clause.

That "due process" would restrict the states regarding criminal and civil procedures, and would include such things as the privilege against self-incrimination and the bar on cruel and unusual punishment, was not a stretch, but the application to substantive rights such as free speech and the free exercise of religion is much less evident. Whether this coverage was warranted as subjects of "due process" is debatable, but I shall take it for granted, since it is solidly settled in existing law and almost no one now believes states should have much greater latitude than the federal government to impose on these basic privileges.[8]

There are two special problems, however, with respect to the Establishment Clause. The first I have already mentioned. If the clause was basically about noninterference, why should states now be restricted? The best answer to this is that by 1865 no state retained a formal establishment; since the clause did bar an actual establishment by the federal government, that could then be seen as a kind of basic value concerning individual freedom of conscience that should apply to states.[9] A second problem concerns the language of the Due Process Clause, which is cast in terms of not depriving "any person of life, liberty, or property without due process." Of course, an interference with someone's "free exercise" would be an interference with "liberty," but that is hard to say about forms of establishment of religion that do not really interfere with anyone's free exercise.

Nevertheless, the Supreme Court's application of both clauses makes practical sense, partly because discerning when an "establishment" does or does not interfere with free exercise, and therefore liberty, would be very difficult. Also, given that very few in present states wish actual establishments of the old sort, the inconvenience of trying to draw this distinction and allowing more flexibility within states is hardly warranted.

A somewhat more subtle question about the Supreme Court's ruling that the Fourteenth Amendment's "incorporates" the basic parts of the Bill of Rights as limitations on the states is how one should understand the actual coverage of those provisions. One *might* say that those who adopted that amendment took understanding at the time of the Bill of Rights to be controlling; but that is not supported by factual evidence and is extremely unlikely. The alternative is that their post-Civil War conceptions were influenced by what had happened since 1791. I will explore these alternatives as they bear on judicial interpretation in the next section. However, a conceivable approach that is not illogical is that coverage should be largely influenced by understandings at the time of adoption. This could lead to a conclusion that the restrictions on states about free speech, free exercise, and cruel and unusual punishment would be greater than those on the federal government, since the restrictions were seen as less when the Bill of Rights was adopted than in 1865. Clearly that resolution would not be practically desirable given the broad power of the federal government. Permitting it to impose punishments and limits on speech not allowed to states would be nearly illogical. If one asked what was wise in terms of latitude, it *might* be to allow states to impose limits not permitted nationally, since objecting citizens are able to move from one state to another, and different kinds of experimentation could be healthy. In any event, once it accepted "incorporation" through the Fourteenth Amendment, the Supreme Court has assumed that for basic rights the same restrictions apply to federal and state governments.

## Approaches to Constitutional Interpretation

In this part, I review very quickly many of the complexities and controversies about constitutional interpretation.[10] These definitely bear on what one thinks about appropriate constitutional resolutions when conflicting values are at stake. Readers who are familiar with this subject, and readers who care about the basic values in play here but not judicial decisions, can disregard this section.

The first point here is obvious, although frequently not mentioned in discussions of constitutional rights and duties. Both legislators and those in the executive arm of government can sometimes violate the Constitution without that being determinable by judges. That can happen in four different ways, sometimes interrelated. The simplest is that the relevant facts are not accessible to judges. That can happen, for example, with many "stops and frisks"; judges cannot really determine how suspicious someone's movements were. A similar inability may exist if individual legislators are constitutionally constrained not to promote a particular religion and violate that constraint in supporting a proposed statute that will help their faith; but all that judges have before them is an adopted law that does not obviously have that purpose. A second possibility is that actual constitutionality is debatable, and courts "defer" to legislators or to an agreement between legislators and the executive branch about what is permissible. Another form of avoidance, one that has not been explicitly used for church-state issues, is that some highly sensitive issues are treated as "political questions" for which judges will not explore whether the Constitution has been violated. A fourth basis for non-determination of substantive constitutional issues concerns standing. Judges resolve substantive claims only if someone has standing to bring a law suit. Given present doctrine, sketched in Chapter 3, no one may have standing to challenge various tax benefits accorded to religious schools or other institutions.[11] This creates the possibility that a legislative choice in this domain may be decisively unconstitutional but effectively beyond judicial resolution.

At various points in the book, I will note examples of possible constitutional violations that, for one reason or another, will be beyond judicial assessment.

Two key questions about constitutional interpretation are the comparative importance of text and intentions in relation to original meaning and how far original meaning should control present resolutions. For basic constitutional issues, the second concern has major importance, but I shall initially offer a few clarifications about the first. In recent years a number of Supreme Court justices, most notably Justice Scalia, have emphasized that what should count in statutory and constitutional interpretation is the relevant text, not what the legislative history reveals about intentions. One can defend this approach as a check on inappropriate exercises by legislators in making that history or abuses by judges who refer to that history in order to rely on their own discretion and arrive at outcomes they think best. But we need to recognize that any core division between textual understanding and intentions is misguided, even silly.

When one person receives instructions from another, he understands those instructions in light of what he takes as the intentions of the person who issues them. If a father tells his daughter, "Go to your room and don't come out for the next hour," she does not assume she should stay in the room if a fire breaks out. When legislation is involved, judges do consider what the objectives were. For example, with a rule that "defendants" could preclude testimony by witnesses when that was likely to be unfairly prejudicial, the Supreme Court, including Justice Scalia, limited application to criminal defendants,[12] since it did not make sense to afford civil defendants a privilege unavailable to civil plaintiffs. In brief, as a matter of principle, no sharp distinction can be drawn between how people understand a text and what they take as the intentions of those who have adopted it. Of course, when many people are needed to pass a law, one may doubt whether a common or dominant intent exists for some possible coverage. A key question here is whether a kind of delegation has made the intent of those most directly involved crucial. If one determines that no crucial intent is discernible, one may have to rely completely on the implications of the text.

When it comes to fundamental constitutional provisions like the religious clauses, it is especially hard to distinguish text from purpose. Because the language is general, it is usually hard to say what exactly are the borders of coverage, and we do not have committee reports that may explain the content of obscure language that is within statutes of excessive length. In the rest of this book, I shall say little about how disagreements about the proper roles of the text and intent should bear on original understanding.

What is very important is the place of original understanding as related to what is the present understanding and how these bear on what would be best conceived as coverage. Of course, on this issue people's present understanding of the constitutional text may vary from original intent and original understanding. And, in fact, present understanding of some key clauses has been largely influenced by well-settled Supreme Court doctrines. There are a number of very strong reasons why with general constitutional provisions like the religion clauses, original understanding should not completely control, and it has not. I shall briefly sketch the reasons here.

The American Constitution is very hard to amend; it carries great symbolic significance, and many aspects of the Bill of Rights are designed to protect those who may be in unpopular minorities. If judges stuck with original understanding not only about the general meaning of the language but also what the terms covered and did not cover, either extremely frequent amendments would be needed, or constitutional protections would become meager in light of modern values, or both. It is much more viable to accept some flexibility and evolution in interpretation as fundamental values develop over time.

It is worth mentioning here that one question raised by all this is "What was the key original understanding?" At the time of the original constitution and Bill of Rights, some flexibility in judicial interpretation was accepted and, in contrast to Article III's enumeration of the age at which a person can become president, the basic rights were cast generally. It is entirely plausible to believe that the dominant original understanding, at least among the minority who actually thought about this, was that the language was designed to allow development in specific applications over time.

I have already noted a particular problem about "original understanding" with the Bill of Rights. If judges really stuck faithfully to that, would not the coverage be different for states and the federal government, given that understandings after the Civil War did not replicate those of 1791? And since in respect to many matters, the coverage of core rights had expanded, the consequence would be fewer restraints on the national government than states, hardly a sensible variation in a federal society.

It is finally worth emphasizing that whatever is the rhetoric of "originalists," the reality is that in many, many areas coverage has changed from an original understanding. A few notable illustrations are these: No one assumed when the equal protection clause was adopted that women were entitled to the same legal rights as men, or that same-sex couples had a right to engage in sex, much less to get married. As far as free speech was concerned, in 1798, Congress adopted a "Sedition Act" that made it criminal to publish, among other things, "malicious" writings designed to bring Congress or the President into "disrepute" or to excite "the hatred of the good people" against them.[13] Never reviewed by the Supreme Court, the law was sustained by lower courts, including ones with Supreme Court justices sitting on circuits.[14] Much broader criticism of government is now protected, as are other forms of speech not originally seen as covered by the free speech clause. At the time of the Bill of Rights, many states imposed the death penalty for ordinary crimes, such as stealing, and some did so for sexual acts between those of the same gender. Across a wide range of topics, it would be both completely inconsistent with what has actually occurred and extremely unwise for judges to return to an original understanding of what was to be allowed and what was not.[15] Whatever may be true for desirable interpretation of recently enacted statutes, the need for development in regard to broad, open-ended constitutional provisions is great.

When we think of the religion clauses, if it was once assumed that communication of general Protestant messages was no problem, we now have a much broader spread of various religious denominations. That obviously makes a difference. A general assumption of the chapters that follow is that both in terms of constitutional determinations and broader assessments, our modern culture should figure in how tensions between the values of free exercise and nonestablishment should be resolved.

I should add two related cautions here. The first is that even if one believes shifts over time are appropriate for the coverage of most generally cast constitutional protections, that still leaves open the argument that the original conceptions better served the basic values involved than does our present legal doctrine. Steven D. Smith, for example, urges that the Supreme Court's extension of constitutional limits on what states can do about involvement in religious practices has actually reduced the degree of American religious freedom.[16] In this book, I do criticize some Supreme Court rulings, but I accept the more fundamental developments of the religious clauses that have occurred since the Bill of Rights and Fourteenth Amendment, without exploring in detail how far they have overall promoted basic values rather than impeded them.

### Key Terms

A final section in this introductory chapter briefly explores key terms that are central in this book. Those are "establishment," "free exercise," and "religion." One question about all these is how they should be understood by judges determining actual constitutional limits. Another is whether these terms should be conceived more broadly by legislators and others making decisions about what laws and practices would be acceptable. These questions are related to the issue whether assisting underlying values should count for constitutional analysis and other purposes even if no direct impairment of the particular provision is involved. An illustration of this last concern is this: suppose that whether or not the government engages in a practice, such as displaying a crèche in a Christmas decoration, will not impair the free exercise of religion. If the concern is that the display might constitute a form of wrongful establishment, should it matter that for many people this kind of recognition of the religion in which they deeply believe can mildly reinforce their exercise of religion?

What counts as an "establishment" is hardly simple. Assuming, as I have indicated, that the Establishment Clause is not only about federal noninterference with states but actually bars establishment, what constitutes that? We can fairly conclude that both when the Bill of Rights was adopted, in 1791, and in 1865, establishment was conceived as affording a special status to one kind of religion or another. Although some may have preferred a stricter approach, for most it did not bar all references to religious truths, such as the existence and support of God. When in the early 1800s public schools grew, those references typically reflected Protestant outlooks. Clearly with increased diversity in the country, explicitly favoring Protestantism is unacceptable now, but does it follow that since no reference will actually be endorsed by every single religion, none should be allowed? And if some very general nonrestrictive references are acceptable, how should legislators and executives draw lines between what to do and what not to do, and how should courts distinguish what is constitutionally permissible from what is precluded?

A particular question about nonestablishment concerns the status of promoting nonreligion. This question ties to what counts as "religion," a subject on which some Supreme Court opinions are highly confusing. Although the Establishment Clause, as it now applies, and did originally to the federal government, bars the establishment of an actual religion, it can properly be understood as barring a definite establishment about religious truth, whether that is positive or negative. The government could definitely not require people to swear, "There is no God or any appropriate religion." With this understanding, we do not need to conceive of atheism or simple agnosticism as themselves religions. As we shall see, some Supreme Court opinions that assume such approaches favoring nonreligion are foreclosed have been unclear about how to cast this. It is, of course, a genuine question whether groups, such as the Ethical Culture Society, without any typical religious views about the universe, are "religious" if their practices closely resemble those of traditional religions. The best answer here is "yes," though that can present a line-drawing problem.

When it comes to the "exercise" of religion, how far does that reach? Most narrowly, one can think of worship services and private prayers. Whatever one concludes about the status of laws that forbid particular behavior, most persons within the Jewish and Christian traditions, and presumably many others, do see their exercise as extending to moral behavior called for by their religion.[17] Aiding the poor, for example, whether called for by church doctrine or individual convictions about religious duty, would be regarded as an aspect of religious exercise. Given that the actual restrictions that had existed within England mainly concerned the core exercise of worship itself, it is possible that that may have been seen as the relevant "exercise" at the time of the Bill of Rights, but it should now be conceived more broadly. That does not tell us what secular reasons the government may need to forbid or require behavior outside worship; but it does mean that such restrictions cannot simply be regarded as having no impact on religious exercise, a reality now embraced by the federal Religious Freedom Restoration Act. That act, which is replicated within many states, is now a key to protecting religious exercise. It grants a right to engage in otherwise forbidden action if a law creates a "substantial burden" on one's religious exercise that is not required to serve a "compelling" government interest.

Another form of religious exercise is advocating one's religious outlooks in public. Not all religions call for this but many, with missionaries as a strong example, do. Given the basic protection of freedom of speech, such advocacy needs no extra protection from the religion clause, but it is genuinely a form of exercise. This can make a difference for a topic considered in the book's final part: the relation of religious outlooks to the acceptance and advocacy of political positions. By coincidence, I was writing the rough draft of this section on the Martin Luther King, Jr. holiday. Dr. King was an extremely important leader of the civil rights movement to promote equality for black Americans. His positions certainly had adequate support in purely secular values, but he did not detach those from his religious convictions, which he expressed openly. For him and for many others who are deciding what moral and political positions to endorse, and possibly to advocate, an aspect of their religious exercise is to further what they see as God's will.

A much more complex issue about "religious exercise" is how far it is appropriate for the government to in various ways assist those who would like to carry out their religious beliefs in certain ways or at least provide them with a kind of public recognition or support. Given that the Free Exercise Clause is cast in terms of not "prohibiting" the exercise of religion, one might reasonably conclude it bears only on unfavorable treatment, not forms of assistance. But matters are more complicated. The clause definitely reflects the perspective that free exercise is a value. If a claimed constitutional violation is about the Establishment Clause, it can be a counter that what has been done helps to promote free exercise, even if the alternative would not prohibit that. And this broader value can clearly come into play when legislators are making choices within the permissible constitutional range.

Later chapters will explore uncertainties about these key terms and their practical relevance in light of specific issues. We need both to avoid oversimplification and perceive how these complexities bear on wise legislative decisions and viable approaches to constitutional limits.

# PART ONE

# Government Use of Religious Practices, Communications, and Symbols

THE MOST STRAIGHTFORWARD TENSION between free exercise and nonestablishment values occurs when, in one form or another, a government at some level actually engages in a religious practice or conveys a religious message. Although the original sense of nonestablishment may have concerned only the government's favoring, or involving itself with, particular denominations,[1] according to the broader modern sense, official religious practices can easily be taken as a kind of "establishment" of religion. However, in at least many circumstances, these can also be seen as a religious exercise for those working for the government or more broadly. Among the relevant situations are prayers within legislative bodies, references to religious truths by officials making public addresses, messages on coins and within the Pledge of Allegiance, and displayed symbols. Public schools are a special kind of government institution within which many of these issues arise. Chapter 1 will focus on these various circumstances, present law and doctrine, and what may be desirable approaches.

Chapter 2 addresses the special situation of the place of religion within government institutions, namely the military and prisons, in which people do not have the liberty to simply engage in religious practices away from the government domain. Soldiers and prisoners are, of course, able to pray on their own and converse about religion, but they cannot simply choose when and where to go for worship services. These special circumstances raise the issue about the role of clergy within the government itself. For prisoners, a particular question about the place of religion is whether their involvement in that properly counts as relevant when discretionary decisions are made whether to grant them parole freedom.

# CHAPTER 1

## Government Engagement in Religious Practices and Messages

A N EXTREMELY STRICT VERSION OF nonestablishment might entail that the government itself and its officials should never convey a religious message—that our political and legal life should take place without reference to religion. On that understanding, President Obama definitely erred when he ended his widely observed 2016 State of the Union Address by saying "God bless you; God bless the United States of America."[1] No doubt, a proportion of our citizens now would prefer that the government, and officials in their official capacities, not involve themselves in such religious messages. On the other side are the following considerations. If officials have religious convictions they believe are relevant, should they not be able to express them? And if most members in a legislative body would like to participate in religious expression, should they not be free to do so? And should the government and its officials not be able to engage in practices and messages that will be embraced by most citizens, many of whom may feel some reassurance at the connection between their government and certain fundamental religious understandings?

Three different factors may bear on whether practices are, and should be, constitutionally acceptable and whether, if within that range, they should or should not be engaged in. As noted throughout this book, the tensions between free exercise and nonestablishment relate not only to desirable constitutional doctrine but also to wise choices within the range of what is permissible. One obvious factor is how specific is the religious conviction conveyed by a message. If the consistent message conveyed by a branch of government is that of a particular religious group, that is much more troubling than if the message is as broad as that of President Obama. For example, within Utah, where the Church of Latter Day Saints has always been very important, it would be seriously disturbing if higher acting officials offered prayers and other religious messages that were distinctly Mormon and at odds with every other religion. Somewhere in between repeated specificity and generality may be prayers for various legislative or other group sessions that are individually somewhat specific but vary in content on different occasions. One troubling aspect about generality is that no religious message is really going to satisfy all religious believers, since some religious persons do not believe in God and others may be offended by a message that is broad and vague.

The second important factor about conveyed messages is how genuinely religious they are, whether in their origin or how they are now conceived by most people. "In God We Trust" on coins provides an example of a formal religious message that most people now do not take as advancing a serious religious claim. "Under God" in the Pledge of Allegiance is more dubious, especially for school children. These are among various messages that are religious on the surface but have been claimed not to raise a serious establishment issue because they constitute "ceremonial deism." Part Three will explore that characterization in some detail. Whether or not one believes that various messages are not genuinely religious despite their language, plainly the intensity of religious assertions can vary hugely, and that may well matter.

The third relevant consideration is historical practice. This can figure in different ways. It obviously bears on what was the original understanding. If a kind of religious expression was uncontroversial at the time of the Bill of Rights and the Fourteenth Amendment, we can conclude that it was not then viewed as barred by the Constitution. Of course, as the Introduction explains, present doctrine should not be completely controlled by original understanding, and historical changes in our population can also make a large difference concerning religion. If general Protestant messages were once widely accepted because the vast majority of those within a state or the country were Protestant, the broadly increasing diversity of religious convictions plainly makes a difference to how inclusive a particular message is conceived to be.

Another historical aspect is that if a kind of message has been consistently accepted for centuries, it may now carry reduced religious significance for many people and may seem less offensive even for those who would prefer that it end. This point is closely related to the claim concerning ceremonial deism.

Related to the appropriate relevance of history is the reality that were the federal Supreme Court or the highest court in a state to declare that a practice long accepted as constitutional is no longer so, that would be much more likely to produce anger and resentment than if a novel religious practice were struck down. This problem may be lessened if legislators rather than judges decide to end a religious message, but abandoning a well-settled historical practice will still be harder than rejecting one that has been newly adopted or proposed.

## Religious Practices Carried Out by the Government

Perhaps the most straightforward way in which the government might be seen as itself promoting religion is by carrying out religious practices within its own facilities. We shall begin with two notable examples of these: prayers beginning legislative sessions, and prayers and Bible reading within public schools. This examination reveals the possible importance of original understanding and continuing historical practice; the relevance of very general versus specific religious premises and the problems of drawing that line; and the unworkability of any single Establishment Clause test of what is constitutional.

From the time of the founding, legislative sessions in Congress, as well as most state legislatures, have begun with prayers offered by clerics. Three days before it approved the Bill of Rights, Congress authorized the appointment of paid chaplains who would open each session with a prayer. The Introduction has explained that the Establishment Clause was perceived as reaching beyond a bar on federal interference with state decisions whether or not to have established religions; it also precluded Congress from establishing a religion within federal spheres. It follows that, whether they really thought carefully about this, members of Congress did not see chaplain-led opening prayers as a forbidden establishment. That practice has continued up to the present.

In 1989, the Supreme Court in *Marsh v. Chambers*[2] reviewed a challenge to such prayers within Nebraska, directed both at the basic practice of prayer and at the hiring of a Presbyterian minister who had served in the position for sixteen years when the suit was brought. To be clear, being paid less than $320 a month while the legislature was in session, the minister was not a full-time employee, but he was compensated for his participation. In response to a challenge by a member of the legislature, a federal district court had ruled that paying the chaplain did violate the Establishment Clause, and the court of appeals determined that the whole practice, which included publishing the prayers, was forbidden.[3] The appeals court rested upon what was then the standard Establishment Clause test developed in *Lemon v. Kurtzman*,[4] a case involving aid to parochial schools. Although, as we shall see with various examples, this test was never applied across the board, it declared that a government practice is invalid if its purpose or primary effect is to advance religion or if it fosters an excessive entanglement in some form. In this case, the court of appeals determined that what Nebraska had been doing violated all three prongs of the test.

The Supreme Court reversed, upholding the manner in which the state provided for its legislative prayers. Chief Justice Burger's majority opinion emphasized history. Without claiming that historical patterns "standing alone" can "justify contemporary violations of constitutional guarantees,"[5] it urged that the history showed that the draftsmen of the First Amendment perceived no real threat to establishment values from this practice of prayer.[6] Importantly, the delegates did not consider opening prayers as a proselytizing activity or as officially approving a particular religious view. Given the unbroken history since that time, invoking Divine guidance on law-making bodies is not an establishment, but "simply a tolerable acknowledgement of beliefs widely held among the people of this country."[7] The Court discerned no particular problem in the Nebraska minister being paid or in his Presbyterianism, so long as his prayers did not proselytize or advance a particular religion. That the prayers were within the Judeo-Christian tradition was not a problem given the country's traditions.

Justice Brennan, raised as a Roman Catholic, dissented, joined by Justice Marshall. Noting that the Court's majority had departed from settled Establishment Clause doctrine, he concluded that official invocation prayers should be regarded as unconstitutional. The purpose and primary effect are clearly religious.[8] Further, choosing a "suitable" chaplain and insuring that he offers suitable prayers involves excessive entanglement, as does the "divisive political potential."[9] More fundamentally, Justice Brennan contended that religion is to be left to private choices that do not involve the government.[10] He noted that no prayer is going to satisfy everyone. In a separate dissent, Justice Stevens urged that the religious beliefs of the paid chaplain are bound to reflect those of most legislators, and he quoted the clearly Christian content of one prayer of Nebraska's chaplain.[11] According to Justice Brennan, what the Court's decision really came down to is a conclusion about a "de minimis" violation.[12]

I am persuaded that some form of "de minimis" understanding is indeed the best evaluation of what was mainly going on in *Marsh v. Chambers*. Those legislative prayers do present a genuine tension between free exercise and nonestablishment. Many people believe prayers are appropriate before they engage in important endeavors, and perhaps legislators should have that opportunity. Further, if most people in the country are religious believers, they may feel a bit better if they understand that legislators begin with prayers, just as they may feel reassured if the President concludes a speech with "God bless you." But how far is "free exercise" actually impaired if legislative sessions do not begin with prayers? This is not really an exercise at all for ordinary citizens, and legislators themselves are obviously free to meet informally for group prayers before the formal session begins. However general the session prayers may be, they cannot encompass all religious perspectives and they are undoubtedly a governmental recognition of religious views. Further, since *Marsh v. Chambers*, serious religious conflicts have occurred over these prayers. These have been frequent and severe enough to generate many lower court cases and persuade Christopher Lund that this post-*Marsh* history should lead to the case being overruled.[13]

Putting all these facts together, the prayers definitely amount *more* to a form of establishment than to a noninterference with, or promotion of, free exercise. Nonetheless, given understanding at the time of the founding and consistent historical practice since then, *and* given the modest degree of "establishment" involved, treating prayers of invocation to be constitutionally acceptable still makes sense, even if it would be desirable for many legislatures to stop using them. This constitutional conclusion does, among other things, show how difficult it is to compose simple standards that will work well in all situations.

A more complicated and more troublesome prayer case, *Town of Greece v. Galloway*, was decided in 2014.[14] It reviewed a challenge to the saying of prayers by local clergy before monthly board meetings at which some ordinary citizens were present. These citizens were not just observing what their officials did, but typically participated with proposals and discussions. Since virtually all local clergy were Christians, for years their prayers had often been made in specifically Christian terms. Once this procedure had been challenged, the local board had reached out to others who might provide prayers. The two basic objections to the town's practice were that many of the prayers were distinctly Christian and that the ordinary citizens in attendance were under a kind of compulsion to be respectful, since they did not want to offend board members, especially if they were there to advocate one position or another. The town citizen who brought the complaint requested an injunction that would limit the town to "inclusive and ecumenical prayers" cast in terms only of a "generic God" that would not embrace any one faith.[15]

Justice Kennedy, who had been the key swing vote in many religion cases, wrote the majority opinion sustaining the town's practice. His opinion asserts that "*Marsh* stands for the proposition that it is not necessary to define the precise boundary of the Establishment Clause where history shows that the specific practice is permitted."[16] Remarking that the prayers of one of the Senate's first chaplains were often explicitly Christian, Kennedy urged that for legislators to require nonsectarian prayers would itself involve the government in religious matters to an unfortunate degree. It is sufficient if the town maintains a policy of nondiscrimination in choosing those who will pray and the prayers do not attempt to proselytize or advance one religion or disparage others. So long as all that attending citizens need do is to stand quietly, that does not count as unacceptable coercion.

Joined by three other liberal Justices, Justice Kagan dissented. While explicitly accepting the approach of *Marsh* for some legislative prayers, she urged that the sectarian content of prayers and the participation by ordinary citizens rendered the town's practice unconstitutional.[17] In contrast to federal and state legislative meetings, these town meetings "revolve around ordinary members of the community," who urge policies and request applications for such things as permits and licenses.[18] In Justice Kagan's view, the majority paid insufficient attention to "the multiplicity of America's religious commitments" and the need for "governing all as united."[19]

Both opinions in this case leave a substantial degree of uncertainty about what they would allow. The majority opinion does not tell us how far specific religious messages might be taken as a form of proselytizing or advancing one religion and whether yet more central citizen participation in a form of meeting would matter. The dissenters were not clear whether any citizen involvement would call for less prayer and how far *Marsh* entails that some sectarian messages are genuinely all right.

If we turn from constitutional borders that limit the range of legislative choice, what *should* legislators do? Clearly they should aim for nondiscrimination in who says prayers and encourage them not to focus on particular religions. They should also seek to assure that ordinary citizens are not pressured in one way or another.

## Public Schools

What follows focuses on public schools, how they differ from legislative sessions, and the special place of moments of silences within them.

For much of this country's history once public schools were created, prayers were said at the beginning of the day and Bible readings were common. Within most states, the Bible read was the King James Protestant version. Although hardly the only basis, the Protestant flavor of public schools, representing the great majority of the population in most areas, was one reason why the Roman Catholic church created many parochial schools and strongly encouraged church members to enroll their children in them.

After the Supreme Court had declared that the Fourteenth Amendment incorporated the religion clauses, it reviewed in *Engel v. Vitale*[20] a challenge to New York's system of school prayers. The Board of Education of New Hyde Park had specifically directed that the following prayer be said: "Almighty God, we acknowledge our dependence upon Thee, and we beg Thy blessings upon us, our parents, our teachers, and our country."[21] This was challenged by parents who asserted that the use of this prayer violated the religious convictions of themselves and their children. Writing for the majority, Justice Black, who was a leading figure in the development of Establishment Clause doctrine,[22] urged that the clause does not require a showing of compulsion and is violated by any laws that establish an official religion, however they are cast. Such laws do constitute a kind of "indirect coercive pressure" on members of religious minorities to conform to the official religion. Beyond this, uniting the government and religion can undermine government and degrade religion.[23] Referring to the Act of Uniformity in England under which people were required to attend the Church of England and were forbidden to conduct other religious gatherings, Black also suggested that government establishment of religion could easily lead to religious persecution.[24] Although the New York law was not a total establishment of one religion, and the prayer was brief and general, it was nonetheless a violation of our liberties for which, as James Madison had urged, we should take alarm.[25]

Only Justice Stewart dissented. He emphasized that the prayer allowed school children to satisfy their wish to say a prayer. He also objected to the basic idea of a "wall of separation" of church and state, which he saw as at odds with "countless practices of the institutions and officials of our government."[26] In a footnote, Stewart did not see how school prayers could be distinguished from other expressions of belief by officials.[27] This brings us back to what became an important a feature in *Greece v. Galloway*. Public schools are not about officials themselves, and the students are not merely observers. They are involved in a practice or are at least being encouraged to accept and favor it. Even if they have the right to leave the classroom while a prayer is being said, many students will hesitate to do so, in order to avoid embarrassment and possible negative reactions from their fellows.

One year later, again with Justice Stewart dissenting, the Court in *Abington School District v. Schempp*[28] treated the religious exercise of Bible reading as also impermissible. It did not matter here that individual students chose what to read from the Bible. Whether the government wrote or selected the text or left decisions to students was not crucial.

Another school prayer case arose three decades after *Engel v. Vitale*. In *Lee v. Weisman*,[29] the Court, 5–4, sustained a challenge to prayers said at junior and senior high school graduation ceremonies. In the specific instance, a rabbi had provided an invocation and benediction. School officials had given him a pamphlet entitled "Guidelines for Civil Occasions" that the National Conference of Christians and Jews had prepared; it recommended prayers composed with "inclusiveness and sensitivity."[30]

When reflecting on nonestablishment and free exercise values, we can see two important differences between the prayers here and those in New York that began the school day. The first is that sending a suggestion not drafted by the government itself to a cleric who was not in fact attached to the dominant religion seems much weaker government involvement than actually dictating what a prayer must be.

More important, I believe, is the nature of this ceremony. Many people feel that when a really crucial occasion for them is about to occur, a prayer that acknowledges God and seeks God's help is appropriate, and perhaps even needed. Although some parents and children may conceivably regard ordinary school days in that way, graduation is a much more critical moment in their lives. They may genuinely feel that if no acknowledgement is made of God, something important is missing. Of course, as with legislators, parents can arrange religious celebrations that precede graduations themselves, but, nonetheless, the free exercise consideration is much greater with graduations than with the beginning of school days. If the vast majority of students and their parents, who, in contrast to school day starts, will actually be present, really want the acknowledgement to God, is it too much to ask the small minority who have opposing sentiments to stand quietly for a few minutes as prayers occur? That can be seen as a form of pressure but it is only a very weak one.

The Court's majority held the practice unconstitutional, with Justice Kennedy writing the opinion. He emphasized the degree of pressure on students, who may feel that even standing or maintaining polite silence might be taken to signify adherence to a view.[31] Justice Souter, joined by two other Justices, wrote that even a nonpreferential approach that involves a religious practice is a form of establishment and that the very act of distinguishing a forbidden sectarian view from an accepted ecumenical one would be a task ill-suited for courts.[32]

Justice Scalia, joined by three other Justices, dissented, urging that the meaning of the Establishment Clause should be much more limited, determined by reference to historical practices and understandings.[33]

Given the Court's division on how cases like this should be decided, it seems likely that will continue when the Court takes on related cases, even given a change in the sitting Justices. The genuine competing values at stake on each side yield different defensible strategies of interpretation and application. I believe it would be helpful for Justices to acknowledge more explicitly the tension between values of free exercise and nonestablishment and how they apply in this context. Given the problem of developing workable principles of what is allowed and what is not with school prayers, I am inclined to agree with the majority about graduation prayers, but I see the case as a very close one because of the more serious concerns about religious exercise involved when major events take place in people's lives.

A final issue about practices within schools concerns moments of silence. Should the pausing for a moment of silence as the school day starts count as a forbidden establishment? Ironically, in the one Supreme Court case that dealt with this issue, *Wallace v. Jaffree* in 1985,[34] Alabama's moment of silence law was declared invalid, but the Justices made clear that most moments of silence were acceptable. The problem in Alabama was that the legislators had amended their law that authorized silence for meditation to include "voluntary prayer." The sponsor had said that the law's purpose was to encourage prayer. That was enough for six Justices to conclude that the law failed the *Lemon* test requirement of secular purpose.

Justice O'Connor, who at the time was the crucial voter on many religion cases, wrote in a concurrence that a law would be all right if it did not "favor the child who prays. [or] convey the message that children should use the moment of silence for prayer."[35] I perceive this formulation as doubly defective. The idea of favoring the child who prays is either misguided or confusing. If all students observe a moment of silence, no one can identify with confidence who is praying and who is not. Thus no practical favoring will take place of those who pray over those who do not. Perhaps all O'Connor meant was that the students who pray will feel they are doing what is being encouraged, but that is hardly a favoring in any ordinary sense.

The second defect is that the notion of a message that a child *should* pray fails to draw a crucial distinction. Suppose a teacher says, "We'll now have a moment of silence. This has been created to provide the opportunity for prayer, but those of you who are disinclined can use the moment to reflect in some other way." This is a kind of encouraging of prayer, but does not suggest a duty to do so. "Should" sometimes, though not always, suggests a kind of duty. If O'Connor meant that sense, she basically may have accepted an encouragement of praying that fell short of indicating a duty. If her notion of "should" was much broader, it may well reach typical moments of silence within schools. In some contexts moments of silence are clearly set aside so that most in attendance will have a chance to offer silent prayers. In other situations, the primary aim is to encourage reflection on events that have taken place or will take place. Often one can identify no clear distinction between these two, as when a moment of silence occurs at a meeting of a group that has lost a member in death. Although for schools this may have changed over time, and it may be different in districts with variant populations and teachers, I believe most school students will assume that a moment of silence is largely designed to encourage, but not require, individual prayer. If so, should that amount to a forbidden establishment?

Without finding the O'Connor formulation helpful, I believe not. This is a form of accommodation of free exercise that does not coerce anyone or require their witnessing religious practices to which they object. Although some religions, such as the Quakers, may favor silence more than others, no religion is being propped up and none is put down by a moment of silence. Clearly a moment of silence carries out nonpreference better than any form of oral prayer. For these reasons, moments of silence should be constitutionally accepted, so long as no one is told she must or absolutely should pray. Local teachers, school boards, and legislators can decide whether the values of a moment of silence are sufficient to warrant its use within public school classes.

## Official Messages with Some Element of Religious Content

Apart from actual forms of worship, what if the government formally, or individual officials, convey religious messages? When are such practices unconstitutional or unwise? I shall treat in turn Sunday closing laws, speeches by officials, celebration of traditional holidays, messages on physical objects or as parts of prescribed statements such as the Pledge of Allegiance, and a variety of involvements with religion. The next section addresses displays of symbols. Without exploring these various forms of message in great detail, I focus mainly on the troublesome notion of "ceremonial deism" and related concepts.

The idea of government declaring Sunday to be a day when businesses cannot be open or employees cannot be required to work has reasonably struck some as a favoring of those who worship on Sunday, and thus as a form of "establishment" of the Christian religion. At its basic core, this constitutional conclusion is usually unwarranted, although peripheral elements of some Sunday closing laws may be subject to this criticism. Since parents want to be with their children on days off, and couples, both of whom are working, will want to be together, having one day in a week during which schools will not be operating and most people will not have to work makes sense. Since the seven-day week is firmly established in our culture, and historically most people in the country have wanted freedom on Sunday to worship, a practice still true for a substantial proportion of the population, that was the obvious day to pick. One could see doing so as a weak form of establishment that promotes free exercise, but even if one focuses on purely secular reasons unrelated to religion, the designation was called for, at least under certain conditions. Of course, if very few owners of businesses would decide to have them operating on Sundays, workers who want that day off could simply choose to be employed by a business closed on Sunday. No law would be needed to protect them. Matters are different, however, if a great many businesses would, if allowed, be open on Sunday, and a significant percentage of employees would want not to work on that day.

Although the closing of businesses could be seen as partly responsive to notions that Sunday, for religious reasons, should be a day of peace, it can also make sense to provide a day when ordinary people are assured they do not have to work. In 1961, the Supreme Court sustained the application of such a law even as applied to an Orthodox Jewish owner of a retail clothing store who claimed a right to be open on Sunday because his religion required that he close on Saturday.[36] In recent years, Sunday closing laws have largely disappeared or been sharply reduced in their coverage. This may well indicate that their underlying bases were largely religious, but it does not follow that they lacked a secular purpose and effect.

Certain narrower closing requirements are harder to defend on such grounds. In some localities, liquor stores cannot open until Sunday afternoon. Given that they can open earlier on every other day, it is difficult to see this limit as other than a message that people should not be drinking seriously before and during the time of worship. One might suggest in response that this allows those who work at the stores to go to worship services, but in that respect it is hard to conceive why those selling liquor should be distinguished from all sorts of other stores, which are allowed to open Sunday morning.

Treating Thanksgiving and Christmas as holidays is not so different from the special status of Sunday. Both these holidays historically have religious significance, and Christmas, along with Good Friday and Easter, is, of course, one of the three most important days within the Christian religion. But Thanksgiving and Christmas are well settled within our culture and people broadly want to celebrate them in one way or another. To declare them as holidays is both consistent with historical practice and helps people who wish to engage in some form of religious exercise. Even if Thanksgiving's recognition of the place of God and the grounding of Christmas in Christian beliefs can be seen as a weak kind of implicit "establishment," their status as holidays is clearly acceptable.

Perhaps the most straightforward form of a religious message is when the President or another official speaks in those terms. President Obama's closing "God bless you" is a simple version of such communication. Can conveying such messages actually be unconstitutional; if not, can doing so at least be unwise? Apart from the status of the communications themselves, can they affect the validity of laws in some way?

I shall start with the last question, for which the answer is clearly "yes." Whether contained in a committee report or uttered by an individual sponsor, a clear message that a proposed law should be adopted to promote a religious objective can matter for its constitutionality. Of course, it is now controversial how much stated intentions should count in comparison with the text of the law, but as the Introduction explains, clearly stated intentions do matter for how a law is perceived. If enough legislators make explicit that a law is designed to further a specific religious objective, those aware of this will understand the law in that way. In the prior section, we reviewed *Wallace v. Jaffree*,[37] a case in which this aim did matter. The Court's majority, although willing to accept most "moments of silence" in public schools, struck down the Alabama law that was amended to include voluntary prayer. It relied partly on the sponsor's statement that the purpose was to encourage prayer.

Putting aside the possible effect on the validity of a law or regulation, could a speech or committee report itself be unconstitutional? Given the basic idea of freedom of speech, which applies to government officials as well as citizens,[38] it is hard to conceive, at least at this stage of history, that a court would say that an ordinary official has actually violated the Constitution by simply conveying a message that reflects his own religious views,[39] even one that indicates a negative view about some other religion. As noted in the Introduction, we can conceive of behavior that might well be seen as unconstitutional even if not directly ruled that way by a court. One could believe that certain speech by officials really does exceed constitutional limits, especially if it threatens negative treatment of those who do not subscribe to the speaker's view. But the serious issue here is primarily what is a wise accommodation of values by officials. In our culture, plainly an official endorsement of a particular religious view is undesirable.[40] More general references to God, on the other hand, although they do not capture the views of all citizens, may help to reassure the great majority who do believe, or hope, that God exists. I do not think we should conclude that such expressions, when made by officials in that capacity, are always misguided.

This brings us to the harder questions about formal religious messages on objects or within statements for which the government is responsible. Our coins and our paper currency both say "IN GOD WE TRUST." This wording is easy to read on the paper bills but is very small on the coins. Most people do not pay attention to these messages; indeed, probably a fair proportion of the population is actually unaware of them. Given their long historical existence, we can reasonably understand them as not now being serious religious communications despite what they actually say.

Is this also true about "under God" in the Pledge of Allegiance, which is the statement people, including children, are called upon to say to express their loyalty to our country? Congress enacted this basic pledge in 1942: "I pledge allegiance to the Flag of the United States of America, and to the Republic for which it stands, one Nation, indivisible, with liberty and justice for all." In 1954, Congress amended the pledge to include "under God" after "Nation"; the sponsor of the addition indicated that the aim was to contrast this country's belief in God with the atheism of the Soviet Union, with whom we were in a "cold war."[41] Among the circumstances in which people say this pledge is when noncitizens become naturalized.[42]

In 2004 the Supreme Court in *Elk Grove Unified School Dist. v. Newdow*[43] had granted certiorari for a decision by the Ninth Circuit that a school district requirement that elementary school children recite this pledge every day was unconstitutional under the *Lemon* test because it endorsed a religious view. The Court never decided the case, ruling that the complaining biological father, who did not have custodial responsibility for his daughter, lacked standing. Three justices, however, did reach the merits, and all would have allowed the pledge. Justice Thomas made clear his narrow sense of the Establishment Clause constraints, expressing doubts about the Court's invalidation of classroom prayers and Bible reading in public schools.[44]

Chief Justice Rehnquist and Justice O'Connor adopted a more nuanced approach, with Justice O'Connor developing the concept of "ceremonial deism." Rehnquist's opinion characterized "under God" as a "descriptive phrase" that allowed public recognition of our country's religious history and character.[45] Justice O'Connor developed a fuller explanation of how "under God" does not really assert a religious proposition. She noted that the Pledge is not a prayer. That, in itself, does not take us very far, given that the Apostle's Creed said in some church services is not a prayer and that a public pledge could include very specific religious details such as "under God the Father and our savior Jesus Christ, upon whom our salvation rests." Like the Chief Justice, Justice O'Connor called "under God" descriptive. However, asserting that God exists and that we as a nation are subject to God's providence and authority are certainly propositions of the kind ruled out by an unqualified bar on government endorsement of religion.

Justice O'Connor's central argument was that saying "under God" in the pledge was an act of ceremonial deism, not religious affirmation. Denying that any "de minimis" violations of the Constitution are acceptable, she urged that "under God" only commemorates the role of religion in our history and solemnizes occasions rather than invoking divine provenance.[46] She relied partly on the facts that "under God" is inclusive, not favoring any belief system, and that it has minimal religious content.

Although this assertion has not disappeared—being accepted, for example, by courts allowing "In God We Trust" to be placed on government buildings all over North Carolina[47]—Justice O'Connor's contention that "under God" does not endorse a particular religious view is actually unpersuasive. As with coins, it may be that many people who actually say the Pledge of Allegiance, do not really pay attention to these two words or feel that they are genuinely asserting a religious truth with which they agree or disagree. Nonetheless, this is not just a handling of coins; people are actually asserting a religious proposition.[48] My intuition that this may disturb some nonbelievers was confirmed by an atheist law student who described how he felt uncomfortable and as an outsider when the Pledge was said at his school.

Both Justices Rehnquist and O'Connor should have carefully considered that the actual case involved elementary school children. Whatever may be true for adults in typical settings, we cannot expect second and third graders to say to themselves, "Yes 'under God' seems to assert that God exists and is important for our country, but this is really only about our historical tradition." Especially in elementary schools, "under God" does definitely entail a religious assertion.

A more realistic approach would acknowledge this and directly face the following question: Given the generality of the phrase, the reality that most people in the country have a belief in God and may feel that including that in a pledge is actually beneficial, should this kind of indirect religious exercise be accepted? Of course, no one should have to utter the Pledge or that particular phrase within it if she objects. This does not itself eliminate the problem for students who may wish to avoid being seen as nonconformists, but it does reduce concerns about unfairness to those whose views are different. Plainly, nonestablishment values do lie in place here against pressure that students say this Pledge, and an honest, careful resolution cannot rely on the idea that this is *just* ceremonial deism.[49] One can plausibly believe that the breadth and inclusiveness of the phrase *and* its historical connection do matter, and further that the Pledge can represent an acceptance of a kind of religious exercise, but on these bases its constitutional legitimacy should depend on a balance of considerations.

It may be helpful here to be a bit more explicit about how I see "In God We Trust" as a national motto on coins and "under God" in the Pledge of Allegiance. Both do involve religious assertions on their surface and both are backed by historical traditions. An extreme version of nonestablishment would simply forbid them both. But certain differences are crucial. When you say a pledge you are much more likely to be genuinely aware of the message you utter verbally, and, at least on the surface, you are committing yourself to what you say. And you are less likely to think, "This is just historical." This becomes much more of a potential threat to beliefs that do not conform than is using currency, and it amounts to a more essential establishment. That concern is especially true for small children who are in circumstances in which they are very unlikely to say, "Oh, this is only ceremonial deism," and they are under genuine pressure to utter the Pledge. Although one could see similar competing values in play for mottos and pledges, the nonestablishment concerns are much greater for the latter, especially in school settings.

One might see these reasons as strong enough to warrant a judicial declaration that the Pledge should not be said in ordinary public school classes, but we can still perceive that the degree of establishment is minor. For the Supreme Court to declare the Pledge unconstitutional would cause significant outrage. Justices do, and properly should, give some weight to how socially disruptive particular decisions are likely to be. They may be wise to leave this issue to decisions made by legislators and state courts.

The government and its officials can involve themselves in subjects concerning religion in ways that do not fit within the previous categories. Some of them concern international relations. In general, these matters are beyond judicial resolution and should not be seen as official violations of basic constitutional standards, but the values of free exercise and nonestablishment are often genuinely in play to some degree.

A straightforward connection between the government and religions was adoption of the International Religious Freedom Act aimed at protecting religious freedom in countries around the world. Some in this country and abroad have objected that this law gives religious liberty a priority over other basic rights generally protected under international treaties and common law.[50] Whether treating religion as special is warranted here really comes down to a matter of judgment. One may believe that deprivations of religious liberty in some parts of the world are especially grave, that these lead to deaths and severe conflicts. Further, one may think that our country's tradition of religious liberty, and essentially equal treatment, warrants concentration on that. Of course, many countries have sharp restrictions on freedom of speech and other basic rights, and one might conclude that all these should be referred to equally. The basic values of free exercise and nonestablishment cannot themselves tell us what legislation should be adopted.

A different kind of connection is involvement of the government and the officials with religious leaders. Since 1959 most presidents have met with the Pope,[51] and in 2015 Pope Francis addressed a joint session of Congress.[52] One might see both of these as a kind of favoring of Catholicism and encouraging Catholic citizens to vote for those who carry out these connections. On the other hand, the Pope is indisputably an internationally important figure with an influence on many people who takes crucial positions on many public issues. These are sufficient reasons both for meetings and for having him address Congress.

A rather different form of involvement is when leading officials, mainly Presidents, meet informally with domestic religious leaders.[53] Most notably, a large number of Presidents met with Billy Graham, a famous Protestant evangelical leader. One might be concerned that such meetings will push official actions too far in the direction of the religious leader's views. But Presidents, like the rest of us, definitely have the right to meet with religious leaders, and whether or not their religious views coincide, the leaders may have insights that could help Presidents and other officials. Again, all this comes down to whether a political official is wisely taking into account a diversity of viewpoints or giving undue weight to one particular religious outlook.

A much more peripheral involvement is Presidents visiting religious sites abroad. Given that many of these sites have played an important role in human history, visiting them is fully appropriate.

### Displays of Religious Symbols

Finally, I turn to displays of religious symbols or messages on government property, including public schools. The Supreme Court did not decide any cases involving these before 1980, presumably because for most of our history these displays were widely accepted. From that time up to 2005 the Court resolved six cases involving challenges, often with the Justices sharply divided about results and about appropriate approaches. Clearly at stake here is some value of nonestablishment if the symbols, as they inevitably do, convey some message regarding religion and do not include every actual religion. The displays themselves do not typically involve the actual exercise of religion by citizens, but one could see them as giving many people some assurance about the importance and place of their religion in this country's history and present composition.[54] Against the establishment concern is the argument that what is involved here is too remote to constitute a genuine establishment. With these observations, we can conclude that according to an original understanding and for most of our history these displays would neither have been conceived as violating nonestablishment nor as genuinely needed for free exercise. As religious diversity has increased and concepts of establishment have expanded, should it matter now for possible coverage that some indirect values of free exercise may also be involved?

The Supreme Court cases on this subject have involved the Ten Commandments, Christmas displays, and the display of a Chanukah menorah, and the setting by private citizens of a cross on government property. In these cases Justice O'Connor developed her "endorsement" test, which proved to be very influential during her time on the Court, since she was then the Justice in the center on many religious issues. Among other things, we will explore just how workable this approach can be and how it may best be understood.

In *State v. Graham*,[55] the 1980 case, the Court reviewed a Kentucky statute that required that all public school classrooms post the Ten Commandments. Although each copy included a comment about the secular adoption of the commandments as the fundamental basis for law in Western civilization, the Court ruled that this was a sacred text and that the law's purpose was "plainly religious."[56] This was obviously correct. Although the Ten Commandments may have had some influence on moral attitudes and affected some legal norms, the first five Commandments concern relations to God that are not a direct concern for modern law, and the other five articulate precepts against such things as killing, stealing, and lying that will be of concern for any legal system, whatever its citizens' religious views.

In 2005, in *McCreary County, Ky. v. American Civil Liberties Union of Kentucky*[57] the Supreme Court considered the posting of the King James version of the Ten Commandments on courthouse walls. By the time the case got to the Supreme Court these displays had been supplemented as a response to earlier legal challenges. The counties involved first responded by including other texts with religious references. When a second injunction was issued, copies of other historical documents were also added, along with an explanation that the Commandments provided the moral background for our Declaration of Independence and legal tradition. At the time of this case, the Supreme Court was also considering the status of a Ten Commandments monument on the grounds of the Texas State Capitol.[58] There were sixteen other monuments on these grounds dealing with assorted subjects, such as volunteer firemen and Confederate soldiers; there were also twenty-one historical markers. A private Fraternal Order of the Eagles had contributed the Ten Commandments monument four decades prior to its being challenged.

The Supreme Court divided 5–4 in both these cases. Eight Justices voted the same way in the two cases; only Justice Breyer did not, so his vote determined the outcomes. In the Kentucky case the majority regarded the courthouse displays as having the predominant purpose of advancing religion. Given the history of why the displays were expanded, the counties had not purged the overarching religious significance of their action. Justice O'Connor joined the majority opinion but also relied in a concurrence on the message of "endorsement," a criterion on which we shall focus shortly. For the four dissenters, Justice Scalia found an adequate secular purpose in the displays, and more sweepingly rejected the basic notion that the government needs to be neutral about religion.[59] In light of the development of these displays over time, it is hard to defend what was involved here as different from the school house displays, unless one simply relies on the fact that within schools, the government is imposing views to a much greater degree than is true in other public facilities.

As noted, eight Justices took similar views about the Texas monument. Chief Justice Rehnquist for the plurality acknowledged the monument's degree of religious significance but regarded its placing as relatively passive and emphasized the role of the Commandments in American heritage.[60]

Justice Scalia wrote that a state's favoring of religion was fine.[61] The four dissenters regarded the basic message as religious and considered irrelevant the fact that sixteen other monuments had different themes.[62] Justice Breyer, the swing vote, acknowledged the religious message of the monument,[63] but also did not doubt that it conveyed a moral and historical message. Its physical setting on the ground among the surrounding monuments did not suggest it was sacred; and its forty years without controversy indicated that people did not regard it as a detrimental favoring of one system of beliefs.[64] Opposed to a "brooding and pervasive development to the secular and a passive, or even active, hostility to the religious," Breyer expressed concern that an invalidation would generate disputes about other displays of the Ten Commandments and create the very divisiveness the Establishment Clause seeks to avoid.[65] Justice Breyer's approach here involved the kind of nuanced appraisal that may well be desirable in these contexts, although that inevitably leaves us without clear criteria about what will be allowed rather than forbidden.

Some of the challenges addressed by the Supreme Court have been to Christmas displays that have included the crèche of the birth of Jesus. Making Christmas a holiday and putting up a Christmas tree, which once had some religious significance that has essentially disappeared, have been uncontroversial, but portraying the birth of Jesus has more obvious religious content. In the 1984 case of *Lynch v. Donnelly*,[66] the Court sustained such a Christmas display owned by the city of Pawtucket, Rhode Island, that had been erected in a privately owned shopping center. The display was alongside a Christmas tree, a Santa Claus house, reindeer, and carolers. Accepting the display, the majority opinion of Chief Justice Burger suggested various theories. After cautioning that the standard of *Lemon v. Kurtzman* was not a simple confining test, Burger noted numbers of government acknowledgements of the place of religion that were accepted. The purpose to celebrate the holiday was secular; the "effect" was acceptable since any benefit to religion was "indirect," "remote," or "incidental,"[67] and no genuine divisive entanglement was involved.

Justice Brennan, joined by three others, dissented. He perceived an approval of Christian beliefs that could have been avoided by having a display without a crèche.[68] Rejecting any idea that historical acceptance could justify a practice, he asserted that the standard should be whether practices "threaten those consequences which the framers deeply feared."[69] Justice

O'Connor relied on a theory of "endorsement" as crucial. She found the crèche acceptable because the government was neither endorsing nor condemning religion.[70]

Because the majority relied on various approaches it is hard to say exactly what *Lynch* stands for. Its reliance on the inclusion of secular displays does not by itself seem very compelling, since those could have been used without the crèche (*unless* one sees the crèche as the most important Christmas symbol). Historical practice alone does not seem sufficient, given that that would protect many acts by the government that the Court has declared invalid. The magnitude of public support should matter if substantial nonreligious purposes are served, but here the presence of such purposes was contestable.

In 1989 the Court considered two more display cases, one involving a crèche. In *County of Allegheny v. American Civil Liberties Union*,[71] a crèche owned by a private religious group had been placed on the Grand Staircase of a county courthouse. Five Justices found this unacceptable, given the religious message. Four dissenters claimed that this fit with the government's latitude to recognize religion's role. In the second case, a Chanukah menorah had been placed next to a Christmas tree and a sign saluting liberty outside a city-county building. Seven Justices voted the same way in this case; for them the different location, the congruence of the menorah with essentially nonreligious symbols, and the fact that its display was related to the religion of only a modest minority did not distinguish the two cases. But Justices Blackmun and O'Connor saw things differently. Acknowledging that the menorah had both religious and secular dimensions, Justice Blackmun saw its place with the Christmas tree and liberty sign as a "secular celebration."[72]

Justice O'Connor relied on a more fully developed version of the endorsement test on which she had rested in her earlier acceptance of most "moments of silence" in *Wallace v. Jaffree*. Since O'Connor was the crucial central vote in many religion cases, this test for years had great importance. In what follows I shall explore her account in more depth, since the basic notion of endorsement is certainly a plausible approach to how controversial establishment issues should be viewed.

Initially suggested in Justice O'Connor's concurrence in *Lynch v. Donnelly*[73] as "clarification" of what the threefold *Lemon* test amounted to, O'Connor employed the standard in cases that followed, sometimes joined by other Justices. In her formulation, an endorsement or disapproval "sends a message to non-adherents that they are outsiders, not full members of the political community, and an accompanying message to adherents that they are insiders, favored members of the political community."[74] Reviewing the public schools' moments of silence in *Wallace v. Jaffree*, she explained that what counted would be whether an "objective observer" who understood free exercise values and the history of a statute would perceive the state as endorsing religion.[75] When applied to the menorah next to the Christmas tree, the endorsement test did not lead her to vote for invalidation because the combination did not convey an "endorsement of Judaism or of religion in general."[76]

There are two problems with Justice O'Connor's formulation of the test, one of which is crucial to how such a standard should actually be applied. The first problem is simply a kind of vagueness. What is it for nonadherents to feel "they are outsiders, not full members of the political community"? Most narrowly someone could feel she really did not count equally in her political and legal rights as a citizen. That was clearly true for women before they had a right to vote, and it is still true for noncitizens who live within the United States. Even if one had all relevant formal rights, one could feel that one's group was effectively put down by certain laws, such as those barring gay marriages or those now creating broad exemptions to allow unequal treatment of gay couples by private citizens and organizations. But suppose none of that is involved. Instead, the government is conveying a message that most citizens are Christian and that the government is essentially in accord with that tradition, although members of other religions have equal rights. This would be seen as a communication that those nonadherents are kinds of outsiders in the dominant culture, but are they actually portrayed as less than "full members of the political community"? One could ask a similar question about individuals who themselves reject certain values of our liberal democracy, such as basic premises of equality, that are explicitly conveyed by the government. Justice O'Connor was never explicit about what counted as "the political community." In terms of what makes sense, the government can convey the message that citizens with basic rights who reject fundamental notions of equality are "outsiders" in terms of our cultural assumptions; but at least if a message is strong, the government should not be able to communicate that religious nonadherents are at odds with the basic cultural community even though they have equal legal and political rights.

The second problem is more troubling and difficult. Whose perceptions should count? Suppose the "objective observer" with full knowledge of background and legislative history would not perceive a forbidden endorsement? In a later case, O'Connor compared her "objective observer" to a reasonable person in tort law, urging that if the focus was on actual observers, a display would mistakenly count as "endorsement" as long as some people perceived it that way.[77] This is non sequitur. One could inquire what a significant percentage of actual people would perceive. Of course, a law or practice should not be invalid simply because a few people see it that way, but what if the vast majority of actual persons do? If that is the overwhelming perception, it should be crucial, even if it is partly based on less than full information or grasp of values.

An even greater concern about the "objective observer" is whose actual perceptions may count. Those in the majority may not perceive a serious endorsement, but those in the minority may see things differently. To take a personal example, in the public school I attended from kindergarten through tenth grade,[78] Christmas carols were sung before the school day began in the week leading up to Christmas vacation, and the more senior students participated in a Christmas pageant. I never saw these as a kind of endorsement of Christianity, but I wonder how my Jewish fellow students, a significant minority, felt. To take a more modern example, when police cars in a Texas county depicted foot-high crosses, the perceptions of non-Christians should have been given special significance.[79] Should an inquiry about "endorsement" take account of how those within different groups are likely to react, and at least sometimes give special weight to the perceptions of most of those in a minority? I believe, as a matter of principle, the answer is clearly "yes."

Although one might defend the O'Connor formulation as representing all that courts are capable of doing, I nevertheless believe judges should not disregard variations in perceptions if they are clearly evident. Beyond this, if local legislative bodies or school boards are weighing their constitutional responsibilities and what is a wise balancing of values within the range of what is permissible, they should definitely take those realities into account even if one cannot expect that of courts.

An issue about displays somewhat different from those yet considered is whether, if it allows private displays on public property, the government can bar religious ones. Ohio had permitted displays in its Capitol Square but had not allowed the Ku Klux Klan to erect a cross.[80] Lower courts had required that such a permit be given. The Supreme Court in 1995 divided 5–4 on whether a religious exclusion was acceptable. The majority ruled that such discrimination was not permissible. In a plurality opinion, one that does not include all those who voted in the majority, Justice Scalia relied heavily on the free speech clause as a bar to such categorization.[81] Justice O'Connor in a concurring opinion agreed, noting that the state could erect a sign disclaiming sponsorship.[82] She did, however, indicate that sometimes such an exclusion might be an appropriate way for the government to avoid endorsement.

At least if religious displays do not dominate *and* the government makes clear that the displays do not represent its own positions, precluding religious content is unwarranted. Of course, on the facts of this particular case, *if* the display obviously indicated that its source was an organization whose values were in direct opposition to core notions of equal rights, that might constitute an independent reason not to permit it. But allowing private religious displays when the government is permitting all kinds of portrayals on government property is quite different from the government itself providing such a display.

# CHAPTER 2

# Religion and Clerics in Constraining Government Institutions: The Military and Prisons

I N THIS CHAPTER WE WILL EXPLORE TWO special government settings in which religious exercise and nonestablishment face a distinctive tension. In brief, unlike normal human situations, the ordinary freedom
to exercise religion in worship services is often unavailable in the military
and in prison life unless the government involves itself in some way. The
issues in the two settings are a bit different. Within the military, crucial questions are how clerics are to be provided for military personnel, how far those
clerics may and should be constrained by restrictions on how they interact
with soldiers and sailors, and how they are to be chosen. Similar questions
arise for prisons, although given variations between prisons and military settings, the answers are not identical. Certain issues about religion also have
a special significance in respect to prisons. Should group religious worship
have a special status over other group meetings? Should involvement in religion be allowed to count as *a* reason in favor of granting discretionary parole?
For the latter determination, should there be clerical recommendations and
actual clerical participation in boards determining whether to grant parole?

A general theme of this book is important here. Although we normally
think of what is unconstitutional in terms of what courts will declare to be
so, in fact other officials should recognize that some possible actions may
be unconstitutional even if judges would not overturn them on that basis.
Beyond this, constitutional values, such as free exercise and nonestablishment, may be in play for what decisions may be wisest and most just even

when alternative choices are within the range of the constitutionally permissible. Of course, conscientious officials who take the relevant values into account and are confident that what they do will not be overturned by courts do not need, themselves, to draw a clear line between what is actually unconstitutional and what is only undesirable.

For both topics of this chapter, we can see three important bases noted in the Introduction on which judges may decline to declare unconstitutional what in principle might be so regarded. (I leave the fourth basis, lack of standing to challenge, for Chapter 3, although it could sometimes play a role here.)

One of the three reasons why courts cannot resolve an issue is that the relevant facts are too hard to determine. Those uncertain facts may be simply what did or did not occur or, more subtly, what are the overall effects given competing considerations. The second kind of obstacle is that a subject is simply too sensitive for deep judicial involvement. This is most striking in the "political question" doctrine, according to which courts will not address constitutional issues but leave their resolution to the political branches. A less absolute assertion is that courts will consider issues but afford substantial deference to official decisions and actions. Clearly *if* substantial deference is given, a decision could be unconstitutional in principle even if accepted by judges. What I have identified as the third obstacle can concern other domains but seems particularly relevant to certain topics here. Some matters are so picky that judges will not see it worth intervening to declare a choice unconstitutional. We could rightly see this as one form of deference, but its basis is a bit different from other reasons for not overturning debatable choices made by legislators or executive officials.

## Military Chaplains

Soldiers' lives within the military are substantially constrained, especially when they are sent abroad as forces in military conflict. And sailors may spend extended time in ships on the high seas or in foreign locations. For these military forces ordinary religious worship in private churches, synagogues, and mosques will not be feasible. The government must become involved to make standard forms of religious worship available. In this balance of free exercise and nonestablishment, virtually all agree that free exercise values should win out for some accommodation, whether or not the provision of chaplains is actually constitutionally required.[1] But that alone does not resolve a number of questions about basic alternatives. Should the government, insofar as possible, use nonmilitary clerics to provide services? When it employs clerics of its own, should these actually be trained and treated as military personnel? How should it, by its hiring decisions and by other measures, make its coverage as equitable and as broad as is feasible? How much should it dictate what its own chaplains do and say? Should any similar accommodations be made to nonreligious convictions and group meetings? In respect to all of these questions, we can identify tensions between free exercise and nonestablishment values and understand both why any precise line of constitutional permissibility is hard to draw here and why courts have reasons not to get involved in debatable details.

Let me start with the significance of religion. Private citizens are involved in a wide range of activities, some of which involve both convictions about what they should do, such as promote equal rights for women, and group meetings that discuss those objectives. Whether persons are volunteers or drafted, they understand that when they join the military the flexibility to participate in such groups will definitely be curtailed if they are sent abroad in combat and are also likely to be restricted if they remain on a base in the United States. Is religion special? For many people the obvious answer is "yes."[2] Their sense of connection to God and to fellow believers is a central aspect of their lives. They expect to participate in group worship once a week or more.[3] Even if a critic is deeply skeptical of any religious truth and the value of religion in American culture, he should understand that treating religion as special in this context is a reasonable step. As far as history is concerned, during the Revolutionary War chaplains of state militia became part of the national army; and in 1791, the year the Bill of Rights was adopted, Congress authorized the appointment of army chaplains.[4]

Whatever one may expect in a distant future in which this country *may* become much more secular and less religious, at present the hiring of religious chaplains for some military settings, without including leaders of nonreligious organizations, is definitely appropriate.[5] That by itself does not tell us how far that practice should extend, a subject I will mention without exploring in depth.

When soldiers are stationed within the United States, they typically have some time off. Why should the government not allow them to use that time to attend religious services in the community or, alternatively, encourage nonmilitary clergy to conduct services within the military premises? Each of these alternatives involves less "establishment" than hiring clerics within the army. On the other hand, it can be urged that having clerics that the soldiers get to know reasonably well may be important, and that it is very valuable to have those already known to the ordinary troops to accompany them when they are consigned to territory outside the United States. These are considerations that Congress and the executive branch should take into account, but it would be very hard for a court to say, at least putting aside retired military personnel and "armchair" personnel who commute to work,[6] that providing military clerics for worship is actually unconstitutional.[7]

More particular questions about military clerics are how they are chosen, what is their training and status, and what instructions and guidance they are given. At previous stages of history, some military branches tried to relate hiring to religious affiliations in the whole population.[8] Now the services have no explicit standards of distribution,[9] but what should be relevant is the percentage of members within the military, not the distribution among the larger population. And some special attention should be given to members of minorities, such as Muslims and Buddhists, who do not fit well in worship with major groups. (I put the point this way to distinguish what is common among many Protestants. Attending a community church, I was confirmed in the Dutch Reformed religion, but, since I would have been comfortable with many other Protestant clerics, as a serviceman I would not have counted as a part of a disadvantaged minority even if no Dutch Reformed ministers had been available.) Of course, not every minority religion is going to have a cleric available in each setting. This is a strong reason for the government to make an effort to see if some other option is available to allow these military members to worship in the way in which they believe.

One concern about the need to aim for neutrality is a credentials requirement. The present approach is that a chaplain must have an undergraduate degree and three postgraduate years of education (what typically leads to a master of divinity degree).[10] A problem with this is that any such strict requirement could work to the disadvantage of less traditional denominations whose clerics need not have so much education. It would be wise here to at least allow possible exceptions for such denominations.

A broader question about "neutrality" is whether or not it is acceptable and wise to hire clerics but not the leaders of other kinds of organizations. Given the special place of religion in the lives of many people, treating clerics differently from the leaders of organizations devoted to public projects such as housing for the poor is clearly acceptable and is sensible in our culture. A somewhat special problem is presented if atheists claim that nonestablishment values should lead to their having leaders who will guide meetings. If atheists were typically involved in group meetings that concentrated on how nonbelief in God enriches their lives, the claim for equal treatment would have some force, but since such involvement is now rare, if it exists at all, the argument for this form of similar treatment is weak. However, atheists should not be pushed into religious acceptance or treated negatively.[11]

Chaplains typically receive military training, other than training in arms, and they are subject to military regulations and orders.[12] In this sense, a form of establishment may not only promote religion, it may actually restrict the exercise of the very persons that it places in a kind of privileged position. Not surprisingly, such a requirement is bound to assure that hired chaplains are not explicitly opposed to government decisions about when and how to employ military force. One might see this as a necessary, or at least appropriate, restraint about what a chaplain directly communicates to soldiers about military orders, some of which demand the risking of the soldiers' lives.

More direct restraints are that chaplains be available for members of all religions and that they not engage in proselytizing. These policies, however vague their application may be, do touch on what chaplains may feel free to say without fear of penalty. Of course, if the government is going to have clerics as a part of its personnel, it does not want them causing tensions and divisions within its troops. Thus, these restraints should be seen as acceptable even if they are a modest restraint on the religious exercise of the clerics.

A more troublesome question is raised by instruction to chaplains that part of their job is to encourage the religious interests of troops.[13] Even if this falls short of proselytizing, it could be seen as a promotion of religion. One may dismiss this instruction as not serious or as merely reflecting what all clerics see as their role generally, but why should the government maintain such an explicit encouragement of promoting religion? A possible response is that, given the severe tensions and risks of military service, it is actually desirable for soldiers and sailors to have religious convictions. In terms of what is actually desirable, that thesis is highly plausible, but I do not think it is sufficient for the government to directly encourage those who have become military personnel to practice religion. And since chaplains are government employees, telling them to do so should not be regarded as appropriate. Even if this is true, whether what is involved here is significant enough for a judicial declaration of unconstitutionality is dubious.

This brief exploration of military chaplains, their hiring, and their instructions, reflects numerous tensions between free exercise and nonestablishment values. It also reveals how complicated many situations creating those tensions can be and shows that even if judicial involvement is appropriately limited in this context, legislators and executive officials should give careful consideration to competing values when they decide exactly how to set things up.

## Questions about Religion and Prisons

When we turn from the military to prisons, some questions are similar, but others are different. Among the similar ones are how far should religious worship services and other practices be accommodated within prisons, how far should clergy be actually appointed by the government, or at least paid by the government to provide those services, how far should the government be able to control what they say, and whether the government should be able to specifically encourage religious participation. Different important questions are raised by the relation between the religious involvement of prisoners and decisions by boards about discretionary parole. Should they take religious involvement into account and what, if any, should be the role of chaplains in those decisions?

The answer to whether religious services should be provided is quite simple. If people have no capacity to leave a prison facility, the government should provide the services and give prisoners the opportunity to participate in them, even if one could see this as a weak form of establishment. Much more important is how far it should assure that members of all religions are provided with this opportunity. I shall not explore various cases that have raised this issue, but the fundamental answer is that prison officials should make every effort to see that services are available as broadly as possible.

Who should provide these services? Although we can imagine facilities that are so isolated the government will actually need to hire clergy who will be full time employees, almost always the better solution, and perhaps one that should be seen as constitutionally required, is for clergy whose main occupations lie elsewhere to enter the prisons and conduct worship services. This is preferable in that it constitutes less government involvement and control of the religious practices themselves. And, in the contrast to the military, we have no deep historical tradition of government-employed prison chaplains. One might go further and conclude that prisons should let the denominations pay those clergy for all they do. This may in fact be preferable if it works, but if the prisons need to provide religious services, it follows that they can actually pay those who expend their time and energy to lead them.

A different issue about the connection of religion and payment concerns state funding for halfway houses that constitute an alternative for parolees who have violated some term of their parole. Can the government fund and recommend halfway houses that include Christianity or some other religious practices in what they do? This is not a simple question, but the basic answer is "yes," so long as nonreligious halfway houses are also available and the parolees are not required, or strongly pushed, to attend the religious ones. If religious practice does reduce the likelihood of future criminality, it would not make sense to preclude all halfway houses from religious practices. In *Freedom from Religious Foundation, Inc. v. McCollum,*[14] the Seventh Circuit rejected a challenge to such funding and accepted that recommendation did not amount to "coercion."

In terms of control of communication by clerics, the government can forbid messages within prisons that actually encourage criminal behavior, including violence against fellow prisoners and escaping from jail. Perhaps this should extend to messages highly likely to create hostility and discrimination among prisoners. Apart from these limited restraints, the clergy should be free to convey the religious messages they believe are appropriate.

Given the basic principle of nonestablishment, officials should not require prisoners to be involved in religious worship or put pressure on them to do so. As with the military, the sense that religion is generally healthy and promotes good social values should not constitute a sufficient basis for that kind of strong recommendation. I should note that a certain tension exists between this conclusion and what follows, but that tension is unavoidable and the best we can do is to seek a sensible resolution of free exercise and nonestablishment values in the two contexts.

As mentioned in this chapter's introduction, two special questions for prisoners are the place of religion in regard to parole decisions and the role prison chaplains may play in those decisions.[15] Sometimes, clear, objective bases exist upon which prisoners must be granted parole before they have completed their sentences in prison. But in many jurisdictions, boards may grant parole based on discretionary judgments about whether the prisoners are likely to fall back into criminal behavior. There are many ascertainable factors that may be relevant, such as the seriousness of someone's crime, prior criminal record, participation in rehabilitation programs, job skills, and history concerning alcohol and drug use. A correlation also exists between religious involvement and a reduced probability of future criminal behavior.[16] Should a board be able to take that into account?

I believe at one level the answer is "clearly yes," but the issue is far from simple. If religious involvement does reduce the likelihood of future crimes, surely that should count as relevant for a parole decision. It is true that knowing that boards may give it weight could encourage some prisoners to get involved in religious practices and may even lead to dishonest statements of belief and commitment. The latter is definitely a genuine concern, but not enough to wipe this relevant consideration totally out of place.

This is my conclusion about religion in general, but what about specific religions? Suppose the evidence showed that those who subscribed to certain, particular religions were less likely to revert to crimes than members of other religions. Let us assume that, putting affiliation aside, two prisoners seem equally deserving of parole. Should one be granted it and the other denied it because of the different faiths of which they are members? Here I believe the answer should be "no." Even if based on factual evidence, so favoring one religion over another should not be accepted. The reasons are that this would be a much more troubling form of establishment and it could even be seen as a kind of interference with free exercise, encouraging a prisoner to join a religion that may fit less well with his actual convictions.

This conclusion relates to more general questions of classification outside of religion. Suppose it can be shown that women and persons over the age of 60 are less likely to recommit crimes than men and persons under 60. Different treatment on these bases does not seem too troubling, but taking race into account would raise much more serious concerns, as it has with "stop and frisk."[17]

A Utah case does raise exactly what should count as the inappropriate favoring (or disfavoring) of one religion over others. In *Granguillhome v. Utah Board of Pardons* it was claimed that a prisoner's parole board favored members of the Church of Jesus Christ of Latter-day Saints (i.e., Mormons) in parole decisions for those convicted of sexual offenses.[18] Although the court granted summary judgment against the claiming inmates based on a lack of factual evidence, the basic complaint had some plausibility, given that the assertion was about the dominant religion within Utah. But the claim about sexual offenses leads me to wonder whether some of those cases involving Mormons concerned practices of polygamy, which are still carried out by a small, split-off branch that has not accepted the rejection of polygamy by the dominant Church.[19] Whatever may have been true here, we can imagine practices actually recommended by a religion that have criminal status. Those who engage in those practices, especially something like forbidden sex that involves mutual consent by adults, may be less inclined toward other forbidden behaviors than other convicted criminals. (On the other hand, they may be more likely to reengage in what their religion encourages.) The point I want to make here is that my claim that people should not be favored or disfavored based on their particular religion is not meant to cover taking account of the precise details of the particular criminal act, how dangerous it was to others, and whether it is actually encouraged by a person's religion. These are factors parole boards should definitely be able to consider.

When we turn to the role of chaplains, one question is whether they should be able to write recommendations to parole boards and testify before them. This amounts, of course, to the government taking account of the views of religious representatives in making decisions. Nonetheless, the answer is that here, that is definitely acceptable and warranted, *if* a prisoner's religious connections can carry some weight for parole eligibility. If chaplains are the individuals who have been most closely connected to an inmate's participation in worship and in other religious practices, and who may well have had conversations with the inmate, they are in a position to have a considered opinion about the frequency and depth of religious involvement. To bar any interaction with the parole board would not make sense, even if that does create some risk of unfair evaluation and could increase slightly the incentive for inmates to get involved in religious practices and be less than honest with the chaplains who are performing them.

In some jurisdictions, chaplains are actually members of parole boards. To give them this degree of authority regarding important government decisions is going too far. They would naturally have a strong inclination to prefer inmates with religious involvement and, in particular, those that have been engaged in worship services they have conducted. This connection of religious practice and its leadership to government decisions is too great. Chaplains who are operating within prisons should not serve on parole boards themselves; and that degree of involvement should probably be declared unconstitutional.

One obvious aspect of prisons that has sometimes, but rarely, arisen in the military is what exemptions should be provided from standard requirements. That inquiry is reserved for the next part of this book, which includes treatment of the Religious Land Use and Institutionalized Persons Act.

We have seen in this chapter many ways in which government control over the lives of persons both within the military and in prisons reflects unavoidable conflicts between free exercise and nonestablishment values. The exercise of religion needs to be accommodated but the government should not require its practice nor push people strongly to engage in it. It should try very hard to avoid favoring some religions over others and should be constrained in how far it tries to dictate what those who lead services should, and should not, do. Within a fairly substantial range officials are going to be left by courts to work things out as they see best. But even if courts are highly likely to accept certain choices, officials should ask themselves whether what they might do is really unconstitutional, or at least unwise, given the values of free exercise and nonestablishment at stake.

PART TWO

# Forms of Government Aid to Religious Institutions and Individuals: Financial Support and Exemptions

THIS PART OF THE BOOK explains two different forms of government help to religious institutions and persons. The most obvious is providing financial help for endeavors undertaken by religious organizations, including parochial schools. The second is granting exemptions from ordinary legal duties that violate the religious convictions of individuals or organizations. This, of course, has become a highly contentious issue related to the constitutional protection now given to same-sex marriage. For these two subjects, we have both an overlap and a notable difference. The central overlap is tax exemptions, which have been long-standing for churches and other religious bodies. Tax exemptions also reach individual contributions, thus indirectly encouraging greater donations and amounting to an indirect form of financial assistance for religious and other institutions.

The crucial difference between direct financial assistance and other exemptions concerns which religion clause is most directly involved. A claim for an exemption cast in terms of religious conviction is an assertion of free exercise, either as a constitutional right or desirable legislative accommodation. The granting of an exemption, however, can be seen as an unjustified establishment of religion, or when the basic duty concerns nondiscrimination, as violating constitutional or statutory rights to equal treatment. The Free Exercise Clause does not directly require government financial support of religious practices, so most constitutional issues about such aid involve the Establishment Clause. But one argument against contentions that this aid amounts to a forbidden establishment is that it furthers the free exercise of religious convictions.

The topics of this part of the book provide strong illustrations of three of its basic themes. The first is that in constitutional cases when the values of the two clauses are in some tension and the claim is that one is being violated, the competing values can count even if they plainly do not entail that what is being challenged is itself constitutionally compelled. This is most evident with the argument that the exercise of religion supports financial aid even though it definitely does not require it. Second, legislatures need to consider whether proposed legislation would violate the Constitution, even if they can be confident courts will not determine that, for example because those objecting will not have standing to challenge. The third theme is that the crucial values definitely should come into play for many legislative choices that are within the range of what is constitutionally permitted according to prevailing doctrine. This is illustrated by many permissible decisions about exemptions and financial assistance.

An important consideration for both of these domains is whether it is acceptable and just to treat religious endeavors and convictions differently from nonreligious ones. Touched on at various points in this part of the book, this issue is explored in more depth in Chapter 8. With most exemptions, the simple argument for equal treatment is that claims of conscience should be treated the same way, whether religious or not; the constitutional contention can be that failure to do so is an unwarranted establishment of religion. Matters are different for financial support. Against the concern that giving that to religious endeavors may be an unwarranted establishment of religion, we often have the counterargument that if nonreligious endeavors receive aid, treating religious groups less favorably would be an unwarranted establishment of nonreligion, an indirect impairment of free exercise, and perhaps a violation of equal protection.

Chapter 3 focuses mainly on financial assistance in the form of spending money; it also includes tax benefits accorded to religious schools.[1] Chapter 4 tackles the general topic of exemptions. Some of these are noncontroversial, but when it comes to same-sex marriage and performing abortions, what people and organizations should be excused from doing is sharply disputed.

CHAPTER 3

# Financial Support

S HOULD THE GOVERNMENT PROVIDE financial support for activities in which religious groups are engaged? That general issue raises
a more particular question that bears on how a chapter like this may best be
organized: How much should the nature of the activity itself matter? Should
hospitals, aiding the homeless, schools, and worship services all be treated
similarly, or not? Put simply, directly financing worship itself would be the
most evident form of establishment; activities that are furthest removed from
outright religious worship or promotion, such as running a hospital without
proselytizing, are at the other end. Educational institutions fall somewhere
in between. From an analytical perspective, it would make sense to begin
with the simpler examples and then move to schools. However, the overarching number of Supreme Court cases on this subject, and indeed involving
the Establishment Clause more generally, have concerned direct and indirect
forms of aid, including tax benefits, for parochial schools. Because these cases
are so important for how to understand Establishment Clause approaches
for this domain, and for other subjects to which the Clause relates, I shall
start with them,[1] before turning to other sorts of endeavors and then reflecting on how far schools are, and should be, treated as special.

## The Supreme Court's Constitutional Approaches
to Aid to Religious Schools

In 1947, the Supreme Court, in *Everson vs. Board of Education*,[2] issued
a decision on a kind of indirect support to religious education, specifically

57

the financing of children's transportation to and from parochial schools. The Court ruled in favor of the actual practice but with a combination of opinions that emphasized a strong separation of church and state. A bit of background may help to explain why this case was important and why the opinions were cast as they were.

For much of American history after public schools became dominant in the early nineteenth century, the overwhelming proportion of private schools were Roman Catholic parochial schools. This was partly because the public schools generally had a Protestant flavor—for example, using the King James version of the Bible—and partly because the Roman Catholic hierarchy regarded education in their own faith as very important and did not favor liberal democracy.[3] Although such an amendment failed to pass within Congress, many states in the latter half of that century adopted "Blaine" amendments that forbade assistance to sectarian schools.[4] Most of these amendments still exist.[5]

The New Jersey law reviewed in *Everson* required bus transportation for children attending schools, including those going to nonprofit private schools. In the district involved in the case, the only relevant nonpublic schools were Roman Catholic. A bare majority of the Supreme Court upheld the assistance. One of the dissenters urged that the First Amendment had the purpose of creating a "complete and permanent separation of religious activity and civil authority."[6] Another emphasized the religious aims of Roman Catholic schools.[7] For the majority, Justice Black relied on a very narrow ground, emphasizing that, as with police and fire protection, this assistance was not aimed at the educational function of schools. Some of the opinion's language might have been taken as more broadly permissive. Black wrote of this aid going to parents, not the schools,[8] and he noted that individuals should not be excluded "because of their faith or lack of it."[9] But Black also indicated that public funds cannot go to religious activities, that a "wall of separation" exists between church and state,[10] and that the New Jersey law approaches "the verge of state power." When one combines this language with the position of the four dissenters, one cannot help concluding that most of the Justices at the time had a highly restrictive view about public aid for religious education.

In *Board of Education v. Allen*,[11] decided two decades later, the Court adopted a less strict approach and approved New York's program lending to private schools textbooks designated for public school use or approved by a public board of education. This was clearly a support to the education itself, not the fringe of transportation, but Justice White's majority opinion emphasized that the benefits went to parents and their children and assisted the public purpose of secular education.[12]

A few years later, the Court decided two cases under the name of *Lemon v. Kurtzman*,[13] and articulated a standard that has remained somewhat vague, contested, and debatable in coverage since that time. In both Rhode Island and Pennsylvania, the great majority of students attending nonpublic schools went to Roman Catholic ones. Pennsylvania had provided payments for textbooks and instructional materials; and both states had authorized payments for part of the salaries of teachers of secular subjects. After remarking that "we can only dimly perceive the lines of demarcation in this extraordinarily sensitive area of constitutional law,"[14] Chief Justice Burger set out a three-part test. A statute's legislative purpose must be secular; its principal or primary effect must not be either to advance or inhibit religion; and it must not foster "an excessive entanglement with religion."[15] Just how this test applies has been both uncertain and controversial; whether it applies at all and, if so, in which circumstances, has also been unclear over time.

Various parts of this book note some of these contexts. Two general points are important. The first is that the Court itself has never really taken the test as dominant for claims of free exercise constitutional rights or for claims of support based on statutory concessions to free exercise, the subjects of Chapter 4. The Court had been granting some constitutional free exercise claims at the very time of *Lemon*. It would take a considerable stretch to say that when legislators afforded similar grants, these had a secular purpose and did not have the effect of advancing religion. The second general point is that despite criticisms of the test as misguided, plainly much of what it obviously covers is relevant for the Establishment Clause. The government should not aim directly to use government resources to further religious endeavors over nonreligious ones, and it should not "entangle" itself in ways that require unwise practical intertwining with religious institutions or demand extremely complex judgements about just what constitute relevant religious convictions. However inapt the overall *Lemon* test may be in some circumstances, the factors to which it refers cannot be totally disregarded.

Returning to the decision itself, the Court found a secular purpose of enhancing secular education in both states. Although not ruling directly about effects, it is evident that the Justices' perceptions about religious effects did bear on their conclusions that the laws in both states demanded unacceptable entanglements. Given their connection to Catholic churches, the aims of religious instruction within the Catholic schools, and the high percentage of teaching nuns, for a state to try to limit aid to secular instruction by separating that from religion doctrine was seen as too entangling. Chief Justice Burger's majority opinion also referred to "entanglement of a different character—the divisive political potential of the state programs."[16] Concerns about divisive political potential should properly play a role in political decisions themselves, but whether courts should ever invalidate legislation on that basis is highly dubious. In no case has that been actually the dominant stated reason for invalidation.

On the same day as the *Lemon* case, a majority of the Court took a different approach to federal construction grants to church-related colleges and universities.[17] The statute itself barred grants for facilities used for sectarian instruction or religious worship. Given that college students are less impressionable and less susceptible to religious indoctrination than those in high school, and that "by their very nature, college and postgraduate courses tend to limit the opportunities for sectarian influence," the plurality opinion of Chief Justice Burger saw less need for intensive surveillance.[18] Such aid was thus acceptable so long as a particular institution was not so sectarian that financial assistance to it would be advancing religion.

In the decade after *Lemon v. Kurtzman* numbers of cases involved invalidation of various forms of assistance, but the Supreme Court did accept the supplying of standardized tests and scoring services used in public schools,[19] reimbursement for pupil evaluation and other expenses connected to state-prepared examinations,[20] and the provision of diagnostic services within private schools.[21] About the *Lemon* criteria, one of the Court's general comments was that they were "no more than helpful."[22]

In 1983 the Court moved decisively toward a more permissive approach to aid. Reviewing a Minnesota law that allowed parents to deduct from their state income taxes what they paid for school tuition, for textbooks, and for transportation for children, the Court held in *Mueller v. Allen*[23] that this was just one of many available deductions, and that the aid went to parents, not parochial schools. That parents whose children attended public schools did not need pay any tuition unless they sent their children outside their own district, and that about 95% of the students attending private schools were going to sectarian ones meant that the overwhelming benefits here did go to parents sending their children to religious schools. However, that did not undercut the program according to the formal approach used in Chief Justice Rehnquist's majority opinion.

Although *Mueller* led many to think that the Court was about to undergo a radical shift toward permissibility,[24] that did not happen in two 1985 cases. These struck down a program for paying teachers at private schools to conduct after-school courses[25] and a program paying public school teachers to offer courses for remedial reading and mathematics, and for English as a second language, within parochial school classrooms.[26] The key to the disconnect with *Mueller v. Allen* was that Justice Powell, who had joined the majority in that case upholding state assistance that went primarily to religious education, regarded these two programs as impermissible.

This difference in results represents a kind of reality that may not be known to all those outside the law, but that has played an important role in a significant number of religion cases. The Supreme Court reviews difficult cases, ones about which lower court judges are likely to have been divided. Often the Justices themselves disagree over outcomes, sometimes 5–4. It is this fact that made the question of the outlook of a successor to Justice Scalia, a leading conservative, of interest not only to many scholars and practicing lawyers, but also a fairly important issue during the 2016 presidential election. When the Court is divided 5–4 in two somewhat similar cases, the outcomes can vary, if only one Justice sees things differently. Thus, eight of nine Justices believe that the correct approach leads to the same decisions in both cases, but the single swing Justice produces a discrepancy, one that is often hard to characterize on a clear principled basis.

In 2002, the Supreme Court in *Zelman v. Simmons-Harris*[27] did render a decision that was significantly more accepting of financial aid that helped religious education. It sustained the operation of an Ohio voucher program as applied in Cleveland. Nonwealthy parents sending their children to parochial schools and private schools could receive vouchers for as much as 90 percent of tuition, up to $2,250. Of the participating schools in the 1999–2000 school year, 82 percent were religiously affiliated and more than 96 percent of the students involved attended these schools. The *Zelman* case presents some difficult and fascinating questions both about the outcome and what is a desirable approach, but before tackling those questions and others concerning aid to schools, we will first turn to aid to other religious institutions. That can help us to see not only what makes sense for them but also what is, and should be, regarded as special about schools.

## The Constitutionality and Approaches of Aid More Generally

When we turn to the broader question of aid to religious institutions that are providing forms of public service, we can see three related realities mentioned earlier that bear on a number of other religion clause subjects. The first is the incredible complexity of factors that can affect the best resolution of relevant values. The second is how hard it may be for the courts to sort out how those will be promoted or sacrificed by general legislative standards and their specific applications. The third is that all this bears heavily on what have been, and should be, adopted as judicially imposed constitutional limits, or left to the determinations of legislators and executive officials. When we reflect on criticisms of Supreme Court approaches to the religion clause cases as lacking clarity and consistency, these complications provide part of the underlying explanation, along with shifts among the Justices about what really counts most.

What I shall first do is to set out the basic competing considerations and then refer to some leading cases that did not directly involve parochial schools. We will then return to the school cases and explore what makes the most just and wise approaches in respect to them.

Consider three different kinds of examples of religious institutions providing secular services: hospitals, the giving of food and shelter to the poor and homeless, and helping people to recover from inclinations that are criminal or are misguided in some other way. Here are some of the factors that are potentially relevant. Is a service being provided that is of genuine secular benefit? Is that service largely detached from a specific religious message? Are those who receive the benefits able to do so without having to comply with religious standards or submit to religious messages? Are potential beneficiaries able to choose the religious institutions without pressure? Are the beneficiaries selected by institutions without criteria of religious conformance? Are employees within relevant institutions selected independent of their religious affiliations? Are nonreligious institutions that supply the same services being treated similarly by the government? Can the services be provided without an intertwining of government and religious officials? Is the financing for religious individuals coming directly or indirectly from the government? Is the government itself now directly supplying similar services, and has it always done so?

Before exploring the more difficult questions here and their comparative importance, I shall note a few that yield straightforward answers for what is both appropriate and clear under existing law. Since, as presently understood, the Establishment Clause does bar direct financial aid to worship and other unmodified religious exercises, the service provided must be one with a genuine secular benefit.

In this area, religious providers cannot be generally treated more favorably than nonreligious ones. This principle leaves open whether officials with a responsibility to choose institutions that are suited to carry forward services may pick those that happen to have a religious affiliation. The key theoretical question here about comparative treatment of religious and nonreligious institutions is whether the religious ones must be treated equally or may formally be disfavored, not whether, as with exemptions, they may be favored. When the main concern is nonestablishment rather than free exercise, it is assumed that religious approaches should not be afforded special benefits.

The third obvious point is that government needs to figure out a way to support help without entangling itself too deeply into what a private religious institution is doing. This is a limit cast by the entanglement prong of the *Lemon* test and has been applied even when the Court makes no direct reference to that test.

Let us now turn to the more troublesome issues. If the secular service is not detached from religious involvement, nonestablishment concerns greatly increase. Suppose a religious hospital required all patients to say Christian prayers and attend Christian services. For the government to finance hospital care would inevitably help promote the religious exercises. On the other hand, if a helpful secular service is actually being provided, do free exercise values suggest that religious groups should be able to do so in the way that their religious convictions tell them is right? Similar competing considerations are in play if the question is who will work for the organization that provides the services. The ability to choose those sympathetic with its outlook can be seen as a form of free exercise for the group, but it also seems to establish those religious bases as favored by government support. Choosing beneficiaries might also be seen as a feature of free exercise, but the use of government funds to pay for one's services makes such a selection properly seen as an unacceptable establishment.

When it comes to choices by individuals for their potential beneficiaries, both free exercise and nonestablishment support the genuine freedom of no pressure to pick a nonreligious or a religious institution. Subtleties about this are presented when the institutions provide different services and some may be recommended over others by government officials.

Concerning the degree of government involvement, should it matter if the funds it provides are coming directly or indirectly to the service providers? That this has made a difference in some actual cases does not tell us how much it should really count. A more subtle concern is whether it matters if the government itself provides a similar service, as is obviously the situation with public schools. We have a potential free exercise argument that people should be able to choose to receive a service from a religious organization if their religious connections and convictions point them toward that. This is one of those instances in which we need to distinguish a plausible constitutional argument from a nonconstitutional consideration. If the government provides a secular service itself, it has no constitutional duty to finance similar religious providers. However, this free exercise consideration can bear on whether such financing is desirable and on whether it may violate the Establishment Clause. A subtle nuance on this issue concerns the government's previous position. If, at one stage, some form of assistance to people, such as hospitals, was left to private organizations, mainly religious ones, and the government then commenced to directly provide the services for little or no cost, this could hurt the financial stature of the private suppliers. This historical development could strengthen the free exercise concerns supporting some financial support for the private institutions.

With these observations, we shall turn to some of the leading cases and how they have dealt with these issues. The Supreme Court's very first Establishment Clause case involved a challenge to Congress's funding the building of a hospital to be operated by an order of Roman Catholic sisters. In *Bradfield v. Roberts* the Court in 1899 rejected the establishment objection on the basis that the corporation had a "nonsectarian public purpose."[28] In that case the Court gave no indication that the hospital should be operated in a way that did not emphasize its religious character, something quite unlikely for Catholic nuns. Of course, displaying a religious character is quite different from actually replacing ordinary medical techniques with distinctive religious practices.

Under many federal and state laws, religious organizations have had to create secular arms to receive public assistance. For example, nonprofit subsidiaries of Catholic Charities U.S.A. have received a large amount of federal money. As one writer has explained, their programs generally do not proselytize, engage in worship, provide religious education, or discriminate in whom they serve and hire,[29] but we have nothing like a full understanding of how they do or do not convey a Catholic identity. Should the requirement of forming a secular arm be generally adopted by legislators making available public money? And should such a requirement be seen as constitutionally necessary? These are hard questions, at least for some services. I qualify the point in this way because when it comes to parochial education, it is difficult to conceive of a secular subbranch running the school.

Perhaps the Court's most important case about the boundaries of what legislation should be treated as invalid on its face or assessed in terms of how it is actually administered was *Bowen v. Kendrick*, decided in 1988.[30] What was involved was a federal Adolescent Family Act offering aid to private organizations for services promoting self-discipline for matters involving premarital adolescent sexual relations and pregnancy. What this act provided actually fell somewhat between school teaching and ordinary services such as hospital care and food for the poor. Under the act, grants could not go to programs providing abortions or counseling regarding them. One funded activity was "educational services relating to family life and problems associated with adolescent premarital sexual relations."[31] Those who challenged the grants not only argued that they created a potential for religious instruction, they offered substantial evidence that that was taking place. The Justices were sharply divided. For the four dissenters, Justice Blackmun urged that religious teachings, as shown by actual examples, were likely to be intertwined with advice about sexuality and pregnancy. He claimed that the result should not depend on whether the organization is pervasively sectarian; the law giving financial support for counseling adolescents about this highly sensitive subject with religious significance should be declared invalid.[32] In an opinion by Chief Justice Rehnquist, the majority disagreed. Since nonreligious organizers were eligible and various approaches to such things as teenager self-discipline were not "inherently" religious, although they coincided with certain religious views, the act was valid on its face.[33] Concurring, Justice

O'Connor acknowledged that, given what this statute was designed to do, it was much more difficult to preclude religious doctrine than with projects like helping the poor or sick, but nevertheless she discerned no constitutional violation.[34]

In 1996, under President Clinton, Congress adopted what was called "Charitable Choice" legislations, aimed to allow religious organizations greater participation in federally funded social service programs.[35] Without setting up secular subsidiaries, religious organizations could receive funding on the same basis as nonreligious ones, so long as they did not use the funds for worship or religious education and did not discriminate against recipients because of their religion or their refusal to participate in religious practices. Such legislation, although neutral on its face, raised the question whether, in its application by federal and state officials, some religious organizations were likely to be inappropriately favored and whether the limits set on what those organizations could do would be enforceable without too much government interference.

An interesting case under the Charitable Choice Act involved Wisconsin's funding of an alcohol and drug addiction treatment program called Faith Works.[36] This residential treatment center characterized itself as a "faith-based program," aiming "to develop a community of believers that would foster religious honesty; first with God, second with oneself, and third with the body of Christ."[37] At mandatory meetings participants were not required but encouraged to discuss their faith. A commitment to Christian beliefs figured as a hiring consideration, and staff members were required to grow in their faith by engaging in religious practices.[38] Characterizing Faith Works as pervasively sectarian, the district court judge initially ruled that it could not receive direct funding because that violated the Establishment Clause. However, Judge Crabb reached the opposite conclusion about a kind of indirect funding. The state's Department of Corrections had contracted with Faith Works to pay for the treatment of offenders on parole and probation who had chosen this rehabilitation program over spending time in jail and over other rehabilitation providers. That independent private choices made the funding acceptable was key. The fact that the Faith Works program for parolees was significantly longer than the alternatives and was often recommended by agents of the Department did not undermine the independence of choice. The Seventh Circuit, in an opinion by Judge Posner, sustained this funding scheme on the basis of free choices by the offenders and the absence of evidence that the corrections agents were influenced by their own religious preferences.

In respect to what is an appropriate constitutional position about these matters and what is actually just, we can identify two fundamental competing positions. One is that the right approach is neutrality;[39] as long as they are providing the services, religious organizations, whether or not pervasively sectarian, should be treated like nonreligious ones and should not have to compromise their religious identity. In a 2000 case we shall consider when we return to aid to schools, three other Justices joined a plurality opinion of Justice Thomas that treated neutrality as sufficient to withstand an Establishment Clause challenge and regarded that as satisfied even if the vast majority of actual beneficiaries were religious schools.[40] Although it then appeared fairly likely that, given the composition of the Court, that position might soon be embraced by a majority, that has not yet happened.

The opposing position is separationist. The Establishment Clause should preclude the government from promoting religious activities.[41] Not only should government funding refrain from directly supporting religious practices, it should not be supporting other activities in a manner that allows the religious organizations to shift their own funds to their religious purposes. Another concern is that, whatever a statute says, officials are likely to apply it in a way that favors dominant religious groups over those of disfavored minorities such as U.S. Muslims.

In contrast to the older notion that religious groups must typically be excluded from aid, some people now support the proposition that their being treated equally might well be seen not only as permitted but as a constitutional requirement. An essay by Nelson Tebbe treats this issue in detail, urging that the balance of considerations depends heavily on context and that legislators financing public services should have broad authority, subject to certain limits, to decide whether or not to include religious organizations.[42] Legislators would then do well to carefully consider the specific factors and values involved.

Of course, between the most straightforward neutrality and separationist outlooks as possible constitutional standards, we can perceive numerous intermediate positions that aim to somehow accommodate the multiple values of beneficial public services, free exercise, equality, and nonestablishment. These positions can figure both in appropriate constitutional requirements and wise choices within a permissible range.

On some questions, a present consensus exists, based partly on Supreme Court decisions. When receiving federal funding for programs, religious organizations should not discriminate on the basis of religion in admitting applicants. The government should not select providers simply because they are religious, and it should not directly fund core religious activities. Potential recipients should be able to choose an alternative secular provider. *If* religious groups do set up separate corporations to provide services, as some federal and state regulations require, and these corporations do not significantly promote the religion, they should not be treated less favorably than other groups.

Three major issues concern the government's implication in religious activity, pressure on protected beneficiaries, and employment discrimination. As Ira C. Lupu and Robert Tuttle emphasize for all the issues, great differences in the kind of programs can matter.[43] Suppose, in a town with many Brazilian families, the city, believing it would be desirable for more citizens to understand the Portuguese language, offers to fund such education. The only entity that steps forward to provide that is an evangelical church that plans to begin its sessions with a prayer and to include as a source of language the Portuguese translation of the Bible. Since no nonreligious organization has offered a program, one might conclude that any religious elements are not attributable to the city, and that no citizen is under any pressure to participate. By contrast, if what is involved in a rehabilitation alterative to jail, the pressure to participate is huge. Even if secular alternates are available, if the program run by a religious organization has strong religious components and also has features that make it more effective in reformation objectives and lead government officials to recommend it, concluding that the government is really not involved in the religious components is much harder.

When one asks about the effect of a program on the participants, it could be relevant whether they are under legal or factual compulsion, whether they had a choice that included nonreligious providers, whether they are required by the religious organization to participate in religious activities, and whether the program has transformative goals.[44] If a program has some religious components, it can matter whether they are separable from secular ones. A soup kitchen may provide food for those in need and, after meals are over, invite those who wish to stay to participate in a religious service. This clearly separates the religious aim from the secular benefits, and it constitutes little or no pressure on beneficiaries to involve themselves in religious

exercises. A strong counterexample is when the very objective of a drug rehabilitation program is to transform those who have violated the law into committed Christians whose religious convictions will lead them to refrain from
drug use.

Although a plurality opinion of the Supreme Court rejected using the test
of whether aided organizations are "pervasively sectarian" for violations of
the Establishment Clause,[45] that remains a crucial standard in some states.[46]
It has been criticized as both too vague and overly simple. A suggested more
detailed breakdown has been between "faith-saturated" providers for which
religious content is extensive and mandatory, "faith-centered" providers
whose religious messages are central but allow participants to opt out, "faith-
related" providers whose programs contain no explicit religious messages but
who have religious symbols and opportunities for religious dialogue, and
"faith-background" providers who have historical religious ties, but whose
program has no explicit religious aspects.[47] This more explicit categorization
is somewhat simpler to apply than "pervasively sectarian," but it also has
some uncertain edges; and it may be hard for courts to conclude in various
cases just what does step over the line in terms of the Establishment Clause.
As indicated in prior paragraphs, it may make a difference how great is the
pressure on people to become involved.

Yet another question concerns employment discrimination. Put very generally, we could see religious organizations hiring their own members or those
with similar beliefs as itself a form of religious exercise or, more importantly,
as promoting the religious exercise in which the organization is engaged. On
the other hand, discrimination in hiring when government funding is used
can be regarded as an unacceptable establishment of religion. If the activity
itself is the provision of a valuable secular service, without religious content,
it makes sense to see religious discrimination in hiring for relevant positions as unacceptable. If all those involved, however, are actually conveying
a religious message, using religion as a criterion for employment is almost
unavoidable. The reality can cut both ways. It can obviously support such discrimination in these contexts. But it can also provide an extra reason for the
government not to fund organizations that plan to provide secular services
with a strong religious content. If the government is the direct and primary
source of funding for a program, religious discrimination by an organization
in its employment should probably be regarded as unconstitutional, just as it
would be for the government itself.

### Religious Schools: Are They Special?

Having looked at government aid to religious institutions that are providing various kinds of services, we now return to aid to parochial education, which, as already suggested, has provoked the most controversy and has led to a number of important Supreme Court cases casting more general approaches to coverage of the Establishment Clause. Looking again at some of these decisions, and concentrating on the one that sustained a voucher program in Cleveland, we will ask what kind of approach or approaches seem constitutionally sound and what considerations legislators should take into account.

Initially we can begin with a simple question: should aid to religious schools be perceived differently from aid to other religiously motivated endeavors providing public services and, if so, why? The most basic point is that if the whole purpose of what you are doing is teaching students, it can become much harder to separate what you are teaching them about ordinary subjects from conveying your religious perspective. On this, one needs to be careful not to put things too generally. If one thinks of universities that are Catholic, such as Fordham and Notre Dame, many subjects will be taught without reference to religious outlooks, and non-Catholic students can go through four years with relatively little compelled exposure to Catholic perspectives. This is also true of many universities with different religious connections. When it comes to elementary and high schools, huge differences exist in just how far they convey their religious perspectives and whether virtually all their teachers share those perspectives.[48]

A concern that turns out to be related in a significant way is the range of particular religious connections. When aid to parochial schools in the United States was most controversial, the vast majority of private schools were Roman Catholic, with many teachers and administrators being nuns or priests. The most obvious concern here was that aid formulated in general terms would in fact mainly assist Roman Catholic schools. And when priests and nuns were involved, it seemed much more likely that religious messages would be conveyed by them than by ordinary teachers. Although most Catholics in this country had a different view, official Roman Catholic doctrine was then very opposed to liberal democratic pluralism. That changed significantly in the 1960s, and the division between Roman Catholics and other Christian groups, and between them and political supporters of liberal pluralism, has sharply diminished. So also has the number of priests and nuns in the United States.[49] That has almost certainly reduced the extent to which most of the schools concentrate on a particular religious message.[50]

Another change has involved the development of other private schools. One sharp cause of this was public school desegregation in the South after *Brown v. Board of Education*, which led there to a growth of private schools. In many other parts of the country, concerns about the quality of public schools[51] has led to more private schools. Despite these changes, it is still true that a religious school will convey a religious message in a more direct and unavoidable form that many hospitals or food services run by religious organizations.

As Part One explains about the Supreme Court's constitutional approaches, its view about aid to religious schools was initially strongly separationist. In *Everson vs. Board of Education*,[52] four Justices thought that the state could not provide free bus transportation for children going to these schools, and the majority opinion indicated that this was at the edge of what was acceptable. In subsequent cases it made a great difference whether the assistance, such as the loan of secular textbooks, did not go directly to the schools and whether aid would be genuinely limited to nonreligious aspects of the schools' education. In the 1983 case of *Mueller v. Allen*[53] the court accepted allowing parents paying a Minnesota income tax to deduct from their income any tuition payments to private schools, although roughly 95 percent of students attending private schools were going to sectarian ones. After *Mueller*, the Court's majority remained rather strict in 1985 about having public school teachers paid by their states to provide instruction within the premises of religious schools. For Grand Rapids, Michigan, this was said by Justice Brennan's majority opinion to be creating a danger that these teachers would conform to the religious environment in their instruction.[54] New York had a system to monitor the teaching to prevent religious instruction, but this was considered an excessive entanglement of church and state.[55] As explained in Part One, Justice Powell's swing vote explained why these fairly restrictive decisions followed *Mueller v. Allen*.

In 2000 *Mitchell v. Helms*,[56] the Court moved a bit further toward permissible aid in a way that might have foreseen a genuinely radical change, one that may still happen but has not yet been embraced explicitly by a majority of the Court. Six Justices approved the use of federal funds to lend educational materials and equipment directly to private schools. Justice Thomas, writing for himself and three other Justices, emphasized "neutrality."[57] So long as aid is offered to a broad range of groups regardless of religious affiliation, it is acceptable even if the main beneficiaries are religious organizations. If these organizations actually divert the aid for religious purposes, that subsequent use of the aid cannot be attributed to the government. Although the case itself involved instructional materials, nothing in the Thomas opinion suggests a different approach to other forms of financial assistance. The two concurring Justices, O'Connor and Breyer, rejected Thomas's broad theory.[58] Were the Thomas approach adopted, it is hard to think of situations in which aid to schools would be treated differently from aid to other institutions providing public services.

Although this is tangential, it is worth noting that Justice Thomas, a Roman Catholic along with two others who joined his opinion, characterized the focus in earlier cases on whether schools are "pervasively sectarian" as "not only unnecessary but offensive," calling for an inappropriate "trolling through … [an] institution's religious beliefs."[59] The exclusion of such schools from aid was "born of bigotry, [and] should be buried now."[60] I have already indicated that it is indeed hard to say just what amounts to "pervasively sectarian," and the call for a less slippery approach makes sense. The "born of bigotry" comment contains a partial truth, but is also misleading. For much of the nineteenth and twentieth centuries, many citizens, including those opposed to aid to religious schools, did have negative attitudes toward Roman Catholicism. To a significant extent, these were based on prejudicial attitudes toward groups of immigrants that lacked any moral justification. But the resistance to aid to Catholic schools was at least partly grounded in that denomination's rejection of ideals of literal democracy[61] and of a political and legal approach that did not afford special status to its true religion.[62] It is a bit unfair to simply cast this negative attitude toward a group with those premises as "bigotry," in the sense that would be fully appropriate for similar attitudes based simply on race or national origin.

A key decision in the march toward permissiveness was *Zelman v. Simmons-Harris*,[63] decided in 2002. The circumstances of the case, and the 5–4 split among the Justices, highlighted some of the most troubling questions about school aid and the difficulties of finding a tenable approach to relevant Establishment Clause decisions. As noted in Part One, Cleveland's voucher program aided low-income families who were sending children to private schools. In 1999–2000, 82 percent of the participating schools were religious and these were attended by 96 percent of the students whose parents were reimbursed.

Writing the majority opinion, Chief Justice Rehnquist emphasized that aid went to the parents directly and only indirectly to the schools and that, given neutral criteria, it was irrelevant that religious schools would receive most of the aid.[64]

Justice Souter wrote for himself and the other three dissenters. He urged that extensive public funding for religious education was unconstitutional. He disagreed about whether the program was really neutral. Since religious schools operated on lower budgets and charged less tuition than other private schools, they were bound to enroll a higher proportion of participating students,[65] and low-income parents typically lacked a genuine choice about how to spend their voucher money, since the added charges at the nonreligious private schools were much higher. In this respect it was notable that two-thirds of the benefitting parents did not embrace the religion of the schools that their children attended.[66] Souter also expressed concern about how public funding would bring about more state control, as evidenced here by a prohibition of a school receiving vouchers if it discriminated based on religious grounds or taught hatred of any religious group. That schools receiving public money should not be teaching "hatred" of any religion seems at one level to be perfectly reasonable, but what counts as "hatred"? A Christian school might teach that modern Jews are somehow to be blamed for the death of Jesus, and centuries ago many Protestants saw the Pope as the Antichrist. Would the teaching of these ideas constitute hatred of another group?

In another dissenting opinion, Justice Breyer suggested that the somewhat vague "hatred" standard could impinge on the expression of religious beliefs and could generate controversial administrative decisions.[67] Justice Breyer also emphasized how substantial funding of this kind differed from what was previously upheld. This supported the core funding of teaching religious truths to young children[68] and was bound to generate divisions among religious denominations.[69]

When we reflect on various objections to the Cleveland program, we can see not only how difficult it is to say which should matter in principle but also how troubling it is to conclude how much they should count respectively for legislative choices and judicial assessments. Here are six possible objections to programs like Cleveland's: (1) the aid is substantial and not really limited to secular aspects of education; (2) the benefits go dominantly to religious institutions; (3) the regulation of religious endeavors is disturbing; (4) divisive conflict is likely to result; (5) the approach is not really "neutral"; (6) the choice for parents is not adequately free between secular and religious alternatives.

Let me start with potential divisiveness. This is obviously a concern that legislators should take into account. As far as courts are concerned, the approaches to general subjects, such as hospitals versus schools, might appropriately be affected by what has or what has not proved divisive over time, but constitutional conclusions should not depend on conflicts that have been or may be created in respect to a particular program. This is both too hard to estimate in isolation, and if it counted heavily, it would encourage opponents of aid to generate extreme opposition in their speeches and demonstrations, hardly an activity to be encouraged.

The regulation of religious endeavors presents a genuine problem. When one thinks of religious hospitals, the imposition of standard medical requirements is an appropriate condition of public funding (and could indeed be appropriate apart from funding) that does not interfere with the religious aspects of most religious hospitals. But when it comes to exactly what religious schools cannot teach, or what their hiring and admissions policies need to be, we can see more of a delving into their religious endeavors. Of course, the government rightly does not want to fund one religious institution's putting down of contrary religions, but regulations to that effect can rightly be seen as an interference with free exercise and free speech.

With schools any general aid is bound directly or indirectly to assist religious aspects of their education as well as secular ones. This of course is also true for general aid to any religious institutions that are conveying religious messages, but for many religious schools the religious content is more central than for hospitals and food services, and it is harder to distinguish from other elements of what they do. The more substantial the aid is, the greater is likely to be the assistance to the religious aspects of education. In this respect, although it has mattered in a number of cases whether aid had been direct or indirect, practically that is an artificial distinction for many forms of aid, including vouchers. The reason is this. If a voucher goes to the parents, because they are both short on resources and are sending their children to private schools, they must then pay the tuition to the schools. If instead the schools were paid directly as a substitute for much of tuition from low-income parents who are sending their children there, the end result would be the same. The schools would receive the amount of the vouchers, and that would still depend on parents deciding to send their children to those schools.

The fact that aid goes dominantly to religious schools cannot matter constitutionally in a particular instance if the authorization is cast neutrally. One might believe that the overall fact that most private schools, as contrasted with private universities,[70] are religious should make a difference for how schools are treated, since it ties both to how much aid will go to religion and how wide, realistically, is the choice of parents.

There were two special features of the Ohio program in Cleveland that complicated this concern. Both are related to the fact that most of the public schools in the city were deficient enough so that parents had a substantial incentive to consider private schools. We can easily imagine a small community with a few similar public schools, and only one private school which is run by a religious institution. If the authorizing law is cast neutrally, is its operation in that community really "neutral" if the only vouchers, ones many parents will seek, will go to the religious school? Matters were obviously more complicated in Cleveland. As the Court's majority emphasized, there was special funding for some public schools to provide education that would help those at a disadvantage.[71] And some nonreligious private schools did benefit to a degree. But the program was formulated so that it would mostly operate for private schools that expended less and had lower tuition. That was obviously going to provide much more help for most religious schools as compared with most nonreligious ones. Further, the fact that two-thirds of the benefitting students were attending religious schools that were not attached to a religion of their own cast doubt on exactly how extensive was their freedom of choice. Concerns like this should definitely matter to a legislature setting up a program and can provide a strong Establishment Clause argument that a program is not acceptable if it will benefit religious providers with a near exclusion of nonreligious ones. Here the concern about "neutrality" ties closely to whether the degree of "freedom of choice" is sufficient.

To summarize, many but not all the concerns about aid to schools involve tensions between the free exercise and nonestablishment values. Their relative force varies in some respects with that relevant for other services. Even though that might not lead to explicitly different constitutional standards depending on the public service being provided, they may well bear on what is a wise policy. For that, of course, other values are also important. If public hospitals cannot provide all needed services or public schools are seriously inadequate, that is a powerful reason to provide funding for private institutions, including religious ones.

It is extraordinarily difficult to see what clear constitutional standards may be called for. If the criteria are simple and straightforward, such as a "formal neutrality is all that is needed," or "no one aid can be given that directly or indirectly may help religious institutions," their applications may accept some inappropriate endeavors and/or condemn ones that are needed. A more flexible approach that takes into account and weighs the significance of multiple factors may lead to uncertainty about what is actually all right and call for judicial assessments that can be difficult or even impossible. Those who are critical of how the Supreme Court has handled some of the relevant cases need at least to recognize just how difficult it is here to have clear, workable standards that best capture the constitutional values. The absence of clear, workable general constitutional standards itself strongly supports leaving a good bit up to legislative choice.[72]

## State Variations and the Standing Problem

Thus far I have largely omitted a major a factor in all this, namely that most states have explicitly stricter constitutional restrictions on this subject than does the federal government. I shall briefly summarize this reality and how what states do can relate here to federal constitutional determinations. The core question in that respect is whether the application of state restrictions should be seen as violating, or possibly even required by, the federal constitution. As noted earlier, in the late nineteenth century most states adopted what have been referred to as "Blaine" amendments, based on the name of the sponsor in Congress who unsuccessfully sought to achieve a federal constitutional amendment prohibiting the use of public money for religious uses.[73] The state clauses are formulated somewhat differently from each other, but their goal is to forbid the use of public money for sectarian education.

Thirty-seven of our fifty states now have such provisions. These raise the central question whether they fall within the range of permissible choices under the federal constitution or violate it, sometimes or always. The obvious objection is that if a state favors nonreligious over religious practice, that impairs free exercise and may constitute a forbidden establishment of non-religion. This is one of those instances in which, at least in one respect, free exercise and nonestablishment arguments can line up on the same side. It should be noted that if judges saw a state conferral of benefits only upon nonreligious educational institutions as invalid, they might either extend the benefits to religious groups or strike down the law conferring the benefits. The latter approach would leave it up to a state legislature to decide whether to reenact the law including religious schools or simply to withhold financial support from all private schools.

The first time the U.S. Supreme Court engaged with a state restriction of this kind was in the 2004 case of *Locke v. Davey*.[74] The state of Washington gave two-year scholarships to students attending college, but these were unavailable for those pursuing a "degree in theology," understood as "devotional ... or designed to induce religious faith."[75] Seven Justices voted to sustain the exclusion, primarily on the basis that it effectively concerned ministerial education, and the state did not have a responsibility to pay for the education of prospective ministers. Chief Justice Rehnquist's opinion did not really resolve whether a more general disfavoring of education by religiously connected institutions would be acceptable. He did refer to "the play in the joints"[76] of the religion clauses, meaning that they do not always generate definite constitutional rules but leave a range of choice up to individual states. Rehnquist dismissed a free speech claim on the ground that, in contrast to the student newspaper denied funding by a university, a scholarship program is not a forum for speech. This analysis was a bit superficial. If the government granted scholarships to those attending classes with controversial messages that the government approved, that would raise genuine free speech concerns. For example, it would not be appropriate to give financial assistance to the student attending courses in Middle Eastern politics only if those courses were sympathetic to Israel and were critical of Palestinian claims for equal treatment. The *Locke* court rejected the claim that the amendment here was invalid because Blaine amendments were based on a malign anti-Catholic purpose. It said this was not a Blaine amendment, disregarding the fact that its actual language was closely similar. On a more general point, it is dubious whether the actual motivations behind a provision enacted more than a century ago should determine its present constitutional status.

Within the states with Blaine amendments, courts have adopted different approaches. Some have taken the provisions in a straightforward way and enforced them;[77] others have construed the language to permit forms of aid, such as grants to parents sending their children to religious schools.[78] We do not yet know whether in the future the U.S Supreme Court will take a decisive and clear approach, such as declaring all such provisions invalid, or will embrace a more nuanced "play in the joints" outlook that will allow states some range to determine the extent of granting aid for nonreligious education and denying it for religious education. A case which the Supreme Court is hearing in the 2016 term and a 2011 decision of the Second Circuit Court of Appeals raise interesting questions in this respect. In *Trinity Lutheran Chruch of Columbia v. Pawley,* the Eighth Circuit Court of Appeals rejected a challenge to an application of the Missouri constitution that bars public money going to churches.[79] In the specific circumstance, all that the church sought was a grant to replace the playground surface of its Learning Center in a way that would be good for children attending the school. This was a situation in which clearly the state could have chosen to treat what was essentially a claim for aid to a religious school regarding a nonreligious activity equally with grants to nonreligious schools. The majority on the Court of Appeals panel concluded that under existing federal constitutional doctrine, Missouri could decline to provide the aid; Judge Gruender in dissent urged that *Locke* required a balancing of interests, and in this situation the disfavoring of religion should be seen as a Free Exercise violation.[80]

In terms of constitutional analysis, I believe the balancing of considerations is the appropriate approach. Since money provided directly to churches or other religious institutions for nonreligious expenses will allow them to use more of their own money for directly religious purposes, my own sense is that states should be left free to decide how to treat these situations; but this is a close, debatable question, which the Supreme Court now faces.

The Second Circuit decision, *Bronx Household of Faith v. Board of Education of the City of New York,*[81] involved the use of public school facilities, not financial aid. New York City's Department of Education allowed use of school facilities by outside groups after school hours, but did not permit worship services. The majority sustained this as a permissible avoidance of an Establishment Clause concern; Judge Walker in dissent regarded it as unacceptable viewpoint discrimination. This is an instance in which I believe the government definitely should be allowed in principle to treat religious worship gatherings the same as other meetings if it sets no limits on what is conveyed in the other gatherings. And it is unwise, and perhaps even unconstitutional, if it precludes worship without a special reason. However, given that students are often aware what is taking place in public school facilities after school, and given that worship services occur on a regular basis, the exclusion of worship so that students will not somehow assume the school is implicitly involved with a particular religion strikes me as a justifying constitutional reason for the line drawn in New York. Whether it is, on balance, warranted in light of actual conditions seems much more uncertain. A peripheral reason not to have such a rule is that it requires drawing a hard line of how much prayer and hymn singing, etc., would make a meeting a "worship service."

A somewhat different kind of case concerning a rejected claim for equal treatment involved a state's allowing pharmacies to decline to provide drugs for various reasons, but not based on religious objections or other concerns of conscience. The Supreme Court declined review, but this triggered a strong objection by Justice Alito, joined by two colleagues.[82] My own sense is that the preferable approach is for courts in these various kinds of situations regarding state standards to examine carefully free exercise and nonestablishment values to decide how much flexibility to leave to states to determine whether treating religious education or other practices differently is acceptable and sensible.

A sharply different question about the relation of federal constitutional decisions and state power is raised by the Supreme Court's development of limitations on standing. The consequence is that when state legislatures decide what to do or refrain from doing, they need to be aware that they should see themselves as subject to genuine limits of the federal constitution that federal courts will not enforce.

I shall not explore the standing issues in depth, but essentially one can challenge a tax funded government program only if he has a special interest at stake. Although the ability to bring Establishment Clause challenges has been treated historically as somewhat broader than other kinds of objections by taxpayers to uses of official funds, in recent years, as explained in detail by Laurence H. Winer and Nina J. Crimm,[83] the Supreme Court has become more restrictive of standing in this domain. In 2011, it ruled in *Arizona Christian School Tuition Organization v. Winn*[84] that a taxpayer lacked standing to challenge a state program that gave taxpayers an actual credit up to $500 if they contributed to organizations providing school scholarships, most of which went to parochial schools. Since this was a straightforward credit, not a deduction from income, the end result was that a donation of $500 would be completely reimbursed; and the government was indirectly paying the $500 to the benefitting schools.

If one focuses directly on the constitutional issue, how far should various forms of tax benefits that clearly have an indirect effect that is not significantly different from direct financial aid be viewed as similar or dissimilar for constitutional purposes? My own sense is that if the effect of the aid really does not vary, the two forms should be treated the same way in terms of constitutionality. But the key consequence of a decision like *Winn* is that federal courts will not resolve this constitutional issue. That means that legislators within states need not only determine whether a proposed law fits with their own Blaine amendment, if they have one, but also whether it complies with the federal constitution. And state courts may take a different approach to standing to challenge state laws than the Supreme Court took in *Winn*. The "no standing" approach thus leaves states substantial flexibility in determining both constitutional acceptability and wise choices.[85] That represents a strong illustration of a basic theme of the book that both the constitutional resolutions and a wise assessment of the competing values of free exercise and nonestablishment are often not settled by dominant Supreme Court resolutions.

## CHAPTER 4

# Exemptions and Other Favored Treatment

## General Observations

Turning from circumstances in which the issue is either whether the government should refrain from engaging in religious practices or effectively assist the conveying of religious messages by organizations providing valuable services, this chapter addresses whether the state should sometimes afford special favor because of someone's religious convictions about what he or she should do. The most straightforward context for this is when the law generally requires behavior that some people believe it would be fundamentally wrong to perform; for example, should an exemption from the draft law be given for religious pacifists? Obviously such exemptions are in part a concession to the religious exercise of the objectors, but, especially if they do not include nonreligious objections in conscience, they can also be seen as a form of favoring religion at odds with nonestablishment values. The force of these competing values can vary considerably depending on just what form of special treatment is involved. Because I have a recently published book on exemptions,[1] I shall not delve into extensive detail, but this chapter, concentrating on conflicts of values, will provide an account of fundamental issues, some of which are now highly controversial, and consider what may be appropriate resolutions.

It is important to be aware that other forms of government action can involve similar values and raise similar concerns, though they are not in the form of "exemptions" as ordinarily understood. The head of a government legal office may allow one of her lawyers who objects to capital punishment not to work on those cases. That lawyer receives the same benefit as what a formal exemption would provide, but it rests on his boss's discretion. In some circumstances provisions may explicitly define the duties of others without covering religious figures. For example, various kinds of counselors must disclose certain forms of revealed information, but clerics may not be required to disclose what has been confessed to them, whether in formal confessions or more broadly. This can be seen as a kind of exemption from normal requirements though provided differently. Finally, a state or locality may have general laws, such as that most businesses may not open on Sunday, that promote freedom from what businesses might require of workers who worship on that day. Such a law, as Chapter 1 explains, can also definitely work to the disadvantage of those, such as Orthodox Jews, with religious convictions that they must not work on Saturday. In what follows, I shall mainly concentrate on exemptions themselves, but it is crucial to understand that the key values at stake can also reach other legal forms. Before looking at particular instances of exemptions, I set out some general facts about their sources and the variety of those in play.

What are the roles of the federal and state constitutions? An exemption may be constitutionally required. Notably, the Supreme Court recently held that the hiring of "clerics," including some schoolteachers, must be free from the application of a nondiscrimination law.[2] For about three decades the Supreme Court set out a free exercise test that supported many more exemptions, but this was sharply cut back in 1990 by *Employment Division v. Smith*, which held that if a law is generally cast, a religious person has no constitutional claim to be excused.[3] Some states have not curbed the coverage of their own constitutions in this way; within those, claims relying on constitutions may still succeed more broadly.

The main sources of exemption claims in modern times are statutes. Laws may provide specifically for particular exemptions or may be cast generally. Congress, after *Employment Division v. Smith*, adopted the Religious Freedom Restoration Act (RFRA),[4] which adopted language that essentially replicated that of the abandoned constitutional standard. A person has a right to an exemption if a law imposes a "substantial burden" and the government lacks a "compelling interest" that cannot be served by "less restrictive means." Many states have similar provisions.[5] The most common exemptions issue facing legislators concerns whether a statutory duty should be imposed on everyone or excuse some who would otherwise be covered. In a great many circumstances, this is a question of state law, although connections to interstate commerce and federal financial support provide bases for Congress to reach many enterprises such as hospitals and educational institutions located throughout the country.

Congress used this financial basis to adopt an important exemptions law on abortion, one that also illustrates another significant variation.[6] Typically laws excuse people from legally imposed duties, but a statute can require that a private enterprise, such as a hospital, excuse its workers from general duties that it chooses to impose. By requiring others to grant exemptions, the government in a sense is actually extending its own requirements rather than constraining them.

How far do constitutional rights create the need for exemptions and possibly preclude them? The determination by the Supreme Court that a constitutional right exists, such as concerning same-sex marriage, does not directly determine how private enterprises and individuals must treat others. Apart from government officials, who do have a duty not to violate the constitution, a ban on unfavorable treatment depends on antidiscrimination laws, adopted by Congress or state legislatures. Most of these themselves contain specific exemption provisions. Many states and the federal government do not now have laws explicitly barring private discrimination against homosexuals or same-sex married couples.[7] However, more general provisions, such as bars on gender discrimination, may be employed by officials to preclude negative treatment of gay and transgender individuals. This has occurred with the federal government, although claimed coverage has not yet been judicially sustained.[8] Without specific laws, or ones more broadly cast that can be construed as barring such negative treatment, enterprises and individuals may treat same-sex couples less favorably than others. Politically, the adoption of such a law against this form of discrimination may depend partly on the providing of exemptions.

May exemptions themselves be unconstitutional? Here Establishment Clause values can be in play: an exemption cast in terms of religious convictions may be seen as unacceptably favoring religious people over others. If all that was involved was the balance of religion clause values, the concession to religious exercise of not requiring people to act against their basic convictions would almost always be strong enough to sustain any such exemption.

That conclusion itself does not tell whether a particular exemption should, or must, be extended to analogous nonreligious claims. My position, explained in different contexts that follow, is that limiting exemptions to religious claims is often warranted, that when nonreligious claims are similar in force they should be treated in the same way, and that sometimes a refusal to do this should properly be viewed as a forbidden establishment and/or implicit denial of free exercise and equal protection. Of course, the Establishment Clause does bar favoring some religions over others, so a law may not grant an exemption to people of one religion and deny it to others who belong to an otherwise similar but different religion. Whether it constitutes a genuine constitutional limit, the nonestablishment value *is* a reason not to limit an exemption to religious claimants. That issue arose with pacifists, and Chapter 8 explains more generally when it is or is not appropriate to treat religious and nonreligious claims differently. It is worth noting that the establishment concern may not be totally eliminated by broadening coverage. If the overwhelming percentage of claims are raised by religious people, and the concession is clearly made to accommodate them, the establishment worry can remain in play even if the formal legal right is cast more broadly.

When it comes to constitutional arguments against legally provided exemptions and policy arguments against their creation, the most powerful objections are not nonestablishment values, but concerns about fairness for those who may be treated less favorably. Insofar as an exemption allows individuals and private enterprises not to provide services of various kinds, that may seem unfair practically and symbolically to those who receive less than equal treatment. This can even rise to a claim that a government concession would constitute a denial of equal protection,[9] an argument now offered against exemptions in respect to equal treatment of same-sex married couples. That argument has its greatest force if the breadth of a granted or proposed exemption exceeds that granted by other antidiscrimination provisions.

It is worth pausing here over a complexity in present controversies and terminology that bears on a number of exemptions issues covered in this chapter. Should a claim for an exemption be substantially weaker, or even unconstitutional, if it is essentially involves "complicity" in the behavior of others, not direct performance of acts that objectors take to be immoral. Two notable examples are providing insurance for contraceptives and refusing social services to same-sex married couples. Douglas NeJaime and Reva

Siegel offer arguments that such objections should often be refused because they involve unfairness to the dignity of others and promote political dissension.[10] Rather than trying to define exactly what counts as complicity, I shall focus briefly on three crucial elements and how they should figure in evaluations. The first is the effect on others. As different sections of this chapter explain, some exemptions have a much more direct effect on outsiders than do others. The second element is whether the refusal to be involved in some way concerns what one takes as the immoral behavior of others. Given that kinds of involvement can vary in degrees, the third element concerns how direct is the participation required. The refusal to provide assistance for an abortion is a much more direct participation than refusing even to give formal notice that a business is opposed to allowing one's insurance to cover certain contraceptives.

It is sometimes suggested that, historically, exemptions did not reach the kinds of actions by private individuals and organizations that are now most controversial. What this mainly fails to take into account is that for most of the history of our country, religious individuals and organizations, and other private entities, were not bound by antidiscrimination laws. They could favor their own members and disfavor others in all sorts of respects. It is the growth of antidiscrimination statutes that makes an exemption necessary for them to now act similarly.

Regarding harm to others, that has been a crucial issue about modern exemption questions, such as those involving same-sex marriage. Without going into great detail, I want to make my own position clear. Whether others will suffer, and the degree to which they will suffer, is definitely relevant to whether an exemption from a duty is warranted and what its scope should be. Harms to others are also relevant to the legal status of claimed exemptions under statutes and the federal and state constitutions. However, we have no absolute principle that the existence of any such harms should preclude an exemption. As I have already noted, prior to antidiscrimination laws, private individuals and enterprises had wide flexibility to deny benefits to some people that they gave to others. And to take a historical example that continues to the present, the privilege of a priest not to testify about what has been confessed to him *could* result in the conviction of an innocent person. And clearly the common law right of religious bodies to reveal private information and even shun former members who have fallen astray could damage those individuals hugely.

Another possible basis for denying exemptions is that their advocacy generates potential conflict, but as Douglas Laycock emphasizes, since religious controversies have often produced such conflict, and that conflict itself is an element of freedom of expression, it should not be taken as a primary basis to bar exemptions.[11]

In summary, the elements that are tied in one way or another to arguments that "complicity" complaints should be treated negatively do figure in what exemptions should be seen as constitutional and which of these seem wise. But whether what is involved is best seen as only "complicity" should not itself be decisive.

For many possible exemptions, certain key competing considerations are in play. Two are the autonomy of people, whether for religious or other reasons, to do what they believe is fundamentally right, and the concern about equality. The "equality" concern is especially powerful if negative treatment is given to a person not because of behavior, but based on fundamental characteristics, such as race, gender, or age, that a person has no capacity to control.

When legislators and private citizens reflect on various competing considerations, it is crucial that they afford genuine concern for others. That concern needs to include a recognition that within our society, and perhaps any healthy liberal democracy, people have radically different views about some moral questions, and that not requiring people to violate their most fundamental convictions is one important value.

A troubling concern about whether to grant an exemption and, if so, over what range, concerns the administrability of possible standards. The law needs standards that can be applied, even if those depart from what one would see as perfect outcomes in principle. Administrability can concern both assessing the genuineness of claimed convictions and the drawing of lines in practice. Illustrations of the latter point are whether, as I suggest, limiting a same-sex marriage exemption to "direct participation" in weddings is workable and whether, as the federal statute provides, one can determine what counts as "assisting" the performance of an abortion.

When one thinks carefully about individual instances, one can see some exemptions as justified and others as misguided. This issue, of course, involves not only whether *any* exemption should be provided, but what its scope should be. One could well see a limited exemption as justified but any broad extension as misguided. In various senses, one can perceive an exemption as not only justified but actually "necessary." The most obvious sense is that it is constitutionally required, according to what either the U.S. Supreme Court or a highest state court has actually decided or in terms of what one believes is the appropriate constitutional standard. A different notion of "necessary" is that given the values at stake, it would be clearly indefensible for a legislature not to provide an exemption even if the constitution leaves it that choice. A third sense of "necessary" concerns political realities. To take the example of same-sex marriage, if a jurisdiction has enough opposition to that so that no law will be adopted that bars discrimination against such couples *unless* exemptions are granted, those will be politically needed to get passage of the basic equal treatment provision.

For at least some existing and potential exemptions, it is worth mentioning a possible alternative. That is to either eliminate the basic duty or not adopt it in the first place, or to give everyone an alternative. In some circumstances, but definitely not all, one may just allow everyone to do what they want. This may be wise if the general choice, such as growing a beard in prison, does not genuinely threaten important values. If, instead, some form of duty remains important, it may be adequately served by giving all those subject to it a choice between options, such as two years of military service or three years of civilian service.

With these general observations, we shall turn to specific subjects on which they bear, first looking at the deep historical tradition of tax exemptions and pacifist exemptions from the military draft.

## Tax Benefits

Given its historical significance, I shall begin with tax exemptions and other tax benefits connected to religious organizations. Analytically, these fall somewhere between most exemptions and the subject of Chapter 3, financial aid. For a church that does not have to pay property or income taxes that are imposed on other organizations, that is one variety of an exemption, but it does not concern allowing some activity forbidden to others. Rather, its consequence is that the church will be better off financially than it would otherwise be, and the costs of government activities will be somewhat higher for those who do pay taxes. This amounts to an indirect form of financial aid. It is interesting that, given the bar on government money going directly for religious practices, no one really doubts that the ordinary tax benefits are acceptable.

We shall look briefly at three forms of such benefits: exemptions from property taxes, and from income taxes, and the reductions in taxable income given to church donors.

Property taxes are mainly imposed by local branches of government.[12] In the United States, churches, hospitals, and other charitable organizations, including private universities, are typically free from those taxes. These kinds of exemptions originated in the historical practice of not imposing them on churches,[13] an approach that could properly be seen as assisting free exercise but also amounting to a kind of establishment. Of course, within England and a number of our states when the country was founded, particular religions were themselves established in some form, but the tax benefit also existed in other early states and in the federal District of Columbia, which could not establish a religion after the First Amendment was adopted.[14] Although nearly all religious groups provided forms of aid to the disadvantaged, the primary basis for the exemption was to preclude official interference with religious practices and to support the exercise of religion.[15]

Our modern laws reach charities more generally, and one could think that the inclusion of religious bodies is now warranted because they help public welfare; but the most important basis probably remains religious worship and related activities, especially since the exemption does not depend on social services religious bodies are providing. One basic religion clause reason is that officials should not be required to assess the property value of religious organizations, since their doing so would create a serious problem of prejudicial evaluations based on their sympathies with particular groups. A powerful "free exercise" reason for an exemption is that within the center of large cities that have highly valuable property, demanding that churches pay taxes according to the actual worth of their locations could effectively remove many of them from these areas. The present breadth of the exemptions reaching many nonreligious bodies does properly eliminate, or strongly reduce, establishment concerns that religion is being inappropriately favored.

For federal law, a crucial exemption concerns the nonpayment of income taxes. These also can be traced back to practices in colonial America and required by early state constitutions. The key provision of the Internal Revenue Code covers entities organized "for religious, charitable, scientific, testing for public safety, literary, or education purposes,"[16] as well as some others. One basis for the general exemption is that this aids the provision of valuable public services and may help reduce how much the government itself will need to provide them. It also promotes an organizational autonomy from general government control that is valuable in a liberal democracy. It has further been contended in a notable article by Boris J. Bittker and George K. Rahdert[17] that these organizations, or many of them, do not have an ordinary income, since donations end up going to the poor and disadvantaged and not those who run the organizations.

I won't examine the details of these arguments, how far they are sustainable empirically, or what critics have claimed; but it is interesting that, although churches often provide broader services, their main objective is to promote the worship of their own members. This means that the inclusion of religious bodies is still rather special, primarily assisting the free exercise of those who belong. One might see that as in tension with nonestablishment values, but any such concern, as with the property tax exemptions, is largely eliminated by the breadth of coverage.

The basic conclusions are similar when one turns to the rule that, within certain limits, individuals can reduce their calculated income by the amount of donations made to religious bodies and charitable organizations. One might see this as simply a financial benefit for being generous, but it can also benefit the organizations to which the donations are made. Suppose, to simplify, a woman who earns $200,000 a year and is in a 30% tax bracket donates $20,000 to her church. Her tax would be reduced from $60,000 to $54,000. This reality might well have led her to donate a bit more than she would have otherwise.

These various kinds of exceptions from taxes for religious bodies and their donors definitely represent a government assistance to free exercise. Against establishment concerns lie a deep historical tradition, the importance of the government not interfering with religious practice, and the modern extension to charitable organizations generally. One might perceive nonestablishment values as being compromised to a degree but here, in contrast with direct financial assistance, it is inconceivable in the near future that the inclusion of religious bodies will actually be declared as unconstitutional or will seem troubling enough for legislators to eliminate them from their benefits.

I should note here a possible exception to this conclusion, addressed at the end of Chapter 3. That involves concerns about some of the special tax benefits adopted in large part to encourage indirect financial help to parochial schools. A tax credit, for instance, may allow a donation without any financial sacrifice by the donor. Whether this should be treated differently from direct financial aid from the state is dubious.

## Pacifism and the Military Draft

The other kind of special treatment deeply embedded in our history is the exemption of religious pacifists from a military draft. Whether, given modern weapons and international relations, our country will ever again really need to draft individuals is uncertain, but both draft registration and the exemption are still actually part of our law. The exemption now operates if a person signs up for two years in the military and then develops pacifist convictions; he or she has a right to be relieved of service according to the standard set by the statutory provision as interpreted by the Supreme Court.

For the entire history of our country and for centuries in other nations, some people have been pacifists, either believing that it is wrong to ever intentionally kill another human being or do so in military conflict. The Protestant Reformation, which emphasized individual conscience, was partly responsible for the development of these convictions. Not surprisingly, men with such a view have had a strong objection to being drafted for military service. One of the English groups that settled early in the American colonies was the Society of Friends, or Quakers, a pacifist denomination that played a dominant role in Pennsylvania.[18]

At the time of the American Revolution, the Continental Congress assured those whose religious principles forbade the bearing of arms that it intended "no violence to their consciences."[19] And the great majority of early states, which collected the military forces for the American Revolution, provided at least exemptions for pacifists, but often one had to pay a fine or special tax to qualify, a practice to which some pacifist groups objected.[20] Interestingly, James Madison's original proposal for the Bill of Rights included a clause that would have barred the government from compelling religious pacifists to engage in military service.[21] The main reason the clause was not enacted apparently was that most of the Bill of Rights applied only to the federal government, and at that stage of history military conscription was carried out by the states.

Before exploring more detailed issues about pacifist exemptions, let us focus on more general questions about how free exercise and nonestablishment values apply here. Clearly granting an exemption is a substantial accommodation to free exercise, understood to include how one behaves toward others. If a man's religion tells him that killing another is deeply wrong, that will constitute one of the most fundamental moral premises in his view. Does an establishment concern exist here? Of course, if many others would prefer to avoid the draft, the religious pacifist is getting a benefit they would like to have. But given that a country with a draft is actually engaging in military conflict, or is setting things up so it will be able to do so, *and* given the reality that pacifist groups have always been fairly small minorities, it is hard to think of them as being "established." When a concession is made to a small minority that is at odds with the perspectives of most religious groups and the overall population, we cannot conceive of this as an aim to "establish" that minority. Not every concession really amounts to an establishment, unless one regards any favored treatment as doing that.

Connected to this point is the absence of a genuine worry of the kind raised with exemptions regarding such things as abortions and same-sex marriage. One concern about those examptions is that their granting may itself convey the message that the behavior those exempted need not assist may be of questionable value. Allowing pacifist exemptions has never been seen as casting genuine doubt on whether military conflict is sometimes justified.

A possible counterargument that can be taken to embrace both nonestablishment and equality more generally is that those who are drafted *because* others are exempted are being disadvantaged by this concession. As generally cast, this counterargument has some power, but it has almost no real relevance for this context. The three basic reasons are these. Typically, an actual draftee will have no idea whether or not he might have escaped the draft had some pacifist been compelled to serve, so no individuals will be fairly sure they would have been treated more favorably absent the exemption. Even more important for what happens to others is that very few genuine pacifists would actually serve rather than going to jail. For those instances of the jail alternative, the exemption does not increase the number of others needed to be drafted. The third basic reason not to give too much weight to the possibility that the exemption may lead to the drafting of others addresses what a genuine pacifist would do if he submits to a draft rather than going to jail. If he finds himself in a genuine battle, he might well decide not to fire his weapon in a way that would likely kill an enemy. This refusal to carry out his military duty could be much more harmful for his fellow soldiers than if he had been exempted from service. In brief, equality concerns, in contrast with some other possible exemptions, do not constitute a substantial reason to deny this one to pacifists.

Equality plays a much more significant role in how genuine pacifists are discerned and what happens to them. Were pacifists just excused from all service whatsoever, they would be treated much better than draftees, a significant number of whom are likely to die or at least undergo physical and psychological traumas. This discrepancy can be moderated by requiring alternative civilian service, as has long been the practice in the United States. For some exemptions we shall look at, it is hard to conceive of fraudulent claims, but given the hardships and risks of military service, that has never been true here. The fact that draft boards and appellate institutions reviewed individual claims fairly extensively satisfied the sincerity concerns to a substantial degree. That made administrability less of a problem than it could be for an exception from a duty that many would like to have and for which government institutions are not really in a position to carefully evaluate individual claims.

It is worth noting that two genuine alternatives are available here to the specific exemption approach. One that is often, but not always, feasible is simply to have voluntary military service, as we do now. If many more people are needed for military service than at present, this may still work if the pay and benefits of service are increased substantially to attract more people, now including women. That approach would not be sufficient for an all-out war, such as World War II. The other alternative is to give everyone a choice, say between two years of military duty or three of civilian service. That largely eliminates the issue of sincerity and administrability. In answer to a concern that the extra year of service would be unfair to the genuine pacifists, this approach would assure that no sincere pacifist who is willing to follow required procedures and do the civilian service would be excluded because he failed to persuade his draft board. Further, given the special risks of military service, it is a bit oversimplified to see the added year of civilian service as really more of a hardship.

With these general observations, we will turn to our laws and relevant cases, and to some special issues raised by "selective objection." The Civil War Draft Act of 1864, which instituted national conscription, excused conscientious objectors whose denominations forbade the bearing of arms.[22]

The World War I Draft Act granted an exemption limited to combatant service for members of "any well-recognized sect" or organization that forbade members from participating "in war in any form."[23] The membership requirement was eliminated in the 1940 Selective Service Act, which remains largely intact. A person qualifies so long as "by religious training and belief, he is conscientiously opposed to participation in war in any form."[24] When courts of appeals divided over what counts as "religious training and belief," Congress responded with a 1948 amendment that these words mean "an individual's beliefs in a Supreme Being involving duties superior to those arising from any human relation, but do not include essentially political, sociological, or philosophical views or a merely personal moral code."[25]

Where do free exercise and nonestablishment values point when one reflects on these various classifications? Both disfavor making eligibility depend on membership. Given that some pacifists belong to religious denominations not themselves committed to that *and* that not all members of traditionally pacifist groups, such as Quakers, are themselves pacifists, nonexclusivity in regard to membership in pacifist groups clearly promotes free exercise. And given that when such a denominational limit exists it may lead people to join the particular groups, that can be seen as at odds with nonestablishment. The only basis here for requiring membership is that it helps ensure someone is a genuine pacifist, but given the number of nonpacifists in pacifist groups and given the detailed examination by draft boards, this limit in modern times was neither effective nor necessary as a required test of sincerity.

Matters become a bit more complicated when one thinks of the line between religion and nonreligion, a subject explored in more depth in Chapter 8. One might think that some religious connection or conviction helps assure the honesty of a claim and the strength of one's beliefs about what it is right to do. With some other exemptions, we have forceful reasons to limit the exemption to religious claims, but they have little or no force here. Some nonreligious people are honestly pacifists. And any genuine pacifist who reflects must believe that it would be wrong to kill in wartime, even were that necessary to defend the country against an invader, like Nazi Germany, that has exterminated millions of people. To have that honest conviction, one must give nonkilling a very high priority in one's mind, whatever one would be likely to do and believe if one actually lived in those more extreme circumstances. Especially since an individual can lie about religious convictions as well as nonreligious ones, substantial reasons support *not* limiting the exemption to religious claims in any ordinary sense.

The reality definitely influenced the Supreme Court's interpretation during the Vietnam War of the 1940 Act with its 1948 Amendment. In *United States v. Seeger*,[26] the Court reviewed the opinions of three court of appeals panels. One had construed the statute broadly. Two, in contrast, determined that claimants who did not believe in a Supreme Being were uncovered. Only one of these ruled that this statutory line was constitutionally acceptable; the other held that the line drawn was unconstitutional. The Supreme Court chose the broad statutory interpretation approach. Seeger, one of the claimants involved, had cast his opposition as "religious" but also referred to "skepticism or disbelief in the existence of God" and referred to "devotion to goodness and virtue for their own sake, and a religious faith in a purely ethical creed." Ruling that it was enough that a belief one holds is parallel "to that filled by the orthodox belief in God," the Court effectively eliminated the "Supreme Being" restriction Congress had chosen to impose.[27]

Five years later the Court reviewed the denial of an exemption for Elliot Welsh, who had struck "religious" on his application and, referring to "readings in the fields of history and sociology," based his objection to the military complex on the waste of human resources and disregard for human ends.[28] A majority granted him the exemption but on different bases. Four of the eight sitting Justices acknowledged that the statutory language did not cover Welsh. Four others were willing to stretch the statute even further than the Court had in *Seeger*, effectively eliminating any requirement of either belief in God or "religious" belief in any ordinary sense. Justice John Marshall Harlan believed that the language definitely did not cover Welsh, but since the line it drew was an unconstitutional establishment of religion, and because Congress would prefer an extension to an outright invalidation of the exemption, he voted for Welsh's entitlement to the exemption with the four Justices who took an incredibly broader view of the statutory provision itself.[29]

Whether one agrees, as I do, with Justice Harlan's constitutional position, Congress's choice of statutory language highlights two basic concerns about free exercise and nonestablishment values. The first is that sometimes the nonreligious claims for exemptions may not be infrequent and may be about as strong as those of religious believers. The second, also explored in more depth in Chapter 8, is that defining exactly what should count as "religious" in various contexts can be very difficult. Both these reasons, when applicable, provide bases not to draw the line at religion, even if constitutional doctrine leaves the legislature the choice whether to do so.

A kind of draft objection that differs from pacifism raises some similar kinds of questions without yielding the same conclusions. What of "selective objectors," potential draftees whose objection is that a particular engagement is unjust? That such a conviction can have force is powerfully supported both by religions, such as Roman Catholicism, that have concepts that countries should only be involved in "just wars" and by various international treaties that set standards for just wars. Since the federal statute requires objection to "war in any form," it clearly did not reach selective objectors. The Supreme Court held in *United States v. Gillette*[30] that this was constitutionally acceptable. Although one can see obvious grounds for providing an exemption for selective objectors, some contrary arguments are much more powerful than in respect to pacifists. One is that if a person objects not to an all-out war but to one conflict in which the country is engaged, such as the use of troops in Iraq, should he be completely excused from all military service? Relatedly, what is "unjust" can alter significantly if circumstances and strategies change, and the judgment of "injustice" often rests on factual premises that themselves may be disputable or even misguided.

Finally, the edge of "conscientious objection" here is much less clear than with a pacifist. If a person believes a war is misguided, and he definitely would prefer not to risk his life fighting in it, would he believe he is doing a deep moral wrong by submitting to a draft? Someone may have a much harder time deciding that than does an honest pacifist. If the right to an exemption *is* extended, a person who has this opposition to the war itself may have a strong tendency to honestly conclude that his sense constitutes a conscientious objection to participation, or at least to phrase his beliefs in that way. Discerning the level of needed conscience is much greater here than with pacifists. A further concern about excusing selective objectors may be that, especially if a large number step forward, the exemption could help convey and support doubts about how the government is engaging itself, something I have urged is not really true about excusing pacifists. Putting all these worries together, it is a deeply troublesome question whether selective objectors, religious or not, should receive an exemption. My own sense is that, on balance, they should despite the various difficulties, but this is properly left to legislative choice.

A final question about exemptions from military service that apply to many other exemptions is how to set the appropriate range of privilege for those who qualify. We have already looked at one key limit here. Those granted an exemption as pacifists had to perform alternative civilian service. *If* a pacifist refused to do this, he would be guilty of a crime and likely sent to jail. All men of draft age have also been subject to registration requirements.[31] If their objection to military force extended so far that they felt they must not comply with registration requirements, they had violated the law and were subject to criminal convictions. Interestingly, in the 2015–16 term the Supreme Court considered, but ultimately remanded to lower courts, the somewhat related issue whether, under the Religious Freedom Restoration Act (RFRA), businesses with objections to giving insurance for contraceptives should be excused from having to provide an application that will aid the government in seeing that an alternative way of giving the insurance works.[32]

In this section we have looked briefly at one of the deepest traditions of exemptions, which both illustrates why some exemptions are definitely warranted and raises critical questions that also reach other exemptions from duties. How extensive should the exemption be? Who should qualify? Should a limit be cast in terms of religious beliefs and practices, and if so, how is the line to be drawn? How far can what makes sense in principle be effectively administered, including assurance that claims are honest and rise to the necessary level of strong conviction? Many of these questions reach beyond concerns about free exercise and nonestabishment values, but those values often have relevance for what approach is just and wise.

### Religious Land Use Protection

In this section and the next, we shall look at rights created by the Religious Land Use and Institutionalized Persons Act (RLUIPA),[33] adopted in 2000. The land use part has a significant resemblance to property tax exemptions, but its justification varies significantly. The provision on prisons connects in different ways to what governments can and should do within prisons and the military. As Chapter 2 explains, after the Supreme Court cut back sharply on constitutional free exercise protections in *Employment Division v. Smith*, Congress sought to reintroduce the prior standard by adopting the RFRA, intending it to apply to all governments within the United States.

The Supreme Court held that Congress lacked this power in relation to state and local governments since it could not overturn the Court's own constitutional resolutions, and it had no other basis to control state actions in this general way.[34]

After considerable analysis, compromises, and discussions, Congress adopted RLUIPA, directed at two subjects for which the members believed they could enact broad coverage. The logic for these subjects differed. The main claim about prisoners and other institutionalized persons was that federal restrictions could be set because the institutions received significant financing from the national government. In regard to land use, the primary underlying basis was to preclude actual constitutional violations by local officials.

In terms of its underlying justification for federal control, the land use section differed significantly from tax exemptions for religious bodies. Congress had apparently received "massive evidence" that land use regulations were frequently enacted or enforced "due to animus or hostility to the burdened religious practices."[35]

A striking example of such a basis occurred in a 1988 case involving faculty and students at the University of Mississippi who wanted to construct a Muslim house of worship. The board of aldermen kept denying this application although they had granted all similar requests by Christian groups. Conceivably things would look a bit different now for those who believe concerns about ISIS justify various interferences with the liberty of Muslims in this country; at the time this was a simple case of outright discrimination. The Fifth Circuit Court of Appeals held it unconstitutional.[36]

As we have explored in earlier chapters, such discrimination violates the Establishment Clause and is also at odds with free exercise values. Given that this is an obvious instance in which the values of the two clauses point in the same direction, why is any statute—federal or state—really needed? The answer here is that most crucial determinations about the application of zoning laws are made by local officials with considerable discretion. Those whose requests have been rejected may find it very hard to prove that the denial rests on unfair categorization; and, especially given that courts have afforded deference to such decisions, actual judicial determinations of forbidden discrimination have been few and far between. This is the dilemma that the federal law was designed to counter.

We shall later explore the basic standards of the Religious Freedom Restoration Act, drawn from the Supreme Court's free exercise approach prior to *Employment Division v. Smith*. Under the statute a claimant must show a "substantial burden" on religious exercise, and the government needs to counter that by demonstrating that the rule serves a "compelling interest" and constitutes the "least restrictive means" to achieve the basic objective. RLUIPA includes these standards for both parts, and the land use provision also contains four more-distinct criteria. An institution cannot be discriminated against on the basis of its particular religion, religious institutions cannot be treated worse than nonreligious ones, religious assemblies cannot be excluded from a jurisdiction, and unreasonable limits cannot be placed on religious assemblies and structures. After the enactment of RLUIPA, claims of the sort it covers have been successful much more often than they were under the constitutional free exercise approach that preceded *Employment Division v. Smith*.[37]

As with virtually all the subjects covered in this book, there are difficult cases at the borders whose proper resolution is far from obvious. Here are a few examples in the land use context, with what seem to me to be the best approaches.

What amounts to a substantial burden if a religious organization wants to build a house of worship within an area limited to housing or agricultural use? The organization is unlikely to think it *must* build in that area in the sense that it might believe it must use wine in communion, but a location that is close to existing and potential members and is not too expensive can be very important. That should be enough for a "substantial burden" if the group can show that a restriction significantly compromises its religious endeavors.[38]

A more complex situation arose over general zoning restrictions for commercial areas that applied to churches in commercial areas. The Seventh Circuit sustained these on the basis that they did not render religious exercise effectively impracticable.[39] Chief Judge Posner dissented on the basis that the restrictions effectively favored traditional religious groups over storefront churches that new groups might use.[40] Should this count as unequal treatment under RLUIPA? Suppose that the enactors had no such favoritism on their minds, but would probably not have adopted the restraints if major religions had been impaired. There is no simple answer, but given the unequal effect, I agree with Judge Posner's suggestion that courts should declare such restrictions invalid *unless* the government's interests are very strong and not achievable by alternative means.

Landmark preservation laws that forbid destruction of historic buildings present yet another problem. These laws apply to a much higher percentage of churches than nonreligious structures.[41] It is hard to generalize about the strength of the government's interest; that depends considerably both on the particular facility covered and how exactly those in charge would like to change the landmark. Prior to RFRA, one district court relied on constitutional free exercise to allow the Catholic Church to demolish an old monastery in favor of new church facilities, calling the ordinance not neutral and failing to see historic preservation as a compelling interest.[42] The actual weight of the government's interest is affected by the facility involved. Preserving a building that is extremely significant in our history does seem important enough, but it may make sense that when a serious religious interest supports destroying or altering the building, the government should have to show that importance to defeat the claim.[43]

Just how RLUIPA should apply to the condemnation of church land is far from simple. If that is apparently done to avoid the application of restrictions on zoning, it would be clearly inappropriate, and courts should probably be willing to get involved;[44] but if condemnation covers a broad sweep of property, religious groups should have no special basis to challenge it.

Two other problems involve regulations that cover the use of property owned by religious groups for public services, such as schools and day care centers, and constraints that reach the carrying out of religious worship in ordinary locations such as homes. Given that religious groups regard the provision of services as part of their religious endeavors, they should be able to make RLUIPA arguments in respect to how they use their property for such purposes. Here it can be a concern tied to nonestablishment values that nonreligious providers of similar services may suffer a comparative disadvantage if special concessions are made to religious ones. This should not itself eliminate the force of a religious group's claim, but it might stand as one competing government interest, and it might more generally underlie decisions to grant concessions to nonreligious groups comparable to those afforded to religious ones. When it comes to restrictions on how many people homeowners can have in their dwellings, a special concession for religious services is called for, unless the basis for the limit set is much more powerful than it will normally be.

## Prison Rights

The other aspect of the Religious Land Use and Institutionalized Persons Act addresses prisons and other institutions in which people are contained against their will. Here the exemptions mainly concern individual religious conscience. Obviously in prisons, as Chapter 2 explains, "residents" are much more sharply restricted than are ordinary people. This can raise great conflicts between what is required of them and what their religious convictions tell them to do. In various respects, free exercise considerations strongly support exemptions from ordinary restrictions. The reasons against most exceptions are prison security and expenses. Although, in application of RLUIPA to particular instances, some favoring of major denominations may occur, nonestablishment is not a major concern here. In respect to such matters as growing beards or eating special food, nonreligious desires are unlikely to carry the force of genuine religious convictions. Not surprisingly the Supreme Court sustained RLUIPA unanimously against an Establishment Clause challenge.[45]

As far as judicial decisions in this general area are concerned, the approaches both under constitutional free exercise law and under RFRA prior to the enactment of RLUIPA were highly deferential. In a case decided before *Employment Division v. Smith*, the Supreme Court had endorsed deference to prison officials and stated that not granting an exemption from a neutral rule was all right if "reasonably related to legitimate penological interests."[46] In regard to the deference point, the Senate Report on RFRA indicated that Congress expected judges to apply the law with "due deference to ... prison and jail administrators in establishing necessary regulations and procedures."[47] Apparently for prisoners making RFRA claims before that law was declared unconstitutional as applied to states, only nine of ninety-nine reported cases were decided on the merits.[48] Such deference is understandable given the difficulty of judges determining just how pressing are the needs of prison discipline, but it is also seriously disturbing in light of the understanding that in many prisons some treatment of convicted criminals is harsh and unfair.

Among the kinds of issues that arise under the more specific protections of RLUIPA are beards and other forms of appearance. Some prisons have sharp restrictions on the length of beards; some prisoners have religious convictions that require the growing of beards. In 2015 the Supreme Court decided the beard case of *Holt v. Hobbs.*[49] In contrast to the great majority of states, Arkansas maintained a strict rule forbidding beards longer than a quarter of an inch unless one had medical reasons. Holt's Muslim religion indicated a longer beard but he was willing to compromise on a half-inch beard. He had been denied the right to do even that. In an opinion by Justice Alito, a unanimous Court found that the arguments that the beard restriction was needed to prevent the hiding of contraband and the disguising of identity were extremely weak. The Court relied partly on the fact that the vast majority of prisons do allow the growing of "half-inch beards, either for any reason or for religious reasons."[50] Justice Alito's opinion stresses the rigor of the RLUIPA standard; Justice Sotomayor, who joined the opinion, emphasized in a concurrence that RLUIPA did not abandon deference when a chosen policy is plausible, nor did the statute require a demonstration that there is no conceivable less restrictive means.[51] Almost certainly, among the Supreme Court justices, some division exists about just how rigorous judicial review of decisions of prison officials should be in this context. Since the requirement they reviewed in this particular instance was obviously insupportable, they did not have to delve into that perplexing boundary.

The beard example and others concerning forms of physical appearance and dress provide illustrations of a general possibility for many forms of exemptions. If the need for a general restriction is not very strong *and* it is clear that some prisoners have a genuine religious objection to it, a simple approach is to make an exception generally available—for example, allowing anyone to grow a half-inch beard. This eliminates both any need to assess the sincerity and strength of an individual's claim, and it answers any worry that some prisoners will be treated unfairly in comparison with others. As I have mentioned, a nonestablishment concern about beard growing is quite weak, but making the exception generally available can effectively eliminate it altogether.

A somewhat different claim for special treatment involves food. Should special food be available to Orthodox Jews who regard themselves as needing kosher diets, and to religious vegetarians? The simple answer is "yes," though here some factors come into play that are unlikely for beards. In respect to the kosher diet, it will cost extra money to provide that, but given all the expenses of running prisons, that does not seem a significant factor. Other prisoners who are not getting the food they would like may feel that the Orthodox Jews are being favored, but they are not likely to perceive a serious injustice in this. For the vegetarians, one might urge that they can just take food available to all and not eat some of it. But they may need a larger helping of the vegetarian elements than is provided in ordinary servings. For a refusal to eat meat, it is much easier to imagine fairly strong nonreligious convictions than is true for growing beards. And since most nonvegetarians do want to eat meat, this is a matter on which, if special vegetarian meals are to be provided, they should simply be made available to anyone who chooses to receive them on a regular basis.[52]

Another topic for RLUIPA is religious practices and meetings. The Third Circuit rightly held that a prisoner should not have been disciplined for conducting an afternoon prayer within a prison kitchen's corner.[53] A district court's ruling that a prisoner who believed in "Judeo-Christianity" could be barred from Jewish worship because Protestant services were adequate seemed misguided, affording insufficient weight to a particular person's convictions.[54]

When it comes to worship services, how far should prisons allow services they do not themselves provide for prisoners? Of course, as have seen in Chapter 2, prisons do make available worship services, given that prisoners lack the freedom of ordinary citizens to attend those and other group meetings when they choose. Plainly, insofar as the religious convictions are sincere, prisons should try to accommodate various forms of worship. A pre-RLUIPA case denied a claim of prisoners to hold "full Pentecostal services," given the presence of other Christian services.[55] The Ninth Circuit held that the failure to show that such services were mandated by the faith fell short of a substantial burden. Given their special practices and physical movements, and their degrees of emotional intensity, Pentecostal services vary a good deal from ordinary Protestant worship. A failure to allow them for those who believe they best promote religious practice and understanding should count as a "substantial burden," and these believers should be accommodated, barring some special contrary reason.

The practice of worship services does present the question whether nonreligious meetings should be treated similarly. Religious worship is special enough that, given free exercise values, it can constitutionally be granted distinctive treatment. However, if nonreligious groups genuinely wish to meet to promote understanding of human life and caring for others, affording them a similar treatment would be wise. One could see nonestablishment values in play here,[56] but a much more straightforward basis is that notions of free speech and association call for similar treatment.

The general truth about RLUIPA and other bases for concessions within prisons are that free exercise values are dominant and nonestablishment concerns are slight, unless one worries that fewer accommodations will be made to members of minority groups, including ones like Muslims, who may be subject to negative opinions for one reason or another. Of course, fair and effective prison discipline should not be undermined, but many concessions to religious practice do not really threaten that.

## Clerical and Organizational Rights Resting Largely on the Common Law

This chapter and the book more broadly have concentrated on constitutional and statutory rights and obligations. But within common law systems we also have rights and legal rules created by aspects of the judicially created common law itself. Some, but not all, of these remain largely subjects of that law. Others have been taken over by specific or general statutes. And, of course, the common law, like statutes, may provide particular outcomes whose constitutional validity may be challenged.

This section concentrates on special privileges that are granted to clerics or afforded to religious organizations in relation to their members. In respect to the latter, the main competing concern is whether the coverage of tort law should allow members or former members to recover for injuries they suffer. It is interesting that this concern is not primarily that benefits are given to one faith in relation to others, or to religious groups in relation to nonreligious ones. Instead, it involves the welfare of members, including their own religious exercise.

Before delving into this, I will briefly sketch the relation of statutes like RFRA to these kinds of claims. The statutes are phrased differently in different states, but the federal law is cast in terms of the government not burdening religious exercise from a general rule unless "it demonstrates" that the application is needed to further a "compelling interest" and is the "least restrictive means."[57] This language raises two questions about private suits that one person or nongovernmental organization brings against another.

In these private suits, the government is not "demonstrating" anything;

arguments are made by private parties.[58] Despite this linguistic doubt, which has persuaded some, RFRA should be seen as applicable to private suits that are brought against the behavior it protects. If the statute definitely protects an exercise of religion against any government requirement that people not act in a certain way, it would be nearly illogical to allow private citizens to demand that the action not be performed or to recover damages if someone has rightfully engaged in it. In brief, insofar as RFRA and RLUIPA do protect a right to engage in behavior, the law of torts should not essentially preclude it by providing damages against someone who performs it. That this is how any of the RFRA statutes should be understood unless they clearly dictate a contrary conclusion is strongly supported by Congress's objective to reinstitute a preexisting free exercise constitutional standard, which definitely covered protections against tort damages as well as statutory limits.[59]

A somewhat more arguable question concerns how RFRA laws relate to behavior that is not generally forbidden by a statute but is left to the common law. One could assert that if that law requires behavior, the government is not then imposing the burden. However, courts and the common law are aspects of our government, so their imposition should definitely count as reached by a RFRA statute, especially since, as just noted, constitutional constraints definitely apply to the common law, and RFRA itself was designed to reinstitute the pre-*Smith* constitutional test. In all that follows, I will assume that religious individuals and organizations can raise RFRA claims against tort law requirements that impair their religious liberty.

Among the practices of religious leaders and group members that might be subject to tort law recovery, unless they count as a form of protected religious exercise, are shunning, disclosures of embarrassing facts, defamation, and practices of internal community life. An important feature of most of these is that one can identify a certain tension between free exercise of the organization and the free exercise of individual members who are in a position to suffer. I shall suggest how I think that tension may fairly be addressed.

Certain religious groups, such as Jehovah's Witnesses and those in the Mennonite tradition, are committed to shunning former members who have violated their standards. If members of a group, including even those in family relations, refuse to interact with a former member, this can create extreme emotional distress and economic disadvantages. Tort recovery is potentially possible under the principle that one person cannot intentionally or recklessly inflict emotional distress on another. The relevant religious group is likely to counter that this practice of shunning can increase an offender's shame and enhance his repentance and restoration, and that it also protects faithful members from contamination. However, if shunning is protected, that itself can affect the religious exercise of disaffected members. When a member whose family and close friends belong to the same group has ceased to believe in some of its key doctrines and practices, the threat of shunning may be enough to silence his present convictions and to effectively force him to continue to practice a religion in which he no longer believes. That is troubling.

Exactly how these situations should be handled is definitely debatable, but I believe a kind of weighing process is needed, one that takes account of the core understandings of the religious group and the harm its shunning is doing to former members. One central element is how well informed are individuals when they join the group. If someone understands that those who deviate will be shunned, he is choosing to belong despite that possible future risk. This reality strongly reduces the force of his complaint if that actually happens to him. With some exceptions involving those who have very close contact with members, a group's right to shun should not extend to nonmembers, and shunning should not be justifiable simply on the basis of causing harm to a former member, independent of how that will affect his possible repentance and the internal lives of group members.

All this should count as to whether the shunning is "outrageous" enough to warrant tort damages for the infliction of emotional distress. In ordinary cases, applying the "outrageous" standard would be left to a jury. However, given the fact that the degree of sympathy of jurors with the religious group involved could make a huge difference, the judge in a case here should initially undertake that evaluation and either make a final determination or submit it to the jury only if she concludes that the religious group does not have a powerful free exercise argument.

Religious groups may believe that the disclosure of personal behavior that has violated their standards, such as committing adultery, is warranted even if such a disclosure would ordinarily be a kind of unjustified infliction of emotional distress. Awareness that this revelation may happen can, again, influence what an individual does and what efforts she takes to conceal her behavior. As with shunning, it should matter here how well a group has informed prospective members that this is one of its practices. Someone who knowingly joins such a group, possibly appreciating this way to keep its members close knit and morally proper, has a much less forceful complaint if his behavior puts him on the receiving end.

Two Oklahoma cases dealing with disclosure ended up with an approach that is defensible in principle but is genuinely unwise in light of free exercise values. In 1989, the state supreme court sustained a claim made by a former member who had recently resigned that the elders in a Church of Christ had committed a tort by informing members of her former church and closely related churches that she had had sex outside of marriage.[60] Three years later, the court indicated that simple revelation was justified if either someone still was a member or the church or the communication implemented a previously announced sanction even if it occurred after the person was no longer a member.[61] The logic for this difference is that those communications, which would not be warranted for nonmembers more broadly, should be tied to a person's actual involvement with the group.

Here is the problem. If a person were aware that, while she was a member, the religious leaders were investigating her behavior, she might well resign *before* a sanction had been authorized. Yet if the investigation was secretive she might not be in a position to do this. If religious groups were aware of the line the court had drawn, they would have an incentive to employ secret tactics to enhance their chance of having a privilege to disclose. This is hardly a healthy incentive. More relevant would be how much time had passed between a person's resignation and the disclosure.

Special rights to disclose information that would otherwise be "private" should involve only disclosures aimed at one's own members and not reach the lives of nonmembers (unless their relation is especially close to members). This privilege is not one that should extend to nonreligious groups, unless they are committed to particular moral objectives, such as vegetarianism, and a member is living in violation of those objectives.

Life within the religious community itself raises two other issues, one closely related to the disclosures of embarrassing facts. If members of a church are choosing a pastor, and the personal life of a prospect is relevant, members have a right to state what they honestly believe, even if they are wrong and what they say would amount of defamation by ordinary tort standards. This privilege resembles what is a more general privilege in respect to statements about public officials and prominent figures.

A different issue concerns internal community life that causes emotional distress for those who participate. A nun might complain that relevant restrictions have sharply curtailed her emotional stability; a woman who has had an abortion might be distressed by religious leaders continually reiterating that this is the intentional taking of innocent life. So long as a religious group or a subsection is clear about how it approaches issues of life, those who choose to belong or to take special positions are responsible for the risk that these may cause distress. The government cannot be in the position of ruling that some of these religious practices are disturbing enough emotionally so that individuals who make those choices can recover monetary damages. Here, the group's free exercise far outweighs any claim that the practices are emotionally harmful. This conclusion would not apply, however, to actual physical injury that is intentionally inflicted and generally forbidden.

A variety of issues arise over what privileges should be given to clerics because of religious premises. The most important of these is the priest-penitent privilege not to testify about what a cleric has learned in confession. I have previously noted that clerics may be given less or no obligation to take the initiative to disclose crucial facts of the kind that lawyers and doctors may have an obligation to reveal. That is not exactly an exemption because there is no general duty to disclose, and it just happens that specific duties are imposed on other professionals. But if clerics are similar in many ways to those professionals, the absence of a duty is closely similar to an exemption. I will concentrate here on the privilege not to testify. Since there is a general duty to testify when called to do so, this is a clear exemption.

The privilege is one that obviously supports the free exercise of religion. Priests and other clerics may believe that they cannot reveal what they have learned in a confession, and members who are told they have an obligation to confess may be much more inclined to do so if they are assured that what they say will not be spread more broadly. In contrast to some other exemptions, we can see here some competing nonestablishment concerns. Does it "establish" religions to favor divulgences made within their practices in comparison with what people may divulge to close friends and secular advisors? And depending on how the actual privilege is cast, may it favor some religions over others? The latter concern definitely bears on how the legal privilege should be cast.

With the exception of marital partners, people generally have an obligation to testify in criminal and civil cases if called upon to do so. According to the Roman Catholic religion for many centuries, priests are forbidden to reveal what they have learned in formal confessions. Those confessions are a crucial element of religious practice since they are believed necessary for God's forgiveness and are supposed to precede participation in a Mass. These premises constitute powerful free exercise bases not to require priests to testify. If everything depended on prosecutor's choices, one might think their thoughtful restraint could make a legal privilege unnecessary, but not all prosecutors would exercise that restraint, and witnesses are also subject to being called by criminal defendants and parties in civil suits. If they had no such privilege, most Catholic priests would nevertheless refuse to testify about confessions made to them, even if the consequence would be time in jail. Thus, the general objective of gaining information would not be greatly served. The argument for such a privilege in thus very powerful, even if on occasion a priest could say something that would indicate that a person being prosecuted is clearly guilty or clearly innocent. Given all this, it is hardly surprising that all states, now by statute, and the federal government, without a statute, provide such a privilege.[62]

Just how to cast the privilege is troubling. That should be addressed by specific statutory language. One might argue that all denominations should be treated equally, but if a religion has no institution of formal confession and further sees no responsibility of clerics not to disclose what they learn, no exemption from testifying should be available. A difficult problem is that many religions fall somewhere between the Catholic approach and one under which clerics have no relevant special position. For most Protestants, key confessions are in private prayers and general worship ceremonies, but many individuals still believe they should talk confidentially to ministers about sins they have been committing and what they might best do about those. Even if not strictly dictated by church doctrine, many Protestant ministers may see the premises of their faith as requiring confidentiality about what they learn in these settings.

Although exactly how to draw lines here is debatable, I believe the privilege should extend to clerics who have a plausible argument that testifying would be at odds with basic premises of their denomination, but should not extend to any cleric who simply indicates he personally would prefer not to testify. Such a cleric should not be privileged over others who, on nonreligious bases, think it would be better to withhold testimony.

A nuance in all this is who should be seen as having a final say about the privilege.[63] If, as in the typical instance, the confessor and the cleric would line up against testimony, that is not a practical question, but what if they disagree, because the person who confessed believes the revelation would be favorable? If religious doctrine clearly forbids testimony, the cleric should still have the right to refuse. *And* if the confessor fears the testimony, she should be able to preclude it if the priest has left the church and is now willing to disclose. If church doctrine precludes testimony *only* to protect the confessor, she should be able to waive the cleric's privilege not to testify.

Two other nuances are who counts as a cleric and what amounts to a confession. Within some religions there are special figures who may often receive confessions although they are not clergy in the strict sense. Roman Catholic nuns are a notable example. The privilege should reach them. In the opposite direction, people in crucial conversations may reveal damaging information to friends or relatives who happen to be ministers, or they may reveal criminal activity when discussing church business with its minister. These should not count as confessions to which the privilege applies, because they are ordinary conversations in which the minister's role to hear confessions does not have a crucial status.

A different question is what should be the tort liability of clerics who give improper advice? Should they be treated like other professionals? Clerics do not receive the kind of official authorization given to doctors and lawyers, and their advice about what an individual should do is likely to be strongly influenced by religious convictions. Much should depend here on what, if anything, is conveyed to the person seeking advice. If a cleric or other religious counselor makes clear that he is not offering a range of advice that would be highly reliable from a nonreligious point of view, he should not be liable. An illustration of this would be when someone is ill or psychologically upset, and the minister recommends prayer and religious involvement, rather than seeing a doctor or therapist. He should not be liable if things work out badly.[64] On the other hand, if the minister assures that the advice will be complete and sound from every perspective, liability should follow. If, in between, he is not clear, the person who seeks it should be aware that, in general, advice from religious leaders is not the same as that from secular experts.

A final point concerns the activities of some clerics that violate ordinary laws. A notable publicized example was the sexual involvement of priests with minors. If a substantial secular reason exists to forbid such behavior, no excuse should be provided for religious leaders, *unless* those who are "harmed" are aware of a clear religious practice and they are old enough to self-consciously accept that.

### Use of Forbidden Substances

When the purchase and ingestion of substances is forbidden, should exceptions be created for religious use, and, if so, how should the exception be cast? Two notable examples are wine and peyote.

When laws generally forbade the sale and drinking of alcohol, exceptions were created for the use of wine in communion, and insofar as present laws forbid minors from drinking, an exception is often made for those participating in communion. At its core, such an exception is clearly warranted by free exercise, and it raises little concern about establishment. According to the Roman Catholic religion, given what Jesus did at the last supper, having wine is an essential element of the crucial ceremony of Mass, and with two minor exceptions, that does not present the dangers of people ingesting alcohol, since the amount parishioners drink is so slight. It is possible that someone drinking a tiny amount will be tempted to want more and will go home and get drunk; and priests sometimes need to drink a fair amount of remaining consecrated wine after the service. But those conceivable worries are far outweighed by the basic reason to allow the exception.

A slightly more debatable issue, which does involve a degree of establishment concern, is who should qualify. Within many Protestant denominations, wine can be seen as preferable but not absolutely necessary; grape juice may be regarded as an acceptable alternative that is consistent with the basic religious significance of communion. If the exemption were cast in terms of wine being "necessary" for a religious service, members of those Protestant churches might see it as favoring Roman Catholicism and any other groups that assert that view. Such a phrasing would also raise the less than simple question of what counts as "necessary" in this context. Given the minimal harm of this drinking of wine, it makes much more sense to allow it for any religious body that regards that as desirable for its services. Since neither individuals nor nonreligious groups believe it is crucial or highly desirable to take a small sip of wine, except when toasting someone, providing the exception here does not raise a genuine worry about religious practice being unfairly favored.

Matters are more complicated when it comes to peyote. Members of the Native American Church have for centuries regarded the ingestion of peyote as central for their worship services.[65] During worship, participants take enough to produce a hallucinatory state that is seen as allowing direct contact with God. Here we have genuine questions whether an exemption is appropriate and, if so, how exactly it should be cast. The desirability of any exemption depends both on how dangerous a drug is and how serious are the risks of fraud if an exemption is created. Peyote is not as dangerous as a number of other forbidden drugs,[66] and it is not one that many people would choose to use on their own. This reduces the practical dangers of granting a specific exemption or allowing a general statute like the Religious Freedom Restoration Act to provide one.

Interestingly, the very issue about religious use of peyote happened to be the one directly involved in the constitutional decision that led to RFRA. In a well-known 1964 decision, the California Supreme Court had ruled that the federal Free Exercise Clause conferred a right to use peyote for the Native American Church.[67] It relied partly on the absence of evidence that that ingestion in worship produced harmful effects or undercut general enforcement efforts by spreading to use outside of services. In 1990 the Supreme Court considered a similar claim. Oregon did not enforce against members of the Native American Church its criminal prohibition on the use of peyote, but the litigating church members had lost their jobs for violating the statute. They urged that they had the constitutional right recognized earlier by the California case. In *Employment Division v. Smith*[68] the Supreme Court rejected the claim, ruling that so long as a statute was generally cast, one basically had no free exercise right to violate it.

Justice Scalia's opinion did offer what is really an illogical exception to accommodate earlier decisions. Free exercise could count, he wrote, if a claim is hybrid, resting on both free exercise and another constitutional claim. One problem here is determining when another genuinely separate kind of claim is involved. When, for example, do freedom of speech or freedom of association count as separate from religious exercise? The more fundamental illogic is this: If a claim can carry actual weight, and it may determine the outcome when another claim is also involved, how can one possibly assume that as a matter of principle it will never be strong enough by itself? That just does not make sense.

As a consequence of this case, whose restriction of constitutional claims has not been adopted within some states, exemptions in this context are now left to specific statutes or to ones like RFRA that are cast generally.

When it comes to drug use, we face legitimate concerns about private unsupervised use and the fraudulent creation of "groups" to allow participants simply to ingest the substance. Especially since this is not an area in which officials are in a position to explore individual convictions in depth, strong reasons exist either to allow general use of a drug that was once forbidden or to limit an exemption to religious group services, neither extending a privilege to individual use nor to nonreligious group gatherings. If the danger of fraud is very great, one might even require that a religious group has existed for a certain period of time, in order to preclude the setting up of a group that claims to be religious simply in order to receive an exemption. Perhaps these worries are not all that great in our society, given the widespread use of illegal drugs and the disturbing number of deaths that result each year.[69]

The existence of distinctive historical groups does suggest a possible standard for extending exemptions beyond religion that we have not yet considered. It has been suggested that persons should have a "cultural defense" to criminal prosecution if, at least for some crimes,[70] they are only doing what their narrower culture takes as an established practice. We could imagine statutory exemptions cast in those terms. My own view is that such an exemption would be too broad,[71] at least if it is not limited to a specific practice; but we can see this approach as a different alternative from protecting "conscience" that does reach beyond a religious exercise limitation.

I will not explore another possible argument favoring the Native American Church in particular. Given both the harsh treatment of Native Americans through much of United States history and the somewhat independent communities that exist on reservations, one might think concessions are appropriate here that should not be granted to religious groups that are composed of ordinary citizens in the general population.

The overall conclusion of this section is that exemptions from bans on substance use are sometimes warranted for key aspects of worship services and that, in order to avoid fraud and the possible undermining of effective enforcement, these should not extend to individual use and nonreligious groups.

## Declining Medical Treatment and Other Benefits: Adults and Children

What we have looked at so far are primarily claims of organizations and individuals not to perform general duties that the government has set for citizens. This section addresses the refusal to accept benefits that are broadly available and which people are, or might be, legally required to accept. These mainly involve various forms of physical assistance, such as blood transfusions and medication. For adults themselves, this turns out to involve few serious practical issues. Matters are much more complicated when we turn to children and what their parents believe is called for.

In our society, people do not have a right to commit suicide.[72] If this is so, would it not be logical to require that they receive crucial medical treatment, such as blood transfusions, needed to keep them alive? Were this the law, we would have a genuine question whether an exemption should be granted to those, such as Jehovah's Witnesses, who have religious convictions against transfusions. One would not worry here about nonestablishment values because virtually no one would have a nonreligious ground to refuse a needed transfusion unless he desired to end his life.

Despite the lack of a "right" to commit suicide, we have a strong reason not to require people generally to receive medical treatment. Individuals properly can decide how far they should endure the risks and pains of such treatment in order to get its benefits, and this is true even if the way they strike the balance is irrational from an ordinary perspective. Perhaps even more important, no one is required to seek medical help. If religious believers and perhaps others thought they might be required to submit to treatment they would want to refuse, they might decide just to stay home. For these reasons, the privilege to refuse recommended treatment is extensive; that makes unnecessary any special exemptions.

The treatment of children is much more complicated. Parents have a general duty to provide decent care for their children. If they are failing to do that, the state can intervene and supply that care. Does it matter if the parents' "failure" is not a consequence of mere recklessness or negligence but rests on religious convictions? And does it matter if the parents inform officials of the physical problems of the children? These are genuinely troubling questions that I shall cover briefly.

If we ask about the relation of small children to their parents and to the wider society, we can see families as having a degree of independence, but plainly the health and lives of children are a concern of the general population. If officials are aware that a child is likely to die because she is not receiving treatment, they properly intervene and see that it is provided. Parents, thus, have a range of choice within reason, but the state will intervene, under a doctrine of *parens patriae*, if parents have engaged in neglect that is indefensible by ordinary standards. Whether parents are relying on religious convictions or are simply acting irresponsibly does not matter here. That is effectively the law in every state.[73]

That, alone, does not tell us how the parents should be treated. Should they be liable criminally or civilly if they do not inform needed persons of the child's situation and the consequence turns out to be serious physical impairment or death? Most states retain laws that include exemptions from criminal provisions that prohibit child abuse and neglect for parents whose decisions are based on religious convictions.[74] Such an exemption grounded in free exercise concerns makes sense in light of the fact that these parents are not reckless or negligent in an ordinary sense. Rather than neglecting their children, they are doing what they genuinely believe is best for them, even if that includes a risk of death that they may attribute to the will of God.

Whether parents should be potentially liable for manslaughter if their child dies presents a very troubling question. If parents are not guilty of the much lesser crime of "neglect," should the highly unfortunate consequence of death yield a much more serious conviction for them? This consequence could be especially troublesome if it seems likely that parents will carry out their deep religious convictions whatever the possible legal consequences may be.

Provision of this penalty can, however, be defended on three bases. One is that even if the parents have not neglected their children, they have acted in a way that was negligent by ordinary standards and has produced death, which is ordinarily enough to be guilty of manslaughter. Yet more important, perhaps, a criminal conviction of this sort from time to time will encourage parents not to conceal information of children's physical condition and may also discourage nonmembers from joining groups that are committed to not seeking ordinary medical treatment. Another reason not to provide an exemption here is that it might induce others to make religious claims if their ordinary negligence leads to their children's deaths. Just what is the best resolution here is arguable. Although the free exercise concern is great enough to provide a strong reason to extend an exemption from criminal coverage to manslaughter, that has not occurred in most states.[75] State legislators need to specifically address this question, making clear just how far parents acting on religious convictions are going to be excused from criminal liability.

A special question about medical procedures involves vaccinations, which are given both to protect those who receive them and to ensure that they will not acquire the illness and pass it on to others. Some religions are strongly opposed to these vaccinations as contrary to God's will, and some people believe, almost certainly mistakenly, that they generally create a risk of some serious personal harm such as autism.[76] All states require that children going to public schools receive vaccinations; all but a few provide exemptions that reach beyond medical reasons, and about half of these are limited to religious bases. One can conceive a nonestablishment reason not to favor the religious claims here but, given the fact that no nonreligious basis really supports an objection in principle to all vaccinations, and the reality that much of nonreligious opposition rests on misinformation about dangers, limiting any nonmedical exemption to religious objections makes sense.

A final complexity about decisions and exemptions in respect to medical treatment for children concerns whose decision should control when an ordinary teenager of sixteen or seventeen is involved. This resolution will be needed only in rare instances, because typically parents and children will reach agreement about treatment. I shall not explore all the various circumstances of possible disagreement but, given that confirmation in virtually all faiths occurs before the age of sixteen, the teenager at that stage should not be denied desirable treatment based on her parent's religious convictions, if she makes clear that she does not now share those convictions. On the other hand, especially given the frequency in which youngsters alter their convictions over time, if the parents' nonreligious assessment calls for treatment, the teenager should not be able to refuse it on a religious basis. Even if the youngster and her parents agree, they should not be able to refuse treatment if that would be afforded to a smaller child against parental convictions.

These resolutions are far from obvious; what is clear is that the variety of circumstances of parental and teenage disagreements present particular questions about whose free exercise is crucially important and at what age, the control by parental religious choices against the convictions of a maturing child could itself be viewed as a kind of establishment.

A peculiar kind of nonmedical benefit was involved in one of the most important free exercise cases: Did the Amish have a constitutional right to withdraw their children from school after eighth grade? In *Yoder v. Wisconsin*,[77] the Supreme Court answered "yes." Education is a special nonmedical benefit that is legally required. Given that most Amish children stay within their community as adults, and the group educates them about how to carry out that life, the free exercise argument was quite strong. And given the infrequency of nonreligious organizations that take a similar approach, the establishment concern was minimal. *Employment Division v. Smith* effectively negated that constitutional right, at least if one puts aside the opinion's insupportable hybrid theory. But similar claims may still be raised under some state constitutions and RFRA's. To be clear, no exemption for education up to a certain level should be granted. Children have to function within a society. But if most of its children do stay within the group and function effectively, an exemption like this one is warranted.

### Being Excused from Aiding Practices to Which One Objects: The Abortion and Contraceptive Insurance Examples

In our era some of the most crucial questions about exemptions have concerned circumstances in which people have a general duty to assist others in various respects. How far should people be excused from performing such a duty if they have a strong convictions that the practice is basically wrong, and should a privilege of this sort be limited to religious convictions or extend to broader claims of conscience? These questions have arisen in important ways in respect to abortions and the provision of contraceptives.

Legislation about abortions has involved not only exemptions from government duties but also requirements about how private hospitals and related organizations must treat employees whose convictions are at odds with those who control the organizations. The relation between employers and workers raises the more general question whether people should not only be excused from performing duties but also be allowed to perform acts in accord with their conscience, even if that violates restrictions set generally.[78]

Prior to *Roe v. Wade*,[79] decided in 1973, a high percentage of states made it criminal to receive an abortion, at least barring special circumstances such as the need to save the life of the prospective mother. Since a number of religions perceive abortion as against God's will, one could have seen this enforcement of religious morality as a kind of establishment, but two reasons did not make this the dominant objection. One, which remains highly important, is that ordinary rational reasoning does not show that life deserving protection begins only at birth or a late stage of pregnancy. Contrary to claims of some natural law scholars, I do not believe that such reasoning demonstrates that life in this sense begins at conception. In fact, it simply does not tell us when life deserving genuine protection begins and whether such warranted protection is either absent or full, or increases as an entity develops from a single cell to an embryo to a fetus to one capable of surviving outside the womb.

This conclusion that rational analysis does not provide a clear answer here is supported by shifting cultural outlooks over time, explored in depth by Carol Sanger, about how fetuses should be conceptualized in relation to human life.[80] The divided outlooks in our modern era have been affected to a significant degree both by increasing emphasis on women's rights and the widespread perceptions of fetuses made possible by an ultrasound technique.

Because a person not relying on religious conviction may either find the natural law analysis persuasive or may intuitively believe that conception is the beginning of life in the relevant sense, moral objections to abortion need not rest entirely on religious premises. Even more important than this is the fact that the dominant concern about prohibiting abortion is not that it favors religious views but that it interferes with the basic right of pregnant women to decide what to do about their own bodies. That was the basis on which the Supreme Court decided that a woman had that constitutional right until the fetus could survive outside her body.

Given this constitutional right, which remains controversial,[81] statutes must resolve the question of when practitioners should be compelled to provide or assist abortions if that would be contrary to their moral beliefs.[82] As with many other exemptions, one question was whether a line should be drawn between religious and nonreligious claims. Two other issues were whether a privilege here should extend to hospitals and other facilities as well as individuals and, as I have noted, whether the law should compel such organizations to grant exemptions to their own workers who have convictions at odds with those of the leaders.

I will begin with some general observations before exploring specific questions and how the key federal statute addressed them. Here, the argument for an exemption is very powerful. People who strongly object to abortions believe they involve the taking of innocent life. To tell someone that she must actually participate in what she regards as the killing of a human being is undeniably harsh. This provides a strong basis not only to grant an exemption from standard requirements of the law, but also to require that privately owned hospitals that perform abortions not insist that all their doctors and nurses do so.

A possible answer to this argument is that if people undertake to engage in a profession, or work in a particular hospital, they should simply be required to perform its basic duties. At the time of *Roe v. Wade*, most hospital employees would have taken their jobs when abortion was still a crime. It would have been unreasonable to say they should then simply have lost their profession or job because the law had shifted to protect a procedure they regarded as deeply immoral. Most of those who presently hold such jobs will have taken them actually, or potentially, aware that broad exemptions have been prescribed. A point worth noting is that a person who believes abortions are basically wrong may not think they should be legally prohibited, given the sharp division of opinion in our society, the fact that many women will seek them whether they are legal or not, and the impossibility of effective enforcement. It follows that a person might approve of legalization but also have a conscientious objection to personal involvement.

A crucial competing consideration about an exemption here, one that is relevant for various exemptions from required assistance to others, is that women should not be denied their basic right to receive this treatment. That must be taken into account when the range of an exemption is formulated.

Given some of the difficult and very important questions about how broad exemptions here should be, it is very important that they be addressed by specific legislation, not simply left to a statute like RFRA. This is especially true if one thinks hospital choices regarding their workers should be constrained. RFRA, like our constitutions, concerns only rights against government requirements; it does not cover what businesses may insist that their workers perform so long as the businesses are not acting at odds with what the law tells them to do.

After *Roe v. Wade* was decided, Congress adopted a Church Amendment, supplemented by a Hyde Amendment, that provided that federal agencies cannot rely on federal funding to require the performance of abortions.[83] Those whose religious beliefs or moral convictions tell them they cannot "perform or assist" with abortions cannot be required to do so. The law not only protects hospitals, doctors, and nurses who object to abortions from being required to perform them by statutes, regulations, and semipublic bodies that set professional norms. It also forbids hospitals that choose to provide abortions from requiring individual doctors and nurses to do so; on the opposite side, hospitals opposed to abortions may not discipline doctors and nurses who choose to perform or assist them outside of their facilities.[84] In practice, no examination of sincerity takes place, as it has with pacifist objectors to military service; a simple assertion is sufficient. Although an insincere assertion is not inconceivable, say by a doctor who wants to please a man she is dating who objects to abortions, insincere claims here will be infrequent enough so that a simple assertion is adequate.

A possible worry about various exemptions is that they authorize a form of unequal treatment and may impede social progress. Here the equality concern is about women; if one respects women, shouldn't women have a right to get an abortion without any exemptions? One cannot deny that the equality worry *can* be a factor, but that does not seem nearly as important as the troublesome question about the beginning of life. It is relevant here that, according to various surveys, the percentage of women who have been opposed to abortions is about as great as that of men.[85]

Social progress can sometimes be a tricky question. Here, if the relevant beginning of life is hard to determine, defining what is genuine "progress" is not as simple as with various forms of unequal treatment, such as race and gender, now declared unconstitutional. But even if we believe social progress here is definitely toward acceptance of abortions, the role of exemptions is far from obvious. Many of those in Congress definitely did disagree with the decision in *Roe v. Wade*,[86] and they may have cast their law broadly partly to reflect that. However, as with many exemptions, this law likely softened objections. Although granting Roman Catholic hospitals their exemption may have created genuine impairment for women in areas in which only a Catholic hospital is present,[87] had those hospitals been forced to provide abortions, that could have led to much more intense resistance to the Court's constitutional ruling; and some of these hospitals, which admitted 17% of patients nationally in 2000,[88] might have gone out of business. Sometimes exemptions may well lead to greater acceptance of the creation of a new, controversial right than would an absolute duty imposed on everyone.

One question about an exemption here is whether it should be limited to religious claims. For individuals, given the reality that some may believe on nonreligious grounds that abortion amounts to the taking of innocent life, the restriction would be inappropriate. When it comes to hospitals, I believe it is much more dubious whether those running the institution will have such a powerful nonreligious objection to any performance within its premises. For this reason, contrary to what the federal law provides, the exemption for institutions from performance might well be limited to religious ones.

Two concerns about the federal statute and some relevant state laws are setting who qualifies for the exemption and when the privilege can be overridden. Looking at the federal wording, it may be somewhat arguable who is "performing" an abortion, but in any borderline instance of performing, a person is at least "assisting"; thus, the border of practical concern is what counts as assistance. Nurses handing instruments to doctors in the middle of the procedure are obviously doing that; a clerk who admits a patient into the hospital and a janitor who cleans all operation rooms are not. The status of a nurse called upon to provide concentrated attention to a woman admitted for an abortion for or after the procedure is more arguable. Although some vagueness exists at the edges, most situations will or will not count definitely as assistance, and that terminology is preferable to legislators trying to specify every degree of involvement that is included or not.

The federal law contains no explicit exception to required exemptions based on the patient's need. Especially for assistance but even for performance itself, a doctor or nurse should be compelled to act if that is critical for the patient. It is, again, hard to draw an exact line of when the risk or inconvenience is great enough; but the phrasing of a Louisiana law that participation is not required if the patient's "access to health care is not compromised"[89] is one sensible formulation.

A different medical practice to which some object is the use of contraceptives. Here, we can hardly imagine a powerful nonreligious objection to the use of all contraceptives, but some religions, notably Roman Catholicism, have claimed that the basic reason for sexual intercourse is the creation of new life. The use of contraceptives can then be seen as unacceptable, "contralife,"[90] and contrary to God's will. This church's basic position was recently qualified by Pope Francis, who accepted such use when women were concerned about contracting the Zika virus.[91]

More common is a belief that a contraceptive should not be used if it sometimes functions after fertilization or even after implantation. Such use is regarded by some as the accepting of an early form of abortion. Various individuals and enterprises may object to providing or assisting in the acquisition of contraceptives. A drugstore run by a devout Roman Catholic might decline to provide some or all of them; or an individual druggist may refuse to do so within a store that treats them like ordinary prescribed medicines. Whether any exemption should be granted from a legal requirement to make drugs available is a hard question, one the Supreme Court avoided in late June 2016 by denying certiorari in a case sustaining a state requirement that regardless of religious beliefs, pharmacists make these contraceptives available.[92] A key claim in the case was that given all the other permitted reasons not to supply drugs, the refusal to allow religious conviction, or conscience more broadly, as a basis amounted to a free exercise violation. The general principles of accommodating religious and nonreligious conscience do support an exemption so long as a woman can go to another drugstore within her locality. But if a woman who has been using a drugstore for many years is told that a prescribed contraceptive is not available, she may be both frustrated and embarrassed, and she may be disinclined to take the steps necessary to connect with a different drugstore. Thus, an exemption here could be seen as frustrating availability more than with an ordinary product one could easily buy elsewhere. Moreover, simply providing a product widely used is a much less direct participation than actually performing an abortion. Some states now do grant a privilege not to supply for "pharmacists" or "health care providers." In some, the privilege reaches conscience generally; in others it is limited to religious convictions.[93] If a state legislature decides to provide such a privilege, it should also reach individual pharmacists, who should be excused so long as another is easily available to provide the contraceptive.

I shall concentrate here on the less direct involvement of insurance. Should an employer be able to refuse to provide insurance for some or all contraceptive purchases? This issue led to the important and highly controversial ruling in the *Hobby Lobby* case[94] on the coverage of the Religious Freedom Restoration Act. That case leads one to consider what exemption is warranted, how specific it should be, and how RFRA should be interpreted. I shall suggest why I think the Court's approach to the statute in that case was seriously misguided in important ways.[95]

According to the Affordable Care Act, adopted under the Obama administration, companies of substantial size had to provide workers insurance that included contraceptives.[96] The relevant regulators under the act, which had been amended by the 2010 Health Care and Education Reconciliation Act, required such insurance from companies with fifty or more employees. The required insurance covered intrauterine devices, ella, and Plan B, which were believed by many[97] to sometimes work after "conception" (a term I shall use to include both operation after fertilization and implantation). The law originally exempted churches but not other religious organizations, such as hospitals and universities. The administration then expanded the privilege not to pay to religious-based enterprises such as hospitals, but for these the insurance companies themselves did have to give coverage to the employees. In the legal case, the owners of Hobby Lobby and another closely held business corporation objected on religious grounds to providing this insurance; they claimed a right to refuse under RFRA. The case directly involved how the statute's language should be understood in this context; lying in the background was whether this kind of issue should be addressed more specifically by legislators and whether here an exemption is really a good idea. As I shall contend briefly, these questions are interrelated because the debatability of an exemption can bear on how general language like that of RFRA should be interpreted.

The crucial language of RFRA is that the "government shall not substantially burden a person's exercise of religion even if the burden results from a rule of general applicability ... [unless] it demonstrates that application of the burden to the person (1) is in furtherance of a compelling government interest; and (2) is the least restrictive means of furthering that ... interest."[98] To succeed, a claimant must count as a "person" who is suffering a "substantial burden"; the claim can then succeed if the government lacks a compelling interest or if that interest can be achieved by a less restrictive means.

I shall touch on the application of these four criteria, but two general observations are of broader importance. When an expansive formulation is cast in terms of competing considerations, it is mistaken to view each as basically independent of the others. Rather they should be viewed in context. Thus, the greater the burden, the stronger the government's interest needs to be to overcome it. Second, when the application of this kind of approach to a highly important topic is debatable from the statutory language and not clear from legislative purpose, it is far preferable to get specific statutory provisions, rather than leaving this to a highly debatable judicial resolution.

Turning to the four standards, was Hobby Lobby a "person"? Justice Alito's opinion relies heavily on an obscure provision in federal law that contains a broad inclusion within the term "person," unless the context indicates otherwise.[99] One could see this conclusion as also supported by the treatment of such groups as churches being included as covered by RFRA. Given that the statute was designed to reinstate the free exercise constitutional standard that had been wiped out by *Employment Division v. Smith*, and the fact that these earlier constitutional decisions had not really focused on whether ordinary businesses qualified, it was impossible to conclude that this was definitely within the statutory purpose. And if one asks how an ordinary or sophisticated reader would have understood the language, it is unlikely they would have said, "'Person' here doesn't mean just persons, it is broadly inclusive." When one considers the aims and benefits of forming a corporation, such as making money and not being personally liable for business expenses or bankruptcy, the notion that owners need not possess all the rights of individuals and nonprofit corporations does not seem odd. Another perplexity, which the Court puts aside by suggesting that such claims are not likely to be raised by corporations with stockholders, is whether a line can be drawn between closely held corporations like Hobby Lobby, completely owned by their leaders, and corporations with public stocks. Some public stocks may be held by various persons with all sorts of religious convictions. Those who create a company *might* make only a minority of stocks available to others. Would it be fair for them to operate on the basis of their own religious convictions, especially if they have not made those clear at the outset? These are troublesome questions concerning whether the Court's concentration on closely held corporations will prove feasible over time.

This brings us to what should be a "substantial burden," a problem that can exist for other claims of religious and nonreligious conscience. Justice Alito's opinion basically says that it is evident that the claimants here perceive a substantial burden. That approach has a certain appeal, but it is not really viable as *the* legal standard. The appeal is this: What really counts as a "substantial burden" in my life is what I feel is such a burden. In this sense, for two people required to do the same thing, one may genuinely suffer a substantial burden and the other only a slight inconvenience or even welcomed involvement. Yet, this does not work as a legal standard for matters as to which persons can have ordinary self-interested reasons to obtain a privilege and are left to state what burden they would experience.

In *Hobby Lobby*, the business owners undertook considerable expenses and risks by bringing their law suits. As I shall explain, their success may well allow them to save some money. Once their right was firmly established, other owners of closely held corporations might have an incentive to make a similar claim; and in contrast with draft exemptions, no one is going to closely examine their sincerity. To make the degree of burden depend solely on personal feeling comes close in many contexts to eliminating "substantial" as a practical requirement. This is a powerful reason to make this standard one that rests partly on more general perceptions of what is a serious burden.

Closely related to this problem is the question of how direct is one's assistance. Providing insurance does not directly involve the purchase and use of a contraceptive by an employee. That is her independent decision. Although insurance could conceivably lead her to purchase something she would otherwise not buy, broadly that seems highly unlikely for contraceptives. These are not very expensive and most people who use them think they have strong reasons to do so. A crucial question about many possible exemptions, including those for same-sex marriage, is whether someone's involvement is direct enough to warrant such a privilege.

In respect to insurance, an interesting comparison, which also relates to possible alternative means, is taxation. When we all pay general income taxes, some of our money may go to endeavors we believe are misguided or even deeply immoral. Pacifist taxpayers will have their money fall into a general pool, part of which will be used for military expenses. In *United States v. Lee*,[100] a case decided after *Wisconsin v. Yoder*[101] (which allowed the Amish to withdraw children from school after eighth grade) and before *Employment Division v. Smith*, the Supreme Court denied the right of an Amish employer not to pay a social security tax. The basis for the objection to paying was that the employees were Amish and that accepting social security benefits was at odds with the Amish religion. The Supreme Court, with only one dissenter, rejected this claim. Although the ground expressed in the opinion concerned alternative government means, one way of regarding the result is that paying taxes did not really seem a substantial burden. In this respect, how different is providing insurance coverage? Is the burden really more substantial?

In *Hobby Lobby*, the majority opinion did not argue that the government lacked a compelling interest in providing insurance coverage. As I have noted in other contexts, the free exercise compelling interest standard has never been taken as demanding as that for interferences with free speech or classifications that disadvantage racial minorities. In any event, the four dissenters and Justice Kennedy's concurrence regarded a compelling interest as definitely involved.

This brings us to the complex question of whether a relevant less-restrictive means was present in this context, which again relates to the Amish tax case. In *Lee* the Court ruled that the government had a compelling interest in collecting taxes and lacked a less-restrictive means to accomplish its objective. This effectively used a fairly relaxed standard of less-restrictive means. If the government granted an exemption only for religious enterprises run by believers who were opposed to the use of Social Security and who employed workers with similar views, the government itself could bear the minimal financial cost for workers who later left the faith and needed public financial support as they aged.[102] Another option, one I have noted about civilian service in the draft context, would be to give any business the option of paying a bit more than it would owe for social security but have their taxes go to a different use. This indeed might be employed for any claimed objections to particular uses of taxes.

The *Hobby Lobby* Court found the less restrictive alternative by resting on how the administration was treating religious organizations. They were freed from paying for the insurance, but the insurance companies had to provide it; thus it would still be available for the workers. It turns out that how this would work is not so easy to discern. A business may pay an insurance company, which gives the money to the individual worker. If the business stops paying for contraceptive insurance and the insurance company must provide that, will that not raise its costs? In one sense, perhaps not. If the insurance was not provided for contraceptives and fewer of these were used, then the costs for insurance for abortions and pregnancies would rise. Thus, bearing the cost may be better than leaving no insurance coverage. But in another sense, the cost for the insurance company has definitely risen, because if the business itself had paid for covering contraceptives, the company would not have needed to do so. In other words, the insurance company would be bearing a cost it would not have were no exemption granted. The end result is likely that the insurance company would raise the cost of providing broad insurance either for that particular business or more generally.

For closely held corporations or religious enterprises like universities that provide their own insurance, the option is that they hire an independent agent who sees that a separate insurance company provides for contraceptives. That company is recompensed by paying a reduced amount to the government for participation in the Federally Facilitated Exchange Insurance. The way this works out is that by indirect steps the government is effectively paying for insurance that the corporation is avoiding. This is extremely close to the option rejected in *Lee* that the government would pay for social security benefits not supported by an objecting business. Just how all this will function is far from clear, but what is certain is that despite the similarity of claims, the Court took a much more generous approach to religious claims here than about tax payments and was implicitly more willing to have ultimate expenses fall on the government.

The various complications I have sketched help provide a sense of why using a general statute like RFRA to protect the indirect assistance of insurance coverage by for-profit businesses is highly doubtful.

In 2016, the Supreme Court was reviewing claims made by religious organizations and some businesses that they should not have to file documents that will be used to make clear their position and provide the basis for acquiring an alternative way to assure coverage. Given that the eight Justices sitting after Justice Scalia's death had been divided in *Hobby Lobby* itself, and the mostly negative decisions by lower courts, it seemed unlikely that these claims would persuade a Supreme Court majority of the sitting Justices. What actually happened was a remand to lower courts to try to work out compromises between the parties,[103] almost certainly a consequence of a 4–4 division among the Justices.

The *Hobby Lobby* case strongly illustrates how difficult it is to conclude just how far religious concessions should be offered to those whose objection to a practice reaches "assistance" that is really only indirect. It also shows crucial problems involved in interpreting a general statute like RFRA, whose application is far from evident. I have strongly suggested that with such a law, taking each criterion as completely separate is a misguided technique of interpretation. Also these complexities strongly favor a more specific legislative focus. Many of those complications are also involved in the subject of the next section—exemptions in respect to same-sex marriage.

## Same-Sex Marriage and Exemptions

By far the most controversial present question about exemptions concerns same-sex marriage. Now that the Supreme Court in *Obergefell v. Hodges*[104] has held that same-sex couples have a constitutional right to marry, should individuals and organizations have to treat them equally or not? Clearly we can see a powerful free exercise basis for granting at least some exemptions for people who believe that such marriages are contrary to God's will; but in thinking about the range of an appropriate exemption, it is important here to consider other situations in which people deal with those who have acted wrongly in their view. As for objections to exemptions here, we can conceive of one as involving resistance to establishing religion against other social values, but the main concern, as with abortions, is the welfare and dignity of those who will not be treated equally.

Because the rhetoric in debates about this issue is not always clear about the relation between the Supreme Court's decision and the status of possible exemptions, I shall begin by sketching the basis for the Court's ruling, how far that directly relates to exemptions, and the degree to which its underlying grounds bear on those.

By a 5–4 margin, the Court ruled that same-sex couples had a constitutional right to marry. Given the consistent historical view in this country that marriage is between men and women, the Court could definitely not rely on a specific original perception of the constitutional text, but Justice Kennedy did claim that when open-ended provisions were adopted, the understanding was that their application would develop over time as the perception of basic values increased. His opinion relied primarily on the liberty values which he treated as aspects of the Due Process Clause of the Fourteenth Amendment, but he also discerned a violation of Equal Protection. The opinion emphasized individual autonomy and how the right to marry and create an enduring bond promotes expression, intimacy, and spirituality. Kennedy urged that marriage is a keystone in our social order carrying many "rights, benefits, and responsibilities," and that the marriage union is obviously beneficial for children, a substantial number of whom in this country are now within the custody of same-sex couples or individual homosexuals. The equality concern rests on past discrimination against gay individuals and the absence of any forceful reason not to afford them this marriage right granted to others.

The basic position of the four dissenters was not that same-sex marriage is really a bad idea, but that it was inappropriate for the Court to effectively legislate this, rather than leaving it to development by actual legislators over time. It is interesting in this respect that, viewed in light of the fact that a substantial number of state legislators had already adopted this right, what the Court did here was less radical than the fundamental abortion decision of *Roe v. Wade*. It is genuinely debatable whether this decision and its constitutional reasoning were convincing. Given that I believe evolutionary interpretation of clauses protecting general rights is both wise and really unavoidable,[105] and my sense that overall values point strongly in favor of allowing same-sex marriage, I regard the result as sound. However, I think equal protection provides a much more straightforward basis for it than "substantive" due process; and I suspect that may be true for some of the justices who joined the Kennedy opinion.[106] With this brief comment I shall put aside the basic constitutional issue. What matters more for exemptions is whether the basic arguments for them are strong, and what is the force of contrary views.

The constitutional decision does not itself tell us how private individuals and organizations must treat same-sex married couples. In many of our choices in life, we can categorize in all sorts of ways that are constitutionally barred for the federal and state governments. Bars on differential treatment depend on antidiscrimination statutes. These have greatly increased over time in what relations they cover and have also extended in terms of forbidden classifications. Twenty states and the District of Columbia now do explicitly forbid discrimination based on sexual orientation;[107] barring any special qualifications, those would include negative treatment of same-sex married couples.

The desirability of a law barring discrimination does not itself tell us when an exemption is also wise. Virtually all of those laws in this country either do not cover close personal involvements or provide exemptions for those. For example, Title VII of the 1964 Federal Act barring racial discrimination in rentals did not include situations in which an owner lived in a boarding house with fewer than five units.[108]

When we turn to same-sex marriage, we need to consider the strength of objections to providing equal treatment, how closely related these are to general rejection of gay sexual behavior, and the force of competing considerations. Many religious persons believe that the Bible tells us that God regards marriage as between men and women, and the historical connection between marriage and the creation and raising of children, emphasized by Justice Alito's dissent in *Obergefell*,[109] can lead to a similar view. Although it has been claimed that objections to same-sex marriage come down to nothing more than prejudice against homosexuals,[110] and without doubt for many objectors these are closely connected, matters are not so simple. A person might believe gay sexual relations are fine or are no worse than heterosexual sex outside of marriage, but still think that gay marriage is not appropriate. *Or* he might have a negative view about these sexual relations but also see extra reasons why a marriage is wrongful. These perceptions about the marriage would not necessarily lead someone to conclude that withholding legal recognition is called for, given present understanding within our society, but he might wish to avoid personal or institutional involvement. This has been basically the position of the Mormon Church, which has not altered its own nonacceptance of such marriage, but did not oppose an antidiscrimination statute in Utah so long as exemptions were provided.[111]

One argument against any exemption is that it would support an unfair, irrational religious claim, a kind of unjustified establishment that supports objectionable inequality. A related argument is that an exemption interferes with equal treatment and impairs the equal dignity of the couples denied services. Not infrequently, an analogy is drawn to interracial marriage, for which many exemptions after the Supreme Court's ruling protecting that in *Loving v. Virginia*[112] would have been gravely mistaken.

Without going into detail, I shall note two unpersuasive aspects of that analogy. The first is that within the South at the time, given the widespread discrimination against Negros, if some services such as hotel use could be denied to interracial couples, they could have found it very hard to find any availability. The more central difference concerns what counted as the "interracial" marriage that would be treated negatively. If you were one-eighth black and seven-eighths white, you counted as Negro in many southern states. You could marry someone who was all black but not someone who was white. And most of those states did not bar marriages between Asians and whites.[113] The state laws, and the public perceptions that survived their unconstitutionality, were really about preserving white superiority, not an aim to keep races separate and equal. Although many people did have religious convictions that "interracial" marriage was wrong, the supposed religious sources of that view[114] really did not support the criteria by which people were classified. Since an objection to same-sex marriage is not likely to favor one gender or another, it is significantly different from a similar view about what Americans have regarded as "interracial" marriage.

Where does this leave us? I believe the soundest approach is to distinguish actual participation in a marriage from subsequent treatment of married couples. Almost everyone in our society relates to, and provides services for, others whose moral views and past behavior may conflict with their views. Hotels whose leaders object to ordinary criminal behavior, abortions, and sex outside of marriage, and do not think remarriage is appropriate for persons who have received merely civil divorce without religious annulment, do not refuse rooms to couples or individuals who have acted contrary to one of these standards. Of course, when a couple seeks to check in, any of these aspects will be less obvious than whether they are of the same gender, but the hotels rarely make an inquiry about these other matters or refuse service to those whose relations or past acts are actually known. I believe that for these kinds of connections, special exemptions for same-sex marriage are unwarranted, although in some jurisdictions they may now be politically necessary to get adopted an antidiscrimination statute covering same-sex married couples or homosexuals or both.

Actual participation in the marriage is different. People should not be required to participate directly in practices they see as fundamentally wrong. As far as religious institutions that perform marriages are involved, they are almost certainly constitutionally protected from having to perform ceremonies they believe violate God's will. This conclusion is strongly supported by the Supreme Court's unanimous decision that churches and religious institutions can discriminate on whatever grounds they choose in hiring clerics.

What should count as actual participation for individuals and organizations that do not themselves perform the wedding? That is not itself simple, and is certainly contestable about some circumstances. But to take the facts of two leading cases, I believe that being the primary photographer, taking hundreds of pictures whose collection is designed to last a lifetime and be treasured by the married couple[115] is sufficiently direct, but to bake a cake for a wedding celebration is not,[116] since cakes are baked for all sorts of occasions that no one considers as approved by the bakers.

To clarify, the line I am suggesting is not simply a matter of "during or after" a wedding takes place. In what follows, I briefly mention the adoption of children, which can be seen as involvement in the wedding much more than providing ordinary services. And some services before or at the time of the wedding itself, such as cleaning a room or turning lights on, should not qualify as participation. The involvement of the photographer is much deeper and more direct. Undoubtedly this line, which somewhat resembles "perform or assist" for abortions, will not always be simple to draw but most forms of involvement will clearly fall on one side or the other.

Once a couple is legally married they have a right to be provided the insurance benefits of married partners. Since this follows after the ceremony and does not affect its taking place, it is even more indirect than providing insurance for contraceptives; and we are not aware of companies with religious leaders that deny such insurance to a worker because they believe he did not undertake an annulment that would end his first marriage but got only a civil divorce that failed to justify a second marriage from the religious point of view. If such a company would provide insurance although it sees a second marriage as a kind of bigamy, it is hard to see why it should refuse it for same-sex married partners.

Should an exemption in respect to same-sex marriage be limited to religious claims? If it is properly limited to direct participation, I think not. Although most objections to being involved will be religious, we can conceive of similar nonreligious ones and, given the narrowness of the privilege, it does not make sense to draw that line and require at least a theoretical need to decide if someone's convictions are genuinely religious. In those states where the convictions of most legislators or the need for a political compromise make a broader exemption necessary to achieve adoption of antidiscrimination provisions, I believe it would be desirable to limit more extensive accommodations to religious grounds. This would reduce the concern that various organizations might simply concede to prevailing sentiments within local communities. If the exemption is broader in this way, firms should also have to provide public notice of their positions,[117] and they should be unable to refuse a service if a couple cannot conveniently find someone else to provide it. The serious problem of determining how accessible services can be if some businesses refuse them[118] is itself an added reason not to extend the exemption beyond direct participation.

Two special issues are raised by government officials and by adoption. For officials, the constitutional ruling has direct relevance. If people have a constitutional right to receive a benefit, government offices that provide that benefit cannot refuse to provide it. Thus, the action of Kim Davis of essentially closing off her entire bureau from providing marriage licenses for gay couples was at odds with the *Obergefell* ruling. However, that does not resolve what should be done about individual workers. Some government lawyers who believe death sentences are wrong but are employed in states that maintain them have not been required to actually work on capital punishment cases. They do not have a formulated legal right not to participate but are essentially granted the privilege by the discretion of their supervisors. Should such a privilege be afforded in respect to performing a civil marriage ceremony or issuing a marriage license for gay couples? I think the answer is "yes," but the strength of the argument favoring this and the extent of its reach varies depending on a central factor.

Suppose a person got employed by a marriage bureau well before the right to same-sex marriage was established. Someone who joined such an office twenty years ago would not have conceived this marriage as likely within her duties. To tell her she *must* now treat it like all other marriages or lose her job is harsh. An office should make a serious effort to set things up so she is not required to do that. On the other hand, if such marriage is already recognized when someone takes the job, requiring her to provide it is perfectly reasonable, unless she can be excused without any actual inconvenience for others. In both situations, anyone's right to decline should not inconvenience or embarrass the couple seeking to get married. For an official to say: "Because I object to gay marriage, please wait a few minutes while I get someone else," should be unacceptable because this can cause hurt feelings, anger, and embarrassment at a crucial point in the couple's lives.

Adoptions present a much more complicated set of questions. Putting children up for adoption can rightfully be seen as much more of an involvement in a marriage than the provision of other services. However, given that the key to adoption is the welfare of children, it does not really make sense to preclude all same-sex married couples, given that many children are now raised by single parents some of whom are homosexual. I believe absolute preclusion of such couples should not be allowed. But can their status be taken into account? Adoption agencies can, and should, consider factors like age and income that are not broadly permitted. And despite the strong diminution in social differences between men and women, one might still believe that, other things being equal, having parents of both genders or of one's own gender is usually preferable to having two of the opposite gender. Religious adoption agencies are not precluded from taking the religious connections of prospective parents into account. In light of these various considerations, I think it makes sense to allow the genders of a couple seeking to adopt to be taken into account but not to permit the complete ruling out of same-sex married couples.

On many of the questions about same-sex marriage and exemptions from antidiscrimination laws we have no simple answers. Some such exemptions are definitely constitutional, since they exist for other antidiscrimination laws; but very broad religious exemptions might be seen as violating both the Equal Protection Clause and the Establishment Clause. In terms of legislative wisdom, the crucial premise is that we need to care for each other and recognize both the force of competing convictions and the strength with which they are held. Those who believe God does not authorize same-sex marriage need to understand why many people now think such marriage is obviously warranted, and why gay couples have a powerful feeling that they deserve equal treatment, both for their practical convenience and their dignity. Those who strongly favor same-sex marriage need to acknowledge that the idea that it is inappropriate is deeply rooted in the Jewish and Christian traditions and in our country's history. They should not be intolerant of those who subscribe to that position. The more those on each side try to understand and tolerate each other, the better can be the resolution of the bases for antidiscrimination requirements and certain exemptions from these. That could help produce a more tolerant and unified society.

In much of this chapter, we have seen how accommodations to religious exercise points toward exemptions from general duties, but competing reasons of nonestablishment and basic equality are also in play. This makes desirable resolutions difficult. Often these should not be left to general statutes like RFRA, but receive specific focus. Sometimes exemptions should include nonreligious convictions, but sometimes not. Nearly always, understanding and tolerating the views of others is extremely important.

# PART THREE

# Discourse Regarding Religion within Public Schools

CHAPTERS 5, 6, AND 7 ADDRESS various issues about how religion may affect teaching and other communications within public schools. We have already considered the basic impermissibility of those schools themselves carrying out forms of religious worship, the allowance of their having simple moments of silence, and the acceptability of students using classrooms after school for religious meetings. Here we shall look at what teachers may actually say about religion and what they can avoid teaching because of people's religious convictions. One illustration of these questions we shall examine is the possibility of not teaching evolution or of suggesting "intelligent design" as a complete or partial alternative to that. Other topics covered are the relation of religions to the teaching of history, literature, morality, and social justice, and how far students and teachers should be able to express personal religious perspectives.

For many of these issues, the relation of free exercise and nonestablishment is considerably more complicated than it is regarding simple Bible reading and prayer at the start of the school day. A decision not to teach evolution does not directly promote "free exercise" or constitute an obvious "establishment" of religion. But it would almost certainly be grounded on religious convictions that the schools chose to accommodate and prioritize over ordinary criteria for educational classes. Teaching objectively "about religion" is in principle not really related to either religious exercise or nonestablishment, but the concern can be that, almost inevitably, some religions may be favored and others treated in a negative, misguided way. This could be seen as in tension with both clauses. However, if schools don't teach anything about religion, is that not effectively an establishment of nonreligion and a subtle inhibition on religious exercise? We will delve into these complexities, but it is crucial to see here that various tensions need not be simple or direct.

Between these variations and what arguably serves religion-clause values lies a constant theme of this book. Even when these values are undoubtedly in play, one needs to distinguish between what courts have, or should, declare unconstitutional, what others, including school boards, administrators, and teachers, should see as constitutionally required even if they are fairly sure a court would not overturn a contrary choice, and what those others should regard as a wise balance of values within the range of what is constitutionally permitted. To be clear, I am not asserting that nonjudicial officials should typically agonize over whether what strikes them as unwise is only that or is actually constitutionally forbidden beyond judicial invalidation. What is important is that officials in all areas and the rest of us should understand that constitutional coverage is not simply a matter of what courts will determine.

How do these general observations relate to public schools? For this, we need to ask ourselves what part these schools play in the lives of our culture and how decisions about their practices are made. Schools are clearly among the most important governmental institutions in our society. They provide education for the vast majority of our citizens.[1] What does this education do? Most obviously, it is a source of vocational training. The capacity to think and to read and write (in whatever form one now writes) is crucial for many jobs. This importance of educational skills has been partly reflected by the insistence of some Presidential candidates that college education should be provided free,[2] or at least at a much-reduced cost, for young people who will otherwise not receive that education or will get it only by falling into serious debt.

A second benefit is that such education increases a person's knowledge and helps her to enrich her life. Related to this is teaching young people to participate in our civic life, to think for themselves, express their views, respect others, and respond to what others believe. Public schools also aim to develop desirable moral convictions and actions. Some have doubted whether schools really should be teaching what is a "good life," in the sense of a desirable way to live; but clearly, teaching students to be honest and respectful, to care for others, to appreciate art and music, and to avoid becoming drug addicts or alcoholics, is basically uncontroversial. Just how far schools should enter into what is a good life and how that may relate to religion is much more complex and is part of the controversy about how public schools should treat religion.

In respect to what should or should not be uttered in public schools, decisions are made in various ways by state legislatures, councils of education, commissioners, state and local school boards, faculties, and individual teachers. The danger that individual outlooks and prejudices will determine what is mandated or permitted may increase as the decisions become more localized and personal. That may seem to call for greater judicial involvement. But local decisions may also be more sensitive to the actual aspects of particular communities and circumstances, making judicial assessment of a possible constitutional violation more difficult. Judges may also doubt how far intervention in a highly particular situation that is not causing anyone serious harm is worth undertaking.

Another factor in play for some of these issues is how free speech is involved. If teachers and students are at liberty to express their views about many topics, can and should religious perspectives be treated as special in regard to having their utterances forbidden?

# CHAPTER 5

# Teaching about Religion

## General Considerations

If public schools should not engage in prayers and religious ceremonies, should they refrain from teaching about religion? As a simple matter of principle, the obvious answer is "no." Religious convictions, organizations, and movements have been a crucial component of history in all parts of the world, and they remain an important aspect in a high percentage of cultures including ours in the United States. In this country religious perspectives and organizations played key roles in the abolition of slavery, the prohibition of alcohol, and the development of civil rights in the era of Martin Luther King, Jr. They continue to affect approaches to abortions, stem cell research, capital punishment, contraceptives, and how same-sex married couples should be treated. To omit reference or minimize the significance of religion for such subjects is to provide a misguided, far from objective account of what has mattered and still counts for a huge proportion of the world's population. How could essential disregard be a defensible approach within history or social studies?

Of course, the Supreme Court's position on forms of worship makes clear that public schools may teach neither the truth or falsity of certain basic religious premises, such as "God exists," "Jesus Christ is the son of God," and "we have life after death." To teach these as true would violate the initial two strands of the basic test of *Lemon v. Kurtzman.*[1] They would have a purpose of promoting religion and would have that effect. Whether an outright rejection of certain religious premises would be seen as actually furthering one or more competing religions might depend on the actual community,[2] but that is not really important since promoting antireligion is clearly now also taken to violate the Establishment Clause. Precluding the public teaching of the truth of specific religious doctrines does not tell us how schools should address the role of religions in human history and how they affect the cultures of our own time.

A failure to teach about religion is not only fundamentally inaccurate; it raises concerns about both nonestablishment and free exercise. Radically downplaying the place of religion could be seen as a kind of establishment of nonreligion. Despite its using a somewhat confusing terminology, the Supreme Court has made it clear that under modern understanding, the Establishment Clause does preclude a government establishment of an antireligious outlook, as well as those that are religious in any typical sense. Although a failure to teach about religion does not directly impede religious exercise, since students and others are still free to worship as they choose, it can have the indirect effect of implicitly conveying to students the message that religion is not really important. That could have a negative effect on the development of religious convictions and discourage religious exercise now or in the future. Relatedly, some parents might see this disregard of religion as impeding their own attempts to teach and encourage their children to become serious religious practitioners. Typically, devout parents will see such encouraging of their children as a significant aspect of their own religious exercise.

When it disallowed the religious practice of Bible reading in schools, the Court also acknowledged that "[I]t might well be said that one's education is not complete without a study of comparative religion or the history of its relationship to the advancement of civilization." Such teaching and study of the Bible "for its literary or historic qualities" can be "effected consistently with the First Amendment."[3] In concurring opinions Justices Brennan and Goldberg made similar points.[4]

Among the related concerns that teaching about religion raises are objectivity, actual effects, and the perceptions of students and their parents. Much depends here on the competence of teachers and book writers and the character of the community in which the teachers are located. Can anyone be fully objective about the place of various religions in the lives of particular cultures and human development? "Fully objective" is in fact an unfair starting point because none of us is fully objective about most subjects in our lives. We can be objective about whether 2 + 2 = 4 and whether it snowed yesterday, but can anyone be completely objective about how far Barack Obama was a good president? Even if no history book or teacher can be completely objective about crucial subjects, in respect to some of these, such as race relations and the bases for certain military conflicts, this is especially difficult. Perhaps books and instructors can be more objective about most things than the nature of religion and its place in history. How important, for example, was the Protestant Reformation in the development of Western history, and how far were serious conflicts that took many lives essentially caused by Roman Catholic or Protestant reactions to their conflicting views? To take a more modern example, what are the core premises of the Muslim religion and how far, if at all, do the terrorist beliefs of ISIS connect to those premises? As an outsider, I assume this is much less simple than understanding that Quaker pacifism is connected to passages in the New Testament.

Apart from how objective a teaching approach may actually be, how will it be perceived? Devout Protestants and Catholics will probably not see the Reformation in precisely the same way; Muslims unsympathetic to ISIS will not be likely to see the religion's basic premises as providing any support for terrorism; some thoughtful non-Muslims may see a bit of support, as they can discern for Quaker pacifism, but far less than leaders of ISIS assert. The truth is that almost any particular presentation of the central premises of a religion and the religion's effect over time may be seen as misguided by many. And in contrast to other assertions about one-sided historical accounts, this "inaccuracy" will be perceived as offensive if it teaches aspects of one's own faith as unusual or bizarre or downplays its positive role in cultural development. People can also be offended by what they see as too much credit being given to a competing religion.

How far the same presentation will seem wrongheaded will almost certainly vary within different communities. These concerns are one reason why the texts used in public schools say so little about religion, even though the text writers, experts within their fields, probably have the ability to be more objective about these topics than the average teacher.

Somewhat related to these concerns about the actual degree of objective fairness and the perceptions of believers and nonbelievers about whether accounts are fair is the likely effect on students who are the audiences of presentations. Let us imagine that two evangelical Protestant couples, who believe strongly in personal interactions with God, have children in public schools. They understand that the schools cannot teach the truth of their faiths or assert that it is the only religion with genuine positive effects on cultures. The first couple may take this perspective: "If religion is nearly totally disregarded in the school, our kids may be brought to feel it is not really important in human life; thus the secular approach of school may lead them to abandon our religion altogether or give it much less significance than it deserves." For them, efforts at objective accounts in history and other courses would be preferable. The other couple may see things differently: "If the school omits treatment of religion, the children will grasp that its importance is understood outside of school; an 'objective' teaching approach, however accurate, to our religion among many is likely to be more destructive of our basic faith in how God affects their lives than the school's disinvolvement in the whole subject." In truth, parents could reasonably perceive things in either of these ways *and* each perspective is probably accurate about the likely effects on some children.

This makes it nearly impossible to draw a comprehensive conclusion about whether the effect on religious life is likely to be greater if schools continue to deemphasize the place of religion in history and culture or attempt harder to present it objectively. A minor point here is that what makes the most sense may well depend on the age and previous education of children. For students in public universities, efforts to include religion fairly does not generate the concerns it might have for students in seventh and eighth grades.

When we see these various complexities, we should not be surprised that courts have had little involvement in the relevant decisions about what to teach. Judges will be hard put to determine how far more or less teaching *about* religion may create a kind of indirect barrier to religious exercise. Not surprisingly, these matters have been mostly left to local choices. As I have noted, that does not mean educators should pay no attention to free exercise and nonestablishment values, and it does not even mean that, if they reflect, they should not see certain choices as possibly at odds with what are judicially unenforced constitutional requirements. With these general concerns, I now turn to specific topics.

## History and Social Studies

Given the place that religious organizations have played in human history and still play within many cultures, disregard of their place within relevant courses is both misleading and misguided. The Protestant Reformation was an important factor in the development of Western cultures, including that of the United States. To understand that effect, one needs at least some sense of what led various groups, such as Lutherans and Presbyterians, to break from the dominant Roman Catholic religion. When one thinks about the development of communism and the treatment of religious groups within communist countries, it helps to understand that Marxism was essentially an atheist philosophy. One can, of course, imagine a religious version of communism, but development within the Soviet Union and its relations with other countries were affected by its antireligious premises.

When one aims to explain the effect of religious or antireligious convictions, one needs to describe, at least briefly, the convictions' content. To take an obvious example, the fact that Protestantism saw relations to God as more individual and faith based and less dependent than Roman Catholicism on a reliable, designated, hierarchical organization certainly bore on its general effect on how the European culture moved forward. Similarly, the settling in many parts of northern America depended on desires to escape the imposition of basic premises about an established Anglican religion within England. For some, what was sought was both separation of government officials from religious institutions and the dominance of a better religion, such as Puritanism in New England; for others, such as the Quakers in Pennsylvania, greater religious freedom was a powerful objective. One cannot really explain such developments without giving some account of what were the relevant beliefs and practices. The same is true in modern times with respect to many of the world's cultures.

If one focuses on more recent cultural aspects within the United States, one can see that tensions between Protestants and Roman Catholics have diminished greatly over the last century, and in the 2016 presidential contest, some Republicans relied on their religious beliefs in seeking support from a large percentage of Evangelical Protestants.[5] To understand the decline in tension between Protestants and Roman Catholics, we can identify many factors. One is that as the Roman Catholic percentage of the Christian population has increased,[6] along with the growth of other religious groups,

Protestants more easily accept that this is not a "Protestant" country. From the late nineteenth century, the Roman Catholic church has become increasingly accepting of liberal democracies that are not governed by its true religious faith. Also relevant, its leaders, notably the present Pope Francis, have reached out broadly to those with other religious views, urging common objectives, such as assisting the poor and disadvantaged.

Any reasonable account of history cannot disregard all this. Although public schools cannot teach that any particular religious view is right or is obviously wrong, they need some account of various views to explain what has happened. To draw on a nonreligious analogue, one could not sensibly teach why left-wing Democrats take political positions at odds with right-wing Republicans without explaining their different positions about human life and about how governments operate. I do not mean to suggest that textbooks and teachers need to go into great detail about various religious perceptions, but an explanation of basic factors is very important for certain aspects of history and is achievable.

As already explained, this intrinsic relevance is more straightforward than the religion clause values that come into play. If religion is disregarded or deemphasized, that can send an implicit message that it genuinely lacks importance or perhaps is even negative for human life. This can be seen as a kind of indirect discouragement of free exercise and as an implicit establishment of secular values over religious ones. An interesting possible response to this concern is that various religions often lead to violent conflicts or more modestly to the putting down of members of other faiths. An objective account of their effects *might* produce a more negative view than total disregard of religious influences. The basic answer to this response is that if one portrays the truth of what has happened in history, the effect that may have on individual persons' beliefs is not the government's responsibility. By contrast, a decision to simply omit relevant aspects does involve a government choice that could be seen as at odds with religious clause values as well as essential historical accuracy.

Within any actual community, just how much should be taught about all this may depend partly on the likely reactions of actual students and parents. Is there a tense division between evangelical Protestants and Catholics? Is there a minority of Muslims disturbed by non-Muslim citizens? Should these circumstances bear on what schools should teach and what they should sensibly omit or how they explain their curriculum to parents and students?

Another concern is how objective one can expect teachers to be. They should do fairly well in explaining in what ways Martin Luther found himself at odds with the Catholic hierarchy, but how many would be able to describe just how far ISIS terrorism is supportable or not by certain premises of Islam? These concerns about objectivity and the actual reactions of students and parents do not only touch on what may be unwise because doing it will create senses of unfairness and possible psychological conflicts among many students; they also count for the limits of appropriate judicial involvement. Judges will be hard put to say just how much coverage is needed, what amounts to an unacceptable deviation from objectivity, and when omissions are appropriate to avoid discontent and strife within a school or the larger community.

## Literature and Music

Matters are fairly simple when it comes to courses in literature and music classes and performance. If a school is teaching students about literature and its effects, it is certainly appropriate to include literary texts that are part of a religious tradition. Here the Bible is the most notable example in dominantly Christian countries. What may not be done is to assert that the Bible is being used because it is actually is the word of God or reflects a foolish view about the basic nature of human existence. It would also be misguided to put the Bible at the center of all literature, spending most of class time on that, since doing so would implicitly convey that the Bible is intrinsically central for human existence, not merely a dominant text in the history of Jewish and Christian populations.

What I have said about literature also applies to music classes and performance. At some stages of Western history, a high proportion of compositions had religious themes. To say that schools could have students listen to Mozart's piano concertos but not to any of his masses would be silly. For some earlier composers, the percentage of religious themes was even greater. Within classes in which students are taught to sing, various church-related songs can also be relevant. A notable example here is carols during Christmas seasons. A third involvement may be actual performances by students within schools of operas, operettas, musicals, and religious music such as masses. So long as the leaders make clear that the objective is not to convey the necessary truth of religious themes and language, these can be parts of musical training and exercise. Of course, as with literature, a public school music class should not focus exclusively or primarily on religious music. Further, with the singing of some pieces, such as Christmas carols, two concerns may be in play. One is that this is not only a response to community popularity of this particular music, but implicitly seems to endorse its basic truth. The second concern is that nonbelieving students may be uncomfortable even singing premises they do not accept, and some may feel they must remain silent. Within different settings, these considerations are ones that those who are deciding what music to use should take into account, but they are probably too uncertain to lead to judicial involvement, so long as it is clear that no assertion is being made about the fundamental truth of the language involved.

### Civic Obligations, Morality, and the Good Life

Things become much more complicated when we turn from domains that are essentially factual or aesthetic to how youngsters should behave now and in the future. These are subjects on which religions take significant positions; unfortunately, we often, but not always, lack any definite resolution about proper actions reachable by ordinary objective appraisals, a subject tackled in Part V of this book. Among the problems here are that it is much harder to distinguish what people subscribe to according to nonreligious appraisals from how far religious bases contribute to what they believe. How much aid should the government provide for those who are poor or otherwise disadvantaged? Using the example of Pope Francis's urging more assistance to the disadvantaged during his 2016 visit to Mexico,[7] how far would the position of a Roman Catholic or another Christian be affected by her sense of what are the objectives of a liberal democracy conceived independent of religious premises, and how far would basic Christian beliefs about what we owe to each other come into play? Although, as the last part of the book will examine, articulating reasons in one form or the other may not be so difficult and may be advisable in some settings, people seeking to arrive at their positions may not experience a convenient separation of the force of religions and broader outlooks.

Because of this difficulty, should schools simply avoid teaching students about how to behave? Although some may disagree about what I shall call the category of the "good life," the basic answer is clearly "no." Part of how we should live our lives in relation to others concerns our civic obligations. We should not deny others their legal and political rights; we should pay our taxes. Plainly schools should teach the basic obligations for citizens that relate to the political order in which they live. I shall turn shortly to certain disputable issues in this domain, but for the most part one can identify and teach these obligations independent of religious convictions and without referring to those. Insofar as teachers see these supported by religious traditions over time, saying so would be appropriate, so long as the historical account does not assert religious truth or falsity.

What about what we owe to others more broadly and conceptions of the good life concerning how we should live? Because how we should treat others more generally is not so easy to distinguish from civic obligations, I shall start with aspects of the good life that are essentially self-regarding, although, of course, all of how we live can affect others. Should we seek to be physically healthy, to find work that will interest us and provide adequate compensation, to use our free time—or at least some of it—in a productive way, to engage in relationships with others—including romantic involvements—that are not merely superficial? Some have claimed that schools should stay free of moral instruction, leaving that to the private sector. But part of what schools are about is helping students to learn what forms of life will be rewarding and satisfying. At least if it does not produce tensions and anxieties, an interesting occupation is more satisfying than one that is boring and tedious. Relations with others are more rewarding when they reach a certain depth. Even if drinking whiskey and using heroin can be appealing for many at some stages, alcoholism and drug addiction are not satisfying lifestyles, and they threaten physical health. More generally, since physical health is preferable to impairment, students should be encouraged to live in ways that will promote that. In brief, even when it comes to a "good life," some teaching that does not rest directly on religious convictions is definitely a crucial part of public education.

What of an approach that is actually at odds with many religious convictions? Although it has faded in popularity, "values clarification" was once embraced by many school educators. Texts based on this theory suggested that students should clarify their values and make informed choices about what they really value. According to one summary, this was a seven-step method by which a "child develops values by (1) choosing his values freely (2) from among alternatives, (3) after giving thoughtful considerations to the consequences of each alternative; the child shall prize the choice by (4) being happy with the choice and (5) affirming the choice publicly; he should (6) act upon his value choice (7) repeatedly developing it into a pattern in his life."[8] Although exactly how this might be presented could vary, the basic idea was that one's values properly depend on what seems the right way to live according to one's own reflective intuitions. This is in obvious contrast to what many religions teach. If a school is to present such a recommendation, the teacher must make clear that this is one encompassing approach and that it is in contrast, at least for much of how we live, from many, perhaps all, religions.

Concerns about how we should treat others apart from our political and legal responsibilities can be seen as intermediate between those obligations and the good life, but in fact this aspect of morality cannot really be separated from the others. Consider the idea that parents should afford care and love for their children. This is directly about how some people should treat others, but almost everyone assumes that genuine caring for one's children is a better life for the parents themselves (and not only because they are fulfilling a responsibility). And it is easy to conclude that children who are well treated are likely to become better, more caring citizens than those who do not benefit from this parental involvement. Thus, genuine caring for one's children can be seen as an aspect of one's civic responsibilities. The idea that men should treat women equally in major respects also cuts across personal morality and the broader social and political life. The belief that a person's life is better for himself if at least some of his relationships have genuine depth and are not superficial bears on what responsibilities one owes toward those with whom is involved.

Although many questions about what is morally right do not have the kinds of objective answers one might find within science and about history, certainly many moral premises, such as it is wrong to kill someone who has irritated you slightly, are easy to defend on nonreligious grounds. Public schools properly teach those premises, even if they happen to conflict or be in tension with religious doctrines important in the community. If such a conflict does exist, teachers do well to provide that information to students.

Much harder questions arise over moral positions that people believe are objectively defensible and correct but lie in opposition to the perspectives of many others who live within the country. Among these topics over time have been racial equality, equality for women, sexual education for teenagers (including condoms), and the basic privileges of gay members of society. In states in which slavery remained legal before the Civil War, we could not have expected public schools to have taught then that racial inequality is seriously unjust. Clearly that is now a central tenet of our liberal democracy, and we expect it to be taught in public schools, whatever is the range of disagreement about what "equal treatment" should amount to. We have also reached a point at which the same can be said about equal treatment of women, although for much of our history, it was broadly assumed that variant legal and social treatment of men and women was totally appropriate. Although teachers in public schools can appropriately note that some standards of morality and civil obligations now widely accepted may be subject to objections and possible change over time, we cannot expect them to teach that basic standards within the country, as contrasted with some particular applications, are fundamentally wrong.

What of sex education and coverage of homosexual relationships? Some religions teach that only those married should have sexual relationships and some, including Roman Catholicism, even teach that use of condoms is generally inappropriate. (As Chapter 4 notes, Pope Francis has qualified this position for women who may have contracted the Zika virus and who run the significant risk of bearing a child who is severely incapacitated.)[9] Is it mistaken for schools to provide some sex education, including condom use? Even though some people may believe nonreligious bases support the idea that it is better to postpone sexual intercourse until one is married or at least has become an adult, the fact is that most American teenagers do have sexual relationships.[10] It may conceivably be true that sex education leads some teenagers to have sex who might otherwise have abstained, but the evidence is that this education more often leads to delay in those relationships.[11] More important is the likelihood that this education will help reduce damaging consequences. The crucial damaging consequences may include AIDS and unwanted pregnancies that lead to abortions or to unwanted children who may not receive adequate care. Given these considerations, providing sex education that includes information about condoms is definitely called for, even though the stances of many religions are that unmarried persons should avoid sex, or that people generally should not use condoms, or both. Concerns about such education can be partly met by giving parents an opt-out privilege for their children.

These religious views were part of the reason why for many years, starting in 1981 during the Reagan administration, federal funds were used for abstinence-only-until-marriage programs. Finally during the Obama administration, Congress eliminated most of this funding and provided financing for programs that are more comprehensive, including information about the use of contraceptives for teenagers engaged in sexual activity.[12] Although choices about the scope of such education are largely within the power of state and local legislators or public schools themselves, the sensible approach, given evidence of actual effects, is to provide students relevant information about how to avoid pregnancy and sexually transmitted diseases even if they choose to engage in sex.

What should schools teach, if anything, about homosexual relationships and same-sex marriage? Certainly they should inform students at the high-school level that in recent decades the Supreme Court has forbidden criminalizing homosexual behavior and has effectively precluded legal discrimination against gay persons. That approach was furthered in 2015 by the 5–4 holding that barring same-sex marriage is unconstitutional.[13] One can certainly discern nonreligious reasons supporting this equality, including a basic right to marry. Chapter 4 deals with the concerns about gay marriage in some depth. But what should public schools teach about all this? They should indicate the strong reasons that support a right of those of the same gender to marry. However, given how children are created and what arguably remain some genuine differences between most men and most women, many same-sex marriages may differ in some respects from more traditional marriages. And, of course, a number of religions believe such marriages are either not in accord with God's will or are less desirable than marriages between men and women. Given both some factual uncertainties and present divisions of opinion, it is probably good for public schools to avoid decisive teaching about whether any difference may exist in the overall desirability of same-sex marriages in comparison with traditional ones. But they should explain why equal legal rights here are fundamentally appropriate. Again, they should also let students know what are the core divisions of opinion and strong religious views on the subject.

What should the schools say about claims for exemptions, the subject covered in Chapter 4? Teachers should not tell students that controversial exemptions are obviously called for or are silly. What they should point out is that religious liberty and deep convictions about what it is right to do should count for what the law requires of people, partly because one aspect of respect for fellow citizens is hesitating to force them to act against their fundamental convictions. Teachers should also make clear that actions and refusals to act that cause harm to others because of an aspect of their status can threaten equality and dignity. Teachers may further explain that certain exemptions can be seen as allowance of free exercise, but ones that reach too far can better be seen as a kind of unwarranted implicit establishment. As with many other issues we have examined, just how schools should teach about these controversial issues is far from simple; and we should not expect courts to get involved unless what is being done seems genuinely extreme on one side or the other.

## Comparative Religion

Given the important roles of religion throughout history and in the lives of many people today, a full liberal education could well include an account of major religious ideas. Plainly a public school should not teach only the premises of the religion then dominant in the local community, but would a course in comparative religion, or inclusion of that topic as a segment of a world history course, be appropriate?

Let us imagine first what such a course or segment would be like. It would explore in more depth various aspects, some of which should be touched upon in history courses, of a number of religions. These aspects would include doctrines, sacred narratives, ethics, rituals, social institutions, and culture. The teaching would be as objective as possible. Not every human religion could be covered but all major faiths should be. Although teachers should not concentrate exclusively on prominent religions in their locality or in the United States overall, it might be appropriate to let these factors play some role on the amount of time spent on respective religions. However, one can also see reasons to spend more time on major religions with which students are mostly unfamiliar, such as Buddhism and Islam. Teaching about a number of religions could increase understanding of common threads of belief, enhance acceptance of diversity in our citizenship, and contribute considerably to a realistic grasp of what goes on in other parts of the world. For example, a sense of basic Muslim doctrines could avoid a seriously misguided view that most of those in that faith are inclined toward terrorism.

It is not hard to see various problems here. These can lead to the conclusion that omitting such teaching is not only constitutionally permissible but could be seen by some as a wise choice for certain circumstances. One problem is that relatively few schoolteachers are actually now equipped to present a wide number of religious outlooks objectively. And however able they may be, they may not be perceived as unprejudiced by some students and their parents. In both these respects, one can think about how fair a teaching about the Muslim religion could now be, and how it would be perceived both by Muslim students and non-Muslims who fear Islamic terrorists. The amount of attention given to various religions could also be seen as unfair by some. Those in minority religions in the United States, such as Hinduism, might perceive only modest attention as a disadvantage, and Christians might see a 20 percent concentration on their faith as a kind of put-down. Although the limited capacity of teachers themselves could be supplemented by having outsiders such as clerics explain their religion, that itself could enhance worries about unacceptable proselytizing.

Given all these concerns, plainly schools have no constitutional obligation to teach a comparative religion course or to include one as a segment of a broader course. However, as a matter of what is valuable in a comprehensive education about human society, that subject is definitely significant. If schools choose to teach it, that is permissible if they seek and obtain a fair degree of objectivity, but perhaps such a course should not be required of all students. As significant as it is, whether providing this education is wise at the high-school level, as it is in public universities, depends considerably on the abilities of teachers and partly on the religious outlooks within the community.

# CHAPTER 6

# Teaching or Not Because of Religion

APART FROM DIRECTLY TEACHING religious truth or teaching about religion, what if religious convictions and connections determine what otherwise might be taught? Chapter 5 touched on this subject with the example of not providing sex education that informs students about condoms. Within a district such education might be provided were it not for substantial contrary religious convictions. However, since sex education is not at the core of public school responsibilities, however valuable it may be, *and* since one might find nonreligious concerns that such education encourages sexual intercourse that is undesirable for teenagers, a failure to teach may not be obviously ascribable to religious grounds. Matters are much more straightforward when it comes to the teaching of evolution as part of the science curriculum. That is the focus of this chapter.

The relevant questions do not simply concern whether evolution should or must be taught; they bear on including possible qualifications and alternatives. We shall briefly explore the fundamental difference between science and some other disciplines, what are the limits to what science has, and can, establish, and how far alternatives that suggest answers to those limits may, and perhaps should, be taught. Does it matter if such alternatives directly convey or imply the truth or falsity of certain religious beliefs? More particularly, would it be appropriate to teach students about creationism or intelligent design as an alternative or supplement to the fundamental scientific basis for evolution? The answers to some of these questions are clear; the answers to others are genuinely debatable.

## Evolution and Its Conflict with Some Religious Beliefs

In the realm of science, which develops factual conclusions based on its methods and criteria of truth, the assumptions most directly at odds with the religious convictions of some people are those of evolution. If one believes that the book of Genesis provides an accurate account of creation, and that its words are to be taken literally, God created the lives of plants, other animals, and human beings within a few days, and he made each fundamental form of animal independently. All this happened, according to what the rest of the Bible says, at least in the estimation of one bishop, about 6,000 years ago.[1] Both in regard to the nature of creation of life and the time that has taken, this account is fundamentally at odds with what the theory of evolution shows; and some features, such as the years of the existence of earth, conflict radically with other scientific conclusions. I, of course, am neither a scientist nor a philosopher of science, but I initially summarize what I understand about evolution and what it may not resolve beyond doubt, and then I turn to various ways that its teaching might be supplemented.

To begin, we should recognize that evolution, and science more generally, cannot answer all questions about life on earth. Notably, science cannot tell us why anything exists at all, that is, why there was some core from which what now lives evolved. That is simply a subject beyond the capacity of human rational thought. Of course, even if someone believes that basic existence in the world was created by God, that does not tell him why God exists. In brief, at some level we have fundamental unanswerable questions about human existence.

Another question is whether human beings experience a further existence after death. Although much of science might lead to skepticism about this, it cannot provide a determinative answer. Certain claims of factual human experience can bear on one's beliefs about this. Those people who believe they have been in actual communication with loved ones or others who have died will perceive these experiences as strongly supporting a conviction that life does continue after death. But this is not the acquisition of knowledge in a scientific way.

A scientist may respond that these examples have nothing to do with how science courses should be taught, because science is only about answerable questions. Nevertheless, it might be helpful for students to understand how far existing science, and its likely future developments, can answer questions that people may have about their existence on this earth.

More difficult questions for the teaching of science are raised about domains in which many people believe that it does now, or will later, yield complete answers, or at least comprehensive convincing theories, for relevant questions, but other individuals, perhaps based on religious convictions, are doubtful whether that has happened or will happen. Evolution falls into this category.

Although others had suggested an idea of evolution, Charles Darwin in *On the Origin of Species*, published in 1859, was the first to provide a systematic theory drawing from various fields of science. His central thesis was that species are not "fixed and immutable .... From one original species, a number of different kinds may be generated."[2] The central basis of change for Darwin was "natural selection"; if a special characteristic in an individual being contributed to survival and reproduction, it was likely to be passed on. Some decades ago there was some division over just how far natural selection determined development,[3] with "neutralists" believing that development by chance, "genetic drift," accounts for change as well. There is now widespread agreement that natural selection does dominate, an understanding characterized as a neo-Darwinian synthesis.

Not surprisingly, evolutionary theory has disturbed some traditional Christians and perhaps other religious believers. If human life can be explained as a link in a long chain and without reference to God's creative hand, perhaps no vast gulf distinguishes our rational and moral qualities from those of other animals on this earth, and creatures far superior to ourselves may even exist elsewhere in the universe. That is strongly at odds with what the Bible says and with many fundamental religious convictions.

In respect to the existence of the earth, the present scientific view, relying on physics and the dating of rock fragments, is that its age lies between 4.2 and 4.8 billion years. It took several million years before life appeared, and only in the last billion years did single-cell organisms develop into complex plants and animals. This timing, of course, is also in sharp contrast with the beliefs of those Christians and Jews who take the Old Testament passages as literally true.

This conflict raises the fundamental questions whether schools should refrain from teaching evolution or should present the students with various alternatives. The answers to most of these questions are clear, and are actually endorsed by Supreme Court constitutional decisions; but the possible status of a version of "intelligent design" is more complex. The concept of "intelligent design" is itself quite vague, and because, when it plays a role in actual controversies over what should happen in schools, it is often taken as a somewhat less specific version of Bible-based "creation science," I want to clarify at the outset what version raises genuine questions about possible use. That is the core notion that God, or some group of higher beings, did create the world and may have had some direct influence on stages of the development of its beings over time. I do not claim that this is a scientific theory; it definitely is not. Nor, from the standpoint of rational thought, is it a sweeping and fundamental alternative to evolution. But it can provide one way to possibly explain what evolution cannot, or may not, be able to tell us.[4]

### Must Evolution Be Taught, and How Should It Be Presented?

Among the subjects of science, evolution is a central explanation of the nature of life on earth. Given modern understanding, that central topic of science would be actually omitted from a school curriculum only because of religious objections. To make such a decision because of religious sentiments within the community amounts to an effective form of establishment. It promotes free exercise, if at all, only by foreclosing what would otherwise be taught according to nonreligious reasons. The Supreme Court in 1968 in *Epperson v. Arkansas*[5] declared invalid a state law that forbade any teaching that mankind descended from a lower order of animals. The Arkansas law was based on "a particular interpretation of the Book of Genesis"; states could not tailor teaching to the principles of a particular religious dogma. Two decades later in *Edwards v. Aguillard*[6] the Supreme Court concluded that requiring that schools either teach both evolution and creation science, or teach neither, was unconstitutional, since it also constituted a forbidden aim to advance religion. Because "creation science" in its traditional form has no genuine scientific support, requiring its teaching within a science course definitely does not make sense. Of course, actually teaching it is a bit different from a teacher noting that some citizens are not persuaded by standard evolutionary theory because of their religious beliefs. So long as the teacher does not refer to such doubts as a way to imply that the science may actually be invalid,[7] that kind of mention is not itself unconstitutional. Whether doing so is wise is doubtful, and it must be phrased simply to be open about the degree of acceptance of evolution within the community, not to cast doubt on the soundness of the theory.

An interesting question about "soundness" qualifications was raised by a Pennsylvania school board requiring teachers to read a statement indicating that Darwin's Theory "continues to be tested …. With respect to any theory, students are encouraged to keep an open mind."[8] How should this message be viewed? Some aspects of neo-Darwinian theory, for example, that the developments of different species of animals have occurred over time, and that that period has been very long, are almost certainly true so long as one relies on rational scientific evidence. Various details are less certain, and given how the theory has developed in the century and a half since *On the Origin of Species*, we can be virtually certain that further discoveries and analyses will produce a theory that looks a bit different in 2117 than it does now. But this is true about all, or nearly all, scientific theories; they encompass details that are likely to shift over time.

One *could* defend the school board's instruction as a reasonable approach to evolution, as well as many other aspects of science. But that misses what the message would convey to actual students. If they study various aspects of science and are told that Darwin's approach is a theory to be tested by new evidence, their natural reaction to the language will be, first, that no aspects of evolutionary theory are almost certainly sound *and*, second, that if only evolution is mentioned, it is less reliable objectively than other aspects of science. Perhaps someone *could* contend that even on the basis of scientific evidence such a difference is accurate, but clearly the school board did not explore that in depth. Rather, it singled out evolution because of dislike for it by people with certain religious convictions. The district court rightly saw this as a form of establishment because, even indirectly, it instructed the students in a way that could only be explained by religious tenets.

As a preface to the conceivable place of intelligent design, it is important to recognize that the fundamental core of a theory of evolution is not necessarily at odds with belief in God the Creator. A powerful God may have created the world, indeed the universe, so that it would evolve in this natural way. And this God may still have the ability to change how things work on earth if he decides to do that. Once we grasp these possibilities, we can understand that a version of intelligent design could be completely consistent with basic evolutionary theory, although some may doubt that any powerful God would accept a system of development that seems to be so much a matter of unpredictable positive and negative features.

In contrast to an account that could fit with evolution, if "intelligent design" asserts that various developments cannot be understood according to what are accepted as natural, reason-based explanations but instead *must* rest on the intervention of a divine source, then it is a religious alternative to at least aspects of the scientific theory. Its only difference from literal Genesis creationism is that it is less explicit about how God acted and may be less at odds with core aspects of evolutionary theory than is the Biblical account that human beings were created shortly after other animals. If such a version of intelligent design were presented as the genuine alternative to evolution, it would still be a teaching of religion lacking a scientific basis, and it would be unconstitutional for the same reason as any requirement that schools teaching evolution must also teach creation science.[9]

This leads to the harder question whether the more accommodating version of intelligent design may be offered as *the* or *a* possible explanation for matters that evolution, and perhaps other scientific subjects, are not now able to explain convincingly in terms of factual evidence and perhaps may not ever be able to do so.

At one stage, the development of eyes was considered by some to fall into this category. Although scientists have since provided answers that satisfy them, I shall outline the possible problem in a simple form and draw a comparison with a medical question in ordinary human life.

Eyes may seem harder to explain than basic intelligence. If one asks how did intelligence originate and grow over time in different animals, the simple evolutionist explanation can be that when animals first developed, their having some capacity to think helped them, even if that capacity was very limited. Because the degree of intelligence mattered for the survival and welfare of those within a species and among different species, the animals with greater intelligence were more likely to survive and pass their abilities on to descendants. This helps to explain why human beings now, despite committing violence toward each other, may have more capacity to survive than other animals. This development could be very slow and progressive over time, and we might expect intelligence in people to increase further as time progresses.

What can one say about eyes? They are critically important for the quality of the lives of people and other animals and for their survival. At some point in the world's history, eyes did not exist. Eyes are complex. If an animal cannot see, how would some simple element of what exists in an eye help at all? That could be hard to understand. Thus, the slow progression over time in which beneficial characteristics tend to survive and develop in combination with other features cannot really tell us how eyes came into being. To be clear, any doubt here is *not* about whether a primitive version of eyes could develop into modern ones. It concerns whether multiple components, none of which are useful standing alone, could evolve into primitive eyes. Intelligent design could be claimed to be a plausible explanation. Evolutionary biologists have countered with what they take as convincing explanations, but can those be factually established? In contrast with the bones of various animals, a good many of which survive for thousands of years, eyes and any predecessors in their development have not existed long past death. In brief, evolutionary theory cannot now establish on a factual basis the precise steps by which eyes came into being. Further, although we cannot rule out that sometime in the future, more detailed evidence of how eyes developed may be discovered, we may never be sure that this is exactly how eyes did initially develop.

If all this seems a bit fanciful, what can doctors say about why people do or do not recover from serious illnesses? Among people diagnosed with a high likelihood of death, some actually recover. Commonly, doctors cannot tell us exactly why. Is this just a matter of chance, or do the patients' brains operate differently, has their emotional status been crucial, have prayers mattered? (Interestingly, according to one study, however dubious it may have been, women seeking to have children were somewhat more likely to do so if prayers were said on their behalf.[10]) Conceivably, at some stage of history, doctors or experts will be able to predict with certainty who will recover and who will not, but this is not now true for many forms and degrees of illness and medical conditions. Is there some intervention from a higher source who generates recovery that cannot be explained by completely scientific bases? We really do not know for certain. This belief in some special role for intelligent design is not contrary to what medical evidence can establish, because that is incomplete. One could see development of eyes similarly.

If all this is true, would it be appropriate for science teachers to include "intelligent design" in evolution courses as a possible explanation for what science cannot yet and may not later be able to establish? So seen, it would *not* be presented as a basic alternative to what evolutionary theory has shown, but rather as a plausible perspective concerning what the boundaries of science are able to discover.

One possible response is that science courses are about science, and intelligent design is not scientific. Given all the mysteries about what constitutes intelligent design and how it may operate, plainly it cannot count as ordinary science. Standard factual evidence does not tell if there is one God or multiple gods, whether he or they are omnipotent or limited in capacity, whether overarching concern with human welfare or something else guides any involvement in our lives. Intelligent design cannot count as genuine science. Conceivably at some stage human beings may get actual factual evidence about supernatural intervention that supports a particular view; and some people do believe that miracles they think are demonstrable fall into this category. But essentially intelligent design is not now a scientific alternative but a possible explanation of what science itself cannot presently tell us.

Seen in this way, it should not be presented as *the* alternative in some domains for standard scientific theory, but as one possible explanation for whatever are the limits of science.[11] Given that science may be able to provide future answers to what is now not discernible, given that intelligent design is not necessarily *the* answer to what science will never be able to resolve, and given that exactly how intelligent design operates if it does play a role is not determinable by ordinary reasoning, we do not have one obvious alternative to scientific gaps. If intelligent design were taught as the definite alternative to broader claims of science, that would amount to a religious account, although not nearly as dogmatic and tied to a particular outlook as "creation science."

What should be acceptable, and may even be wise, is for teachers to provide students, especially those in high school, with some sense of what science now can or cannot resolve with confidence, and with some grasp of what is likely for science in the future or is probably beyond such explanation. In doing so, they may well mention "intelligent design" as possibly filling in some gaps, but it should not be presented as *the* alternative. Further, the science teacher should not delve into the details of a dominant intelligent design theory, such as whether the intervention comes from a single God who acts out of love for human beings.

In this treatment, I have put aside the relevance of the fact that many actual proponents of teaching intelligent design do see that as an indirect way to promote more traditional creation science. This reality can constitute a good reason to forego what I have suggested would be a sensible and acceptable reference to intelligent design while teaching evolution. It certainly constitutes an important reason why any schools that do include intelligent design need to be very careful about how it is presented.

# CHAPTER 7

# Individual Communication by Students and Their Teachers

I N THIS CHAPTER, WE SHALL explore certain related issues about public schools that are not about what is actually taught or about actual forms of worship carried out by the school. A primary focus will involve choices by students to communicate religious ideas either as part of their responsibilities within classes or on school facilities outside of class. We shall also consider how far students should be relieved of engaging in school work that offends the religious convictions of themselves or their parents. That, of course, is one particular issue about exemptions, the subject of this book's Chapter 4, but given the special setting of public schools, I have reserved its analysis until this chapter. We shall also look briefly about what teachers may properly communicate about their own particular religious convictions and affiliations.

As with other subjects involving public schools, a crucial issue when legal suits are brought is how far judges should actually involve themselves in trying to determine what should be done in particular school settings. Given competing values at stake, which can have different power in different situations, we should not be surprised that courts very often leave choices to school officials.[1] These officials should themselves recognize and take account of competing values, and both they and outsiders should understand that some choices may properly be seen as unconstitutional even if beyond judicial declarations of that.

A distinctive aspect of most of the topics here involves the relevance of freedom of speech as well as the exercise of religion. That can have two different effects. The most obvious is that both can support the right or privilege of people to say what they believe. The highly dubious approach of *Employment v. Smith* suggests that if a claim is hybrid, that is, resting on two constitutional provisions, it generates a much, much stricter standard of review than does a simple claim for special treatment limited to the free exercise of religion.[2] If courts really followed this indefensible hybrid approach, freedom of speech could make a constitutional claim to assert one's religious convictions much more powerful than it would otherwise be.

The second way freedom of speech can work is to preclude distinctions based on kinds of speech. That approach can favor claims that religious communications should not be treated worse than others, but it can also disfavor claims that religious speech should be given a special concession. The broader question of when religion should be treated as special is addressed in Chapter 8. We have touched on it in earlier parts, and, of course, much about public school teaching does assume that religion is special in terms of what school choices should be made.

## Teacher Disclosures

Before turning to students, let us briefly consider what teachers may say that does not really count as teaching in the ordinary sense. Suppose what is being taught is some instruction about religion, or a sensitive moral and political issue, such as same-sex marriage or disagreement about the completeness of a theory of evolution, including perhaps a mention of intelligent design. A teacher may decide to mention that she is a Roman Catholic or Orthodox Jew. So long as she does not assert that her religion is definitely the right one or try to convince students that that is so, she is not formally making a claim about religious truth. We can reveal many aspects of what we care about—such as what we like to eat or watch on television—without telling others they should be doing the same thing.

Is religion special here? In one sense "yes"; but it is crucial to recognize that revealing one's religious convictions can work in two different ways. Religion is special in the respect that most people with religious convictions believe on some basis, whether grounded rationally or in faith, or in some combination, that their religious outlook is true, or at least more likely to be true than competing perspectives. (I put the point this way because I think many religious people do feel degrees of uncertainty about some crucial topics their religion covers.) Thus, one could suppose that any disclosure by a teacher of her convictions about religion, including atheism and agnosticism, *does* implicitly convey the message that this is the right outlook, that students would do well to consider accepting that view. On this approach alone, one might say that teachers should never say anything about their religious beliefs and involvements. This extreme view is defensible, but it is peculiar in a significant way. If teachers are permitted to reveal other aspects of what they care about, should this one aspect be precluded?

This question ties to how personal revealing can, not infrequently, work differently. Stating one's religious convictions may alert the students that one's efforts to be objective about a topic, such as same-sex marriage or intelligent design, may in fact be affected by personal subjective factors. It provides a warning that students may choose to discount some of what one says on this basis. To take an obvious example, I indicated at the beginning of this book that I was a "liberal Protestant," with more skepticism about human nature than is often associated with that label. The point was to acknowledge that a presentation of issues in ways that do not purport to rest on particular religious convictions can often be very difficult, and readers in assessing my claims about how religion should be treated might wish to know how the conclusions *might* have been affected by my own personal beliefs. The truth is that over time I have made more mentions of personal experience than most legal scholars do, mainly because I believe that experience does bear on what any individual perceives as objectively sound in respect to various moral and political subjects.

Putting these considerations together, we have no simple answer to what teachers should reveal about their own religious convictions, but the following conclusions make sense. Teachers should not try to persuade students their religious views are sound; that would be unconstitutional. They should not go into great detail about how the tenets of their faith bear on particular issues. A good deal should depend on the age and sophistication of the students. The more mature students are, and the more they are aware of various religious perspectives, the less a disclosure will convey the implicit message that the particular perspective is best. And the more it may help to reveal a way in which the teacher may be less than completely objective about a sensitive topic. If we are talking about the first grade, teachers should perhaps say nothing about their own religion and if they say anything, it should simply be a brief mention. When it comes to high school seniors, and especially students at public universities, teachers should feel freer to reveal their connections to religion, so long as they do not go too much detail or convey the message that their view is right.

## Student Communications

I turn now to communications by students. I begin with communications outside of class, because one of the most important cases involving public educational institutions and students concerned this topic. *Rosenberger v. Rector and Visitors of the University of Virginia*[3] involved a challenge to that state's university creating an exception for its funding of independent student publications. Its guidelines said that funding was unavailable for a religious activity that "primarily promotes or manifests a particular belief in or about a deity or an ultimate reality."[4] The organizers of a Christian evangelical journal, *Wide Awake*, claimed that the preclusion violated the principle that the government should not discriminate among speech based on its content. The university responded that its categorization was supported by the principle of nonestablishment. The Supreme Court ruled 5–4 that the university could not deny funding on this basis.

A key theoretical issue was whether this amounted to "viewpoint discrimination," which is rarely, if ever, permitted under the Free Speech Clause. Justice Kennedy for the majority said "yes"; nonreligious messages were being favored over religious ones. In dissent Justice Souter claimed the contrary, since equal treatment was being afforded to religious, atheist, and agnostic writings, all writings concerning beliefs about "a deity or ultimate reality."[5] At the most straightforward level, Souter had the better argument. If funding were only for scientific writings, we should not characterize that "content" classification as "viewpoint" discrimination against literary or moral presentations. But matters here were more complicated. Among the subjects in the *Wide Awake* journal were the addressing of moral and political issues, such as abortion, homosexual behavior, and military engagement. If students are free to publish views about these issues, so long as no reliance is made on a religious or antireligious perspective, this does amount to a kind of discrimination based on supporting viewpoints. What should be perceived as the boundaries of "viewpoint discrimination" is far from clear, and categorization is quite important for freedom of speech. It can obviously matter a great deal for whether religious messages can be treated differently from others. In many contexts the narrower question about what constitutes viewpoint discrimination can be cast in terms of the competing values of free exercise and nonestablishment.

An issue about student activities outside of classes that relates significantly to the *Rosenberger* case is whether it is acceptable for public schools to have their facilities available or not available for religious meetings after school. Plainly it would not be appropriate to allow only religious meetings and no other kinds, since that would be an obvious promotion of religion. And treating meetings of all kinds similarly is clearly acceptable. The harder question is whether schools should be able to say that religious meetings in particular are precluded. In line with its *Rosenberger* decision, the Supreme Court has not accepted that line, ruling that such a restriction violates freedom of speech and is not justified by nonestablishment.

In 1990, the Court decided *Board of Education v. Mergens,*[6] in which a high school had denied permission to students to form a Christian club that would use classrooms after school, since the school policy required any club to have a faculty sponsor (and that involvement in a religious club would not be proper for a faculty member), and also barred clubs sponsored by political or religious organizations. The Court considered this denial in light of the federal Equal Access Act that forbade discrimination in respect to access to a "limited open forum" on the basis of religion or other content of speech. Discerning the school's policy as in violation of the federal statute, the Court rejected the claim that complying with it here would violate the Establishment Clause. The ruling in *Mergens* fit with a similar decision involving a public university, which was rendered nine years earlier on constitutional free speech grounds.[7]

In 2001, the Court decided *Good News Club v. Milford Central School,*[8] which I believe raised a more troublesome issue. The club sought to hold weekly after-school meetings for children of ages 6 to 12 within the school cafeteria. The meetings included Bible reading, how Bible stories relate to the lives of club members, and prayers. The Court's majority regarded the school's precluding of teaching of morals and character from a religious perspective as constituting viewpoint discrimination that violated the Free Speech Clause. The dissenters disagreed. This division over whether a special treatment of religion amounts to viewpoint discrimination shows that exactly what that term covers has remained rather vague and disputed over time.

When Justice Thomas's majority opinion turned to Establishment Clause concerns, it omitted what I believe is a key element. His main point was that, in respect to possible coercive pressure, the relevant community would be the parents, not elementary school children, since attendance would require parental permission. Further, even if one asked about the minds of the children, they would not perceive an endorsement of religion any more than they would perceive hostility if the Club were excluded. On the latter point, it seems much more likely that most third-graders will continue to perceive weekly meetings carried out over time as a kind of support than to sense that the school's denial at one time of the privilege to hold meetings amounted to a continuing hostility. This would be especially likely if there were few or no nonreligious gatherings.

The more crucial point concerns the "pressure." Of course, Justice Thomas is right that if we focused on *simple* parental choice, pressure would not be a concern. But let me suppose this is a community in which many residents share the Christian view of the Good News Club, and a significant number of the third-graders are going to the Club's meetings. Joseph has two close friends who are attending; they tell him how pleasant and encouraging the meetings are, and they try to persuade him to join them. Joseph decides he would really like to do so, partly because he likes being with friends and is feeling like a bit of an outsider. He urges his parents to give him permission. Parents generally like to satisfy strong wishes of their children unless they have strong reasons to refuse. In this setting, parents might well agree unless they have really powerful objections to what goes on at the meetings. This genuine kind of pressure, not addressed by Justice Thomas, rests on a combination of reactions by both the children and their parents.

The exact force of this concern can depend greatly on the school and its surrounding community. In contrast to the Court's decision, this worry strikes me as having enough of a potential influence regarding elementary schools to raise an establishment concern, one that should allow local officials to refuse facilities for religious meetings in those schools. If this is right, a court should intervene only if such a claimed concern seems exaggerated and implausible.

Free speech concerns play a role not only in terms of group meetings but also individual communications by students. These can occur in student behavior within classes, in written papers to be read only by teachers, and in what students do outside of classroom settings. I shall start with what occurs inside classrooms. Here we have in play both verbal remarks and the ways in which students dress.

Really deep questions are posed by religious communications students make to their fellows, whether within class or in school facilities outside of class. Here are the competing positions, in a somewhat simplistic form. Individuals have free speech rights to communicate what they care about so long as they are not engaging in defamation or hate speech. The freedom to express religious belief is not special in this sense.

On the other side is the claim that schools are somehow special in this context. Two arguments for this perspective rely on concerns about the avoidance of the schools themselves regarding religious matters and on the need for them to minimize hurt feelings and potential conflicts. The first consideration provides a good reason for teachers not to have classes that involve competing claims about religious truth and its implications.

As I am writing this draft, we have had extensive television coverage of Pope Francis's statement that if someone, namely Donald Trump, wants to build a wall at the border instead of welcoming immigrants who are in need, he is not really Christian.[9] In subsequent messages, the Pope's office suggested that his assertion was not that someone who insists on such a wall is not himself actually a Christian but that his position on immigration is not Christian. Donald Trump responded that the Pope's assertion about his failure to be a Christian was "disgraceful."[10]

Should a public school teacher allow students to discuss in class who has the right stance here according to a specifically Christian understanding? Clearly the school can allow students to express their views about key political issues, but this disagreement involves fundamental questions about what constitutes true Christianity. If one is a genuine Christian and discerns what the messages of Jesus entail, could one support excluding many immigrants? And if a person fails to understand the implications of Christianity here, could he at least be a genuine Christian who happens to have made a mistake about this particular issue? Given wide disagreements among practicing Christians about many issues, including the status of same-sex marriage, it would strike me as really harsh to assume that any sharp disagreement shows that those on one side are not really Christians in a broad sense. But a person *might* believe that for certain concerns, such as how those well off should relate to those suffering, a person's position fundamentally at odds with basic Christian premises does show that he is not a genuine Christian. Although the Pope almost certainly meant to convey the more modest view that one is not really acting as a Christian by adopting the Trump position on building a wall, we can imagine a lively discussion among more senior public school students, however the Pope's statement was taken.

Would that be appropriate? Although one could try to carve out political wisdom here, a serious discussion could not avoid what it really takes to be a true Christian. Whether allowing this would actually be unconstitutional is debatable, but school officials sensitive to nonestablishment values should not encourage such a class discussion, even if the teacher herself will carefully stay neutral on what is genuine Christianity.

Harder problems are raised by student choices about what to talk about or how to dress. If students are told they can pick a topic for which they will make a ten-minute presentation in class, should one of them be able to choose an explanation of why evangelical Protestantism represents acceptance of the true God, saying "I am born again," or why Roman Catholicism is fundamentally misguided? The position favoring such a freedom is this: People are aware that those exercising rights of free speech will often say things with which they personally disagree and may even find offensive. They must simply accept this as an aspect of free and open discourse and try not to be offended.

The competing position acknowledges that schools and classes constitute communities in which individuals are in continuing contact with each other, and generating mutual friendship and respect is an important value. To take an analogy, those who work together in a particular office will not be free to say everything there that they could say in public. This is true for those within government offices and faculty members of public universities, as well as those within private enterprises. Students differ from government workers in that they are compelled to attend instead of joining voluntarily, but that does not eliminate the importance of building a community and avoiding offended feelings. From the free speech point of view, religious assertions would not be distinguishable here from the expressing of other views that could offend fellow students; but one's outlook on the free speech domain could be highly relevant to how far schools should allow religious discourse. A recent study by Catherine J. Ross[11] shows how greatly many schools inhibit speech beyond what is warranted and impose penalties that are blatantly exaggerated, but recognition of these concerns does not tell us to what degree schools should be able to constrain religious assertions.

In oral interactions, others have told me that I am much too sensitive to possible negative reactions students may have to comments made by their fellows. It may well be that as our history has evolved over the past decades, students, as well as most others, have become accepting that others within a community which includes close and continuing contact may express ideas sharply at odds with their own ways of life and convictions. But I still see the concern about emotional hurt and conflict as great enough to allow schools to curtail various controversial expressions, so long as their punishments for violations are not excessive, such as excluding the "offender" for weeks or months from school.

Two related but somewhat different issues are these. Suppose what the student does is to engage in a form of communication outside the classroom but within school facilities, or the student seeks to write on a religious subject in an assigned paper that will be read only by the teacher? Cases have arisen involving both these situations. In *Settle v. Dickson County School Board*,[12] ninth-grade students were to choose their subject for a research writing assignment. The teacher, Dana Ramsey, declined to allow Brittney Settle to write on the life of Jesus, although she did allow others to write on reincarnation, witchcraft, and spiritualism. One stated reason for the refusal was that Settle had not obtained permission by the deadline, but we can be nearly certain that in this context that would not have operated as a bar had the teacher had no problem with the topic itself. The substantial reasons included these: Settle's personal views would preclude a dispassionate paper and would lead to her taking Ms. Ramsey's comments as a criticism of the religion itself; personal religion was not an appropriate subject for public schools; and Settle's knowledge of Jesus would prevent her from learning something new. Although not all of Ms. Ramsey's reasons were persuasive, some were, and she was in a much better position than a judge to determine what the potentialities and risks were for a particular student. The Sixth Circuit accepted her decision, noting the "broad leeway" for teachers to determine their curriculum.[13]

Although the concern about reactions of fellow students was not in play here, a teacher clearly should have some flexibility based on her sense of a student's ability and of her own capacity to review a manuscript without offending the student. This again is another illustration of why judicial involvement is appropriate only when what the teacher is doing is obviously wrong, but the teacher should thoughtfully take into account both concerns about establishment and the values of free speech and free exercise.

When it comes to dress regulation, courts have consistently upheld dress codes against free speech claims. In *Chalifoux v. New Caney Independent School District*,[14] however, a district court did rule that the constitution protects students' wearing rosaries. The court relied on the theory in *Employment Division v. Smith* that heightened scrutiny is called for when a religious claim is "hybrid," (the doctrine whose overall theory I have claimed in Chapter 4 does not really make sense). Drawing upon an earlier Supreme Court decision protecting the wearing of black armbands to protest the Vietnam War,[15] the court used heightened scrutiny and found no strong reason to preclude the wearing of rosaries. It did not provide a definite answer to whether the religious conviction reflected here warranted more protection than would a nonreligious message conveyed by the way a person is dressed.

On this point, I believe two things should be in play. One is whether people have more powerful reasons to wear a rosary or cross than to convey some nonreligious idea. I believe the general answer is "yes." Some people feel that it is a genuine aspect of their religious faith to represent that in how they appear. An individual could have a similar feeling about a nonreligious message, but that would be much less common and intense. The other question is whether the message will disturb others or generate conflict. The wearing of simple religious symbols by some students is unlikely to do that. If one conveys a fundamental message about a controversial issue of morality or politics, such as the legitimacy of same-sex marriage or the sinfulness of abortion, the concern about hurt feelings and tensions is much greater. For these reasons, I believe overall greater protection of religious symbols is appropriate, although courts may rightfully defer to any substantial reasons offered for restrictions that cover that.

One qualification, however, is crucial here. No school can accept traditional religious symbols dominant in the community and deny others. In that respect, France's law banning the wearing of "conspicuous" religious symbols, which was clearly directed at head-scarves worn by Muslim girls,[16] is deeply troubling. Schools must treat religions equally. The only exceptions to this can be if one's dress genuinely undercuts what the school needs of its students, or a symbol is directly antagonistic to some other religion. If messages are effectively hostile to the convictions of fellow students, schools should be allowed to forbid them.

What of religious speech engaged in by students that are not part of class activities? In one case, the district court ruled that a principal's refusal to allow a fourth-grade student to hand out invitations to a religious meeting at a church was not acceptable.[17] As long as such handouts were allowed generally, those for religious meetings could not be barred. This requirement of equal treatment makes obvious sense, so long as teachers make clear that allowing students to hand out invitations does not represent a school's endorsement of a religion.

More difficult problems are raised if students' choices outside of class activities have a carryover that involves display. In one such case, *Gernetzke v. Kenosha Unified School District No. 1*,[18] student groups had been invited to paint murals that would remain on the school's main hallway. The Bible Club submitted a sketch involving a large cross and a key passage from the Gospel of John. The principal approved all but the cross, which he claimed might lead to a lawsuit and require him to approve murals of a Satanic or neo-Nazi character. The Seventh Circuit rejected the club's challenge that the principal's decision violated the Equal Access Act and suggested, without quite deciding, that it was acceptable under the First Amendment. The basic position was that judges and jurors were not in a good position to oversee the "day-to-day control of our troubled public schools from school administrators."[19]

This overall conclusion makes sense, although some puzzles about the principal's decision and reasons are worth examining. First, it was a bit odd that he refused the cross but accepted the display of a famous biblical passage that clearly asserts that Jesus is the only son of God and that those who believe in him "may have eternal life."[20] One might see the cross as more obvious for observers passing by, but it is hardly more assertive about the truth of Christianity. A second point is more significant in its general implications. The principal draws the comparison with neo-Nazi murals. I assume that, even if it has a religious component, neo-Nazism is essentially political. Plainly for displays within a school building, desirable political messages such as the Declaration of Independence, can be accepted, and those critical of the core values of American democracy can be rejected. So within this domain, some forms of viewpoint discrimination are obviously all right. It may well be that acceptance of a religious message that is not heavily political must lead to allowing competing religious messages that fall within that category and are not directly antagonistic to other religions. But the possible acceptance of a cross has no apparent relevance to whether a neo-Nazi message would need to be treated the same way.

A somewhat similar case involved parents of slain students and others associated with the tragic killings at the Columbine High School. Members of the community were invited to paint tiles for the renovated school but were told not to use religious symbols. The restriction of religious symbols was challenged. Reversing a decision by the district court, the court of appeals held that because the tiles carried the imprint of the school and related to pedagogical concerns, and because having religious references on the walls could lead to religious debate disruptive of the learning environment, the restriction was appropriate.[21] Although I am skeptical that tiles on the wall simply referring to religious premises would be likely to cause disruption, legitimate concerns could include a worry that permanent fixtures on the wall would appear to convey school endorsement and that students should not be forced to submit to continual exposure to religious messages. These concerns were sufficient to support the school's decision.

## Being Excused from Ordinary Requirements

A different issue that involves students and their parents is when, if ever, they should be excused based on religious objections from standard school requirements, and whether this should indeed rise to a constitutional right in some circumstances. Given how closely this topic ties to the more general concerns about public schools, it seemed wise to postpone examination from Chapter 4 until this chapter. Should public schools ever excuse students from ordinary requirements based on religious convictions? If the requirements are fringe aspects of the education, the answer is clearly "yes." If a high school student or parent of a younger child believed that dancing or some form of athletic activity was against God's will, relief from doing everything other students have to do in a dancing or gym class would make sense, and in many states this could be seen as required by a Religious Freedom Restoration Act or the free exercise clause of a state constitution.[22] The difficult questions concern the core aspects of public education. These questions were sharply raised by *Mozert v. Hawkins County Board of Education*,[23] decided by the Sixth Circuit Court of Appeals before *Employment Division v. Smith* had essentially knocked out a federal free exercise basis for this kind of claim.

Like most others within the county, a mother of a sixth-grader was a fundamentalist Christian. She was dismayed to hear that her daughter's reader had a story involving mental telepathy. When she and like-minded neighbors inspected more of the Holt, Reinhart and Winston Reader series, they found much else that was objectionable. That included the positive view of magic in a play based on the *Wizard of Oz* and scant attention given to Protestant Christianity in comparison with stories presenting non-Christian religions favorably. Urging that the series promoted secular humanism in violation of the Establishment Clause, the protestors first urged removal of the Holt book at a school board meeting. That issue quickly shifted to whether children could be excused from having to use the books. Two elementary schools refused; a third let a child sit in the hallway while objectionable stories were read; another school allowed students to leave class and read an alternative text in the library. The school board then responded by dictating use of the Holt readers without any individual accommodations. This led to the lawsuit. Many of the more specific objections—such as against the teaching that some values are relative and vary with different situations, and that human beings and apes evolved from a common ancestor—could obviously have much broader import.

What are the competing state interests? Plainly it becomes much more complicated to have different students reading different texts. And within classes, references are often offered to what was read yesterday or last week. Teaching a collection of students, only some of whom have read the standard texts, would be complicated. One can also see desirable education as teaching children tolerance, respect for others, and critical thinking. These objectives could be less achievable if students with some frequency are leaving class because they or their parents object to texts.

A conceivable, additional argument against any exemption is that parents have the options of home schooling and private schools. If they choose public schools, they should accept what those are doing. This simplistic argument is unpersuasive because many parents do not have the time and ability for home schooling and because local private schools may not fit with their beliefs and may be too expensive. Their children's attendance at public school is not simply a voluntary choice for a great many parents.

In their resolution of the constitutional issue, the three judges on the court of appeals agreed that the school board's decision could stand, but their theories were in some ways quite different. Chief Judge Lively wrote a majority opinion. He asserted that exposure to offensive materials was not actually a burden on free exercise.[24] As Judge Boggs noted, this is an evident oversimplification, as illustrated by an earlier Roman Catholic view that the reading of a book on a proscribed index could be a mortal sin.[25]

The heart of the opinions of Judges Lively and Boggs concerned the burdens officials would have to bear if required to make these accommodations. Lively apparently thought that the only way to satisfy the parents in this case would be to use materials that adopted their own perspectives. Boggs thought accommodations were often appropriate, but took existing constitutional doctrine not to preclude the choices of school authorities so long as they did not violate the Establishment Clause.[26] Although joining Lively's opinion, Judge Kennedy also wrote separately, emphasizing the state's compelling interest in achieving educational skills and avoiding disruption and religious divisiveness.[27]

As with many of the subjects of this book, we here have genuine competing interests of free exercise and nonestablishment. And accompanying the nonestablishment concern is also a worry about harm to others, here the other students within classes from which objecting students would periodically be excused. In contrast to other exemption claims, there is also a concern about whether an exemption will have a kind of negative effect on the basic education of those who receive it. Given the complexity of all this, and how the costs and other effects of an exemption can vary greatly depending on the particular accommodation sought and the capacity of the school to provide it, judges leaving these choices primarily to school officials is warranted, unless what they do is clearly unreasonable.

If one asks what choices about standard courses[28] are unreasonable, my conclusions are that authorities should accommodate exceptions like those requested by the Hawkins County parents *if* the following conditions are present: (1) the schools should not have to pay high costs to finance alternative programs; (2) parents will assure that excused children can develop adequate competence; (3) other students using the standard texts will not suffer serious disruption or interference; (4) granting an exemption will not lead to a wide range of exemption claims which might render a coherent program unmanageable. Exactly when these conditions are met will often be hard to say, and this helps to illustrate why court involvement should be limited even if a RFRA statute or free exercise constitutional provision is potentially relevant.

The conclusions reached in this section conform with those that concern a number of other involvements of schools and students, and indeed many other subjects covered in this book. Genuine conflicts often exist between free exercise and nonestablishment values. Just how those should be resolved is often difficult to say and can differ depending on variations in circumstances. For many subjects, judicial declarations of unconstitutionality may not be called for, but school officials, like legislators and executive officers, should carefully consider those values when reaching decisions and further understand that constitutional limits may apply to them even if they are beyond enforcement by judges.

# PART FOUR

# Considerations and Questions that Cross the Range

I N ALL PARTS OF THIS BOOK, two important considerations are what counts as "religion" or "religious," and whether that should receive special treatment. This part, in a single chapter, explores these general questions in a more detailed way. It delves into debated standards for how to draw the line for religion, and how that bears on whether special treatment is justified.

CHAPTER 8

# Religious Beliefs and Endeavors Distinguished from Nonreligious Ones

WHETHER CONCESSIONS SHOULD be made to religious convictions and practices, and whether they should be treated as special, are controversial questions addressed throughout the book. The best answers depend partly on what should count as "religious," which the latter part of this chapter explores in greater depth. As with the chapters on particular topics, this one resists both the idea that the state must, or should, always be "neutralist," never treating religion as special, and the competing idea that singling out religion is always acceptable and never unwise.

In certain areas, including public school teachings and the government financing of secular services, the core question is whether religious practices and messages should be specially avoided by the government. In these areas, the constitutional issue is whether the Establishment Clause precludes the government from treating religious messages and institutions like nonreligious ones. At least in some of these contexts, we can identify competing free exercise values even if these do not definitely compel government promotion or assistance. Relatedly, it can also be argued that to preclude religious groups or subjects is to create a kind of establishment of nonreligion. That, for example, might be said about the effective omission from public school teaching of what religious beliefs and denominations have meant in human history.

A different claim about religious convictions and practices is that it is fine in some contexts to treat them more favorably than nonreligious ones. That is a central issue about many exemptions from ordinary legal duties and is presently one element about any possible exemption from equal treatment of same-sex married couples. Within U.S. history, certain exemptions have consistently been cast in religious terms, and that is now true of the federal Religious Freedom Restoration Act and the Religious Land Use and Institutionalized Persons Act, as well as many state laws. At one stage, some exemptions based on religious convictions were seen as constitutionally required. That doctrine was sharply curtailed by *Employment Division v. Smith*,[1] but still exists for certain central religious practices such as the hiring of clerics, broadly defined.[2] When it comes to legislated exemptions for religious behavior, free exercise values, as Chapter 4 has explained, provide strong support; but treating that more favorably than similar nonreligious activity may seem at odds with Establishment Clause values.

It is significant here to differentiate a nonestablishment argument from one grounded in equal treatment for those directly disadvantaged by an exemption. Same-sex married couples who are not treated equally can urge that since the objections to their marriage are mostly religious, granting a legal privilege amounts to a regrettable establishment, but their overarching contention will be that the law should simply not authorize their being treated unequally, whoever is doing so. On the other hand, an argument that a nonreligious objector cannot, or should not, be denied a privilege given to a religious one relies more centrally on nonestablishment values, which can be seen as also tied to equal protection concerns.

In what follows, I will start with the core question of unequal treatment for exemptions, and then look briefly at government financial assistance and practices.

## Religious Conviction and Nonreligious Conscience

A central concern for many aspects of whether it warrants distinctive treatment is whether religion really is special. In this respect, things may look a bit differently when one focuses on religious denominations and religious convictions, although the two obviously connect. In much of Western history, countries had established churches, with the state treating other religious practices and individuals in a different, negative way. That history also has included direct conflicts between religious groups that have resulted in many deaths. When the Bill of Rights was adopted, six of the original states of this country still had established religions of one form or another.[3] All this helps explain why nonestablishment of religion is seen as special, even when nonreligious analogues exist, and does not embrace some broader notion of what groups and beliefs our governments cannot favor over their competitors. It also tells us why the free exercise of religion is an explicit part of the First Amendment, although the amendment's inclusion of freedom of speech and association would by themselves protect many aspects of religious practices. When it comes to individual convictions underlying behavior, the singling out of religion is more debatable, at least if we can imagine a nonreligious analogue. Some believe that should never occur in the law. I urge that view is mistaken, but that just when special treatment is appropriate is a difficult question, one for which the tensions between free exercise and nonestablishment may come into play.

A key element in all this is what is special about religion. Most religious believers in this country have faith in a higher authority, God, who both cares about how we live our lives and has indicated in some way a great deal about how we should do so. For the devout believer, this actually carries more genuine authority than secular law, and telling her that she must violate what she takes as God's instruction is both deeply unsettling and likely to generate violation of what the law itself or officials are telling her to do. Individuals with nonreligious convictions about what they should and should not do may face similar conflicts, but perhaps they will be less certain of their positions and more willing to adhere to enacted law, since they are not submitting to a higher authority. Such perceived conflicts may also be less frequent, because these people are not typically relying on authoritative organizations that have positions that depend on what they take as sacred texts or upon settled historical premises, which may be substantially at odds with certain modern values. All this might lead us to believe that exemptions are specially needed for religious individuals. On the other hand, the Christian belief that God forbids sins, and that we all sin frequently, may reduce the sense that one absolutely should not act against what one believes the Higher Power has instructed us to do.

A troublesome subquestion about much of this is what exactly is "religious." Is that always, sometimes, or never a viable category for the law? This particular question was one raised sharply by draft exemptions. Although these now have little practical importance,[4] I shall begin with them, both because they illustrate central problems and show how these have been treated in important Supreme Court decisions.

As Chapter 4 indicates, from the beginning of our history draft exemptions for religious pacifists have existed, initially within many states, which at that time provided military forces, and then as a part of the draft laws of the federal government. Sometimes the laws required membership in a pacifist denomination such as the Society of Friends, but in the 1940 Selective Service Act the exemption reached anyone who "by religious training and belief, is conscientiously opposed to participation in war in any form."[5] Two courts of appeals divided on what counted here as "religious training and belief." For the Second Circuit an individual's response "to an inward mentor, call it conscience or God" qualified.[6] The Ninth Circuit required belief in a "responsibility to an authority higher and beyond any worldly one."[7] Congress responded by including statutory language that still exists: "Religious training and belief in this connection means an individual's beliefs in a relation to a Supreme Being involving duties superior to those arising from any human relation, but does not include essentially political, sociological, or philosophical views or a merely personal moral code."[8] Two important Supreme Court cases followed, sharply posing questions about treating religion as special in this context.

One crucial concern is whether that special treatment here is defensible in principle and constitutionally acceptable. Another is how to draw that line. What should be seen as the borders of religion, and is the category of "religious" administrable in practice? As Chapter 4 explains, the Court's two cases on this arose during the Vietnam War, which over time developed intense opposition within this country.

In the first case, *United States v. Seeger*,[9] decided in 1965, the Supreme Court reviewed decisions by three courts of appeals panels. Two panels saw the statute as requiring belief in a Supreme Being; they divided on whether that was constitutionally permissible. One panel read the statute more broadly, and that was the approach chosen by a unanimous Supreme Court. That included Seeger, who did characterize his opposition as based on a "religious" belief but expressed "skepticism or disbelief in the existence of God," claimed a "devotion to goodness and virtue for their own sakes, and a religious faith in a purely ethical creed." Such an account was extremely hard to square with the language Congress had chosen in 1948, especially given the fact that the statute was responding negatively to one circuit's broad construction of religion.

*Welsh v. United States*,[10] decided five years later, involved a statement of belief that was even further removed from the statutory language. Welsh had stricken the word "religious" from his application for exemption; he referred to "reading in the fields of history and sociology" and relied upon "wastes" in the military complex on human resources and "disregard" for human needs.

The Supreme Court divided in three ways on how to deal with his claim. Only eight justices were sitting. Four concluded that Welsh did not fit within the statute as formulated. Four others read the language broadly to cover any registrant whose beliefs "play the role of a religion and function as a religion in the registrant's life," including deeply held "beliefs that are purely ethical or moral."[11] This construction was diametrically at odds with the statute's explicit exclusion of philosophical views and personal moral codes. Among the four Justices who declined to stretch the statutory language this far, three accepted the distinction Congress had drawn. Justice Harlan took a different view. He did not believe it was constitutional to favor religious pacifists over equally sincere nonreligious ones.[12] Since Congress definitely wanted the exemption for most pacifists, Harlan voted for a constitutionally required extension of statutory coverage rather than a striking down of the law itself. This amounted to a fifth vote to support the plurality's taking the statute to include Welsh. Given how far they extended the actual language that Congress had adopted, it is likely that some of the Justices in the plurality were troubled by the concerns of Justice Harlan, although they did not rely on those explicitly. It is a standard judicial practice to construe statutes in a way that does not generate serious constitutional issues.[13]

Whatever one concludes about the constitutional issue and exactly how this statute should have been construed, *Welsh* presents two fundamental questions. Is it appropriate here to distinguish between religious and other bases for an exemption? And how can one draw the line in this context? In contrast with some other topics we will address, the draft exemption involved individual convictions, and these were carefully delved into by draft boards and appellate agencies. As Chapter 4 explains, two reasons to provide a draft exemption are that genuine pacifism is not a good reason to stick someone in jail, and that if a pacifist happens to submit to draft, he may then prove ineffective and dangerous to fellow comrades when involved in actual military conflict. Although most genuine pacifists may be resting on underlying religious convictions, clearly, as the two cases show, some people may become pacifists on bases that are not religious in any standard sense. One concern about including nonreligious claimants in various contexts is that it may well increase the opportunity for fraudulent claims. Here, among the important factors are the individuality of the key beliefs that do not require formal religious connections, the careful review of individual claims by draft boards, and the likelihood that most members of those draft boards will be more sympathetic with religious claims. All this strongly reduces the likelihood that someone would lie about nonreligious bases rather than religious ones. In brief, in this domain, the argument is very strong that an exemption should not be limited to claims that are religious in an ordinary sense.

The second problem, which also arises in other contexts, is line drawing. What should count as "religious"? Not all religions include a belief in God, and they take very different approaches to all the elements of determining what is right and what is wrong. If a statute clearly requires belief in a Supreme Being, that could well disqualify some pacifists who are relying on genuine religious convictions that do not connect to belief in God. Then we would have an inappropriate distinction among religions, not just a division between religion and nonreligion. If the statute is more open-ended, as was the 1940 Act and as the 1948 revision has been judicially construed, then it becomes extremely hard to say who falls on one side or the other, *unless* one says that all objections in conscience are "religious." That approach effectively relies on the inappropriateness of drawing the line at religion by interpreting religion so broadly the line is eliminated.

When we think in terms of nonestablishment and free exercise values here, they point strongly in favor of not requiring religion. To treat genuine nonreligious pacifists unfavorably seems deeply troubling from the nonestablishment point of view, and extending the exemption to those pacifists is hardly an interference with the religious exercise of the religious ones. Indeed, one may best see the treatment of all equally as actually promoting a kind of "free exercise" by taking away inclinations to lie about one's religious beliefs and possibly even to get formally involved with pacifist religious groups just to avoid the draft.

When one reaches beyond wise legislative choices, these reasons underlie a powerful argument that, despite the country's history, any limiting of an exemption to religious pacifists should be seen, as did Justice Harlan, as an unconstitutional establishment. The serious line-drawing problem with any such categorization can add strength to the argument of unconstitutionality as well as bearing on what is statutory wisdom.

We shall now look at a few activities for which singling out religious practices is actually appropriate, before turning to the more difficult questions about abortion and same-sex marriage. Two of the more straightforward are uses of wine as a central element of Roman Catholic Mass or another Christian communion and the ingestion of peyote for worship services of the Native American Church. Given the Biblical account of the Last Supper, the Catholic Church has always regarded wine as a central element for the transformative effect of Mass. Some Protestant groups believe grape juice is an acceptable substitute but that use of wine is preferable. If, as occurred at one point in U.S. history, the sale and ingestion of alcohol are forbidden in order to prevent the harm that heavy drinking can do, should an exception be granted for use in religious services? That was in fact provided when the prohibition was adopted,[14] and it clearly made sense. Except for priests, who may need to ingest a fairly large amount of left-over consecrated wine, nobody drinks a substantial amount because of communion. Drinking at that time may encourage a few worshippers to go home and drink more, but that risk seems very modest as compared with the value of permitting this core element of the religious service. When it comes to nonreligious use, it is hard to conceive of people who believe it is crucial to drink a very small amount of wine. Here free exercise points strongly toward a particular exemption, and since it is hard even to conceive of a comparable nonreligious use, a broader extension would be unwarranted.

When we turn to ingestion of peyote in worship services of the Native American Church, matters are a bit more complicated. Enough peyote is consumed to create a "hallucinatory state" that is believed to cause direct contact with God. Many other drug users seek a somewhat similar hallucination that will enrich their experience and their grasp of human existence. Is it warranted to limit an exemption to religious services? The answer is still "yes," but for somewhat different reasons. Notably if an exemption here covered nonreligious use, or even religious use in private, it would make enforcement of the law nearly impossible. How would enforcers determine why someone is taking a drug, and how would they determine at modest cost whether claims of conscience and religious conviction are genuine? If an exemption was limited to group sessions but included nonreligious ones, the problem would still remain that friends who liked ingesting peyote might get together, form a group, and have sessions designed fundamentally to allow individual use. A conceivable intermediate position would be to allow a "cultural" exemption based on a distinct group's tradition. Nevertheless, whatever one can imagine about a conceivable nonreligious alternative, limiting an exemption to a religious group's worship services, and perhaps even specifying relevant groups, is justified here to avoid undermining general enforcement. The basic limit to religious services is thus definitely constitutionally acceptable.

A similar conclusion applies to allowing the killing of animals in ways that are generally prohibited and to the growing of beards in prison. According to Orthodox Judaism, kosher meat must come from the killing of animals in a manner that is prohibited in some states by laws designed to make the killing less painful. As long as the killing is not significantly worse from the animal's perspective, the created exception for this minority religion is wise. Because it is nearly impossible to imagine any nonreligious conviction of similar force, a limitation to religious practice is really uncontroversial. Beards in prison are essentially similar. Prisoners may on nonreligious grounds want beards longer than permitted, but it is hard to conceive a very strong conviction that this is crucial in their lives. As I have suggested earlier, what makes the most sense here may be simply to relax the general requirement, but if that is to be maintained, it is not crucial to extend the exception to nonreligious reasons.

When we consider tax exemptions, matters are a bit more complicated. If the exemptions go to groups providing public services, such as hospitals and schools, religious groups should definitely not be given more favorable treatment. What about property tax exemptions, which have existed throughout U.S. history for church property and other property used primarily for religious services? One might argue that other groups using property for nonreligious gatherings designed to enhance the lives of people who attend should get a similar exemption. Here are some competing reasons. There are few such groups and identifying them would be hard. Also, not only free exercise but also nonestablishment support the religious exemption. If religious property had to be valued for tax purposes, an obvious concern is that officials might favor some denominations over others. And, as Chapter 4 explains, if value is based on what others would be willing to pay for property, we could easily lose virtually all churches in rich districts of large cities. One would, of course, see a similar concern if large chunks of property were mainly used for nonprofit, nonreligious gatherings, but given both the rarity of these and the fundamental concept that the government should be detached from religious practices, a limitation to religious institutions is appropriate.

That conclusion does present a particular problem that has a wider scope. Determining if a body or personal convictions are "religious" is a genuine and difficult question that I shall further explore in what follows. However, when it comes to property tax exemptions, few institutions are actually on the border; most organizations are definitely religious or not. This makes the categorization less troubling than if a significant percentage of genuine examples in real life are hard to put on one side or the other.

When we look at the most controversial exemption issues of our era, whether religion should have a special status is a genuinely debatable feature. Just how it should be resolved does, I believe, depend partly on the bases people have for objecting to compliance with the general requirements and partly on the range of the exemption. These can bear on the balance of free exercise and establishment values, the likely comparative strength of religious and nonreligious objections, and the concerns about equality for those disadvantaged by refusals of services.

When the question concerns the comparative strength of convictions about behavior, we have no general answer that applies across the board. A person claiming that religious convictions should be treated as special, even when nonreligious analogues exist, might refer to their perceived importance, certainty, and consequences. A true believer may think that following God's will, especially on something significant, takes a very high priority, that we have a clear indication of that will on many moral subjects, and that a failure to comply may have very bad consequences for oneself, such as being condemned to hell. This perspective does suggest a special strength, but it omits certain important elements. Not all religious practitioners believe in God. Among those who do, many may not believe it is obvious what God wishes us to do about some matters. For example, many Protestants definitely think we have a responsibility to care for others, but that itself does not tell us whether early fetuses deserve some protection. Uncertainties are likely to be more extensive if one has doubts about the extent to which what the Bible suggests should be followed. Within a denomination, such as Roman Catholicism, in which church doctrine plays a more central role, many members may nevertheless not accept that doctrine as right about everything.

Another crucial factor for Christians here is the belief that God forgives sins. That reaches both importance and consequences. The consequences connection is obvious. If we see ourselves as committing sins with some frequency, we may not believe that doing wrong about one matter will lead to God's punishment, such as committing us to hell. A person who understands God's forgiveness as central to human life may not perceive doing a wrong as having worse consequences in his life than will a person moved by nonreligious moral convictions. In respect to intrinsic importance, a believer who is convinced that we often do not act in accord with God's wishes may fail to see one instance of that as having more importance than a nonreligious person feels about acting immorally. In summary, although a central aspect of many religious convictions is that we should not knowingly violate God's will, especially when it comes to crucial subjects, nevertheless, no easy basis underlies concluding that the moral outlooks of believers always are weightier than the outlooks of those moved by secular morality.

Abortion provides an illuminating example here. Plainly the liberty of women supports their having a choice whether to continue a pregnancy. As former New York Governor Mario Cuomo urged, our culture has a powerful reason for making that a legal right even though a fair proportion of the population thinks abortions are morally wrong. But the wisdom of allowing abortions does not itself answer how we should see the moral issue as it relates to what exemptions should be granted from performance. A person who believes that, at a certain stage, a fetus is a human life warranting protection may see abortion as the wrongful taking of that life. Given that we have no rational answer to when such life begins, we can certainly perceive both religious and nonreligious outlooks that are similar here. The federal statute that tells medical facilities not to require staff members to perform or assist in abortions does not draw a distinction in terms of religion. One factual explanation for this breadth may be that many members of Congress disagreed with the Supreme Court's creation of a constitutional right to receive abortions; but this statute also provides an illustration of when not drawing the line at religion makes sense.

My conclusion is different about insurance for contraceptives that sometimes operate after conception. I have suggested in Chapter 4 that, given the indirectness by which insurance helps people to purchase and use contraceptives, the Supreme Court's decision in the *Hobby Lobby* case that the Religious Freedom Restoration Act required an exemption for businesses run by those with opposing religious convictions probably went too far. Here the question is different: If one thinks such an exemption is warranted, whether given by a specific statute or under a general provision like RFRA, should it extend to nonreligious objectors? I believe that the answer is "no." Although some Roman Catholics may believe natural law provides nonreligious reasons why the use of all contraceptives is wrong, that conviction has little plausibility for most others. Further, insurance coverage is so indirect, it is really hard to imagine someone without religious premises believing that it would be deeply morally wrong to provide that for a contraceptive that can work after fertilization. An extension of the exemption would probably produce very few genuine nonreligious claims for avoidance and might well lead to fraudulent claims offered in order to further economic interests. Here, *if* any exemption should be granted, its limitation to religious claims is definitely warranted.

When we get to same-sex marriage, matters are more complicated and debatable. Why is this so? Let us start with a simple religious perspective. Some Biblical passages clearly indicate that sexual relations and marriage should be between men and women, that homosexual relations are seriously wrong morally. For a person taking a nonreligious approach, intergender sex and marriage might seem more natural than homosexual relations, given the sexual inclination of most humans and how children are created. But what follows from that? Making homosexual acts criminal has never been really justified, and the Supreme Court's reasons why the right to marriage should be extended were very powerful, whether one thinks the Court rightly created a constitutional right or would better have left the extension to state legislatures—a number of which had already taken that step.

It is hard to conceive of nonreligious objections to same-sex marriage that are nearly as strong as the belief that it simply violates God's will. However, given the country's historical condemnation of homosexual behavior and the understandable sense that traditional marriage is somehow more natural, and given also the reality that some nonbelievers are still influenced by the moral standards of the religious traditions in which they grew up, we can certainly conceive of some nonreligious persons who either disagree with the law's protection of same-sex marriage or who object to personal involvement, or both.

This is a point for which the extent of an exemption may be critical. I have urged that some exemption should be granted, but one that is quite limited. People should not be compelled to participate in practices they believe are deeply wrong. Even if religious objections here are almost certainly going to be much more frequent and powerful than nonreligious ones, a privilege not to be directly involved in the marriages themselves should not be limited to religious objectors. Given that all of us provide unrelated forms of assistance to others whose moral convictions and practices differ from our own, I have suggested that in principle the exemption should not extend to other circumstances. Others will disagree with this conclusion *and* in some political settings an extension may be needed to achieve passage of the relevant antidiscrimination law itself. Insofar as an exemption is extended to subsequent services, such as selling property, providing hotel rooms, and treating couples as married for insurance, it does make sense to limit that to religious claims, given that nonreligious ones will be less strong, less frequent, and more likely to be fraudulent. (I am putting aside here free speech claims put by nonreligious bodies about messages they are communicating.)

For at least certain circumstances, the argument that religion should not be given preferred treatment in exemptions can be cast in terms of the Establishment Clause; Justice Harlan, a crucial vote in the *Welsh* case, did reach that conclusion about pacifists and the draft. More commonly, there will be enough special reasons for a religious exemption so that a specific one cast in those terms or one conferred by a general statute like RFRA will be acceptable and not require the kind of extension that underlay Justice Harlan's position. However, legislators should recognize that, even if most of those seeking a particular exemption are religious organizations and individuals, a statute they adopt should not be specifically cast with that limit, denying the privilege to nonbelievers, unless genuine substantial reasons support drawing that line. Extending an exemption beyond religion largely answers establishment concerns; it does not burden free exercise in any way and can even be seen as supporting freedom not to be pressured into a religious position. If the exemption involves less favorable treatment of others, such as those receiving abortions, the extension will not mean a significant actual disadvantage, since the vast majority of those seeking it will have religious bases, and statutory qualifications should protect the basic rights of those needing help.

## Government Messages and Assistance

When we turn to government messages and assistance to projects, the essential Establishment Clause questions are, as we have seen in Chapter 3, primarily whether the religious authorities or ideas may be put to a disadvantage or should be treated equally with nonreligious endeavors. If an organ of government has a choice what to do about that, I have urged that free exercise and establishment values can still come into play for what is wisest.

For formal government messages the answer about religion is fairly simple. Government institutions are essentially free to communicate ideas on almost any subject, no matter how controversial they may be. Government officials when acting in that capacity are not supposed to articulate the truth of one religion as opposed to all others, and statutes may not do so. Simply put, a line definitely exists between religion and nonreligion, and the constitutional restriction on government messages is much greater in respect to religion. That restriction is a core value of nonestablishment and actually indirectly supports free exercise.

Two qualifications are worth noting, however. The first is that, of course, the acceptance of prayers for government events and reference to God by Presidents and others do convey at least fairly general religious messages: These are solidly grounded historically and are treated as constitutionally acceptable. And, of course, more specific religious convictions are expressed by military and prison chaplains, whose behavior helps the free exercise of those whose ability to choose worship services on their own is sharply curtailed.

The second qualification involves an intertwining of political and religious factors. Donald Trump, while a leading candidate for the Republican presidential nomination, stated that "I think Islam hates us."[15] When asked to explain just what he had in mind a day or two later, he made clear he did not mean every Muslim, but he did regard what he said as true for a high percentage of them. This could hardly be taken as an encouragement for an American to convert to Islam, and the ordinary person could well regard it as a form of condemnation of that religion. But the remark's main relevance, of course, concerned political matters, such as whether we should be very careful and restrictive about admitting Muslims into this country. Even if Mr. Trump had already been President at this point, his communication should not have been taken as primarily religious, although I believe that even as a candidate for that office he would wisely have been much, much more careful about how he formulated his actual belief about this.

Within public schools, the wise constraints on conveyed messages are much broader. Schools should generally not tackle in their classes many highly contentious issues about which the premises of liberal democracy provide no clear answer. But in terms of what is constitutionally acceptable, religion remains special. Schools cannot assert what is religiously true or false. It is important in this context to understand that the constitutional principle covers negative assertions as well as positive ones. School teachers can no more say "there is no God" or "Jesus was just an ordinary person" than they can say "Jesus Christ was the son of God." When the question is what schools must, or should, allow student groups to do, the general principle, as we have seen, is that they must ordinarily treat religious groups similarly to nonreligious ones.

In respect to government assistance, the two basic ideas are these: Putting aside historic property exemptions for churches, and perhaps income tax exemptions for donations to churches etc.,[16] the government cannot provide financial support *if* what the benefitting organization does is mainly to communicate a religious message. More broadly, the state cannot favor religious providers over nonreligious ones. In each of these situations, religion cannot be preferred over other messages and organizations. The key questions are when religion must be disfavored and when it may, or must, be treated equally. On the last question, covered briefly at the end of Chapter 3, if all an organization does is provide valuable services, a fairness argument supports not treating religious providers worse than others. This argument gains some strength from both free exercise and nonestablishment values, although the government can probably respond that financing any religious group would implicitly help it convey its religious message and so is not constitutionally required.

A concern I have not mentioned here is the relation between formal requirements and likely administrative choices. Laws are administered by individuals, sometimes with substantial discretion. Obviously, administrators should not engage in forms of discrimination that are forbidden for formal laws. Legislators need to think about how appropriate the administrative choices are likely to be. Thus, one plausible argument against granting equal treatment for religious bodies that are providing public services is that in a particular jurisdiction they are likely to be unjustly favored by those who have choices about which organizations to finance.

In brief, in this area the general issue about religion and nonreligion is whether religious messages and activities must constitutionally be treated less favorably than others or may be treated equally, and, if the latter, whether a wise choice does or does not involve equal treatment.

## What Counts as "Religion"?

As we have already seen what counts as religion may not be simple. Since that matters greatly for whether a line should be drawn in those terms, I will briefly explore various possibilities and indicate why I think an analogical approach makes the most sense. Under statutes that provide special status for religious exemptions, and according to rules that either require or allow religious messages and organizations to be treated worse than nonreligious ones, being able to distinguish what counts as religious from what does not is critical. Drawing a clear line here is very difficult for virtually all categories of what may or should be done. Before delving into these complexities, I want to make two very important points.

The first concerns the status of essentially antireligious and nonreligious bases for action. We have seen that an explicitly antireligious message made by the government is properly seen as a violation of the Establishment Clause. A similar view, which was taken by Justice Harlan about preferring religious pacifists over nonreligious ones, could be viewed as applicable more broadly to claims for exemptions. Some analysts who have taken this perspective, as well as the confusing language in certain Supreme Court opinions, suggest that the best approach is to see these claims as themselves "religious." Simply speaking, any genuine claim of conscience for an exemption *could* then be seen as "religious," and an assertion of atheism could be similarly perceived. This approach essentially eliminates the relevance of any ordinary sense of what is "religious," although, of course, there will still be questions about what amounts to a claim of "conscience" and whether Donald Trump's assertion about Muslims hating us was a religious assertion. I believe these broad categorizations of "religion" are intrinsically judgments that actual religious claims should not be treated as special. However, these assertions opposing special treatment should be so understood and addressed directly, rather than being put aside by an extension of the term "religion" beyond any plausible boundaries, and far beyond what was the original understanding in the constitution.

The second preliminary observation concerns the relation of the vagueness of a boundary to its workability. A legal standard is best if it clearly demarks categories *and* provides definite, desirable answers to the vast majority of circumstances. Unfortunately, that is not always possible. To take an obvious example, if a person is liable for "negligently" causing injury, it can often be genuinely debatable whether his behavior fell within the bounds of "reasonable" or was "unreasonable." When it comes to possible categorizations, I do not believe any plausible approach to religion will have a clear application across the board, and that is definitely not true for the approach I shall suggest. That concern can constitute a basis for not casting a legal line in that way, and, in at least some contexts, can provide a genuine reason for *not* treating religious convictions and organizations differently from nonreligious ones. But it is important here to understand that, in the vast majority of circumstances, what is involved clearly does fall on one side or the other of "religion." Rather than being uncertain in virtually all possible applications, an approach that is vague at the edges can be fairly obvious for something like 95 percent of actual circumstances even if it is uncertain for one situation in twenty. I believe something like this is true for many proposed categorizations of "religion," including the analogical one I defend.

A final preliminary thought is this. Given the complex values of free exercise and nonestablishment, it may be that exactly what should count as "religion" appropriately differs depending on what the topic is. I believe this view is probably sound, although no simple categorization between free exercise and establishment works here.

When we consider how "religion" may well be categorized, we should understand that an approach needs both to be manageable by judges and other officials and be consonant with the underlying values of the religion clauses.

Before turning to analysis of various conceptual approaches, I will briefly survey some leading cases addressing this topic, although the Supreme Court has rarely tackled it in any systemic way. It did, in 1890, speak of "one's views of his relation to his Creator, and to the obligations they impose of reverence for his being and character, and of obedience to his will."[17] Chief Justice Hughes, in a 1930 dissent, referred similarly to a belief that one owed duties to God "superior to those arising from any human relation."[18] A much broader account was offered in the 1961 *Torcaso v. Watkins*,[19] in which the Court invalidated a state law requiring officeholders to declare a belief in God, on the basis that that improperly preferred theistic religions. Justice Black's majority opinion indicated that Buddhism, Taoism, secular humanism (at least in the organized form of the Fellowship of Humanity), the Ethical Cultural Society, and similar groups counted as religious. As we have seen, when it came to individual pacifist conscience, the Court's majority in *United States v. Seeger* and a plurality of four in *Welsh v. United States* interpreted the federal statute very broadly. These various decisions have led courts generally to a highly inclusive sense of what counts as religion. For example, when the question was whether the Ethical Society qualified as "religious" under the District of Columbia tax code, the U.S. Court of Appeals for the District of Columbia held "yes."[20] Although propounding no theist beliefs, the society held Sunday services with Bible readings, sermons, singing, and meditation, and also had services for naming, marrying, and burying. A California court reached a similar conclusion about the Fellowship of Humanity.[21]

In two cases Judge Arlin Adams of the Third Circuit provided a careful and sophisticated account of the concept of religion. In the first case, the court determined that, contrary to what its teachers in public schools maintained, Creative Intelligence–Transcendental Meditation, which had students receive individual mantras at a *puja*, at which teachers made offerings to a deified "Guru Dev," did count as religion.[22] In the second case, the court held that a state prisoner's membership in MOVE, a "revolutionary organization opposed to all that is wrong" did not entitle him to a "religious" diet of raw food, because the organization lacked the structural characteristics and ideology of a religion.[23] Concurring in the first case and writing for a unanimous panel in the second, Judge Adams concluded that cases had established a new definition of religion that was by "analogy."[24] The elements that were key were concern with "fundamental problems of human existence," a claim to comprehensive truth, and the presence of formal or surface signs similar to those of accepted religions.[25]

With this sketch of what has been said in judicial opinions, we shall turn to various possibilities, starting with single factor approaches, none of which stand up in my view.

The simplest approach would be to require belief in a Supreme Being, one that connects to organizational practices and to what people believe they must do. Although that concept is perhaps consistent with the understanding when the First and Fourteenth Amendments were adopted, it faces the major problem of being too restrictive, favoring Western religions over others.

One possible categorization of claims of conscience would be to make free exercise depend on belief in extratemporal consequences.[26] This would exclude practices that people believe are required or strongly encouraged by their religion but do not involve a threat of those consequences. As explained earlier in this chapter, if a woman believes God forgives sins, she may both believe in extratemporal consequences and that in the end she will not really be penalized for committing wrongs. Many Christians are actually unsure about the precise relation of sins in this life and what will happen after death. To delve into someone's views about extratemporal consequences would seriously complicate assessments of sincerity. That this test is inapt for the Establishment Clause is yet more obvious. Public schools cannot teach the truth of religious views that do not relate to extratemporal consequences nor may the government financially support prayers and worship services of such faiths.

"Ultimate concern" is a broader approach to what counts as religion, one suggested in *United States v. Seeger* and drawing from the writings of Paul Tillich. The basic idea is that a person's ultimate concern is really his God. This approach effectively includes someone's deepest conviction which may not be religious in a traditional sense. So understood, it would possibly work more for individual claims of conscience, like those of pacifists, than for what schools may teach or what assistance government can provide for organizations. Yet even in the free exercise realm, I believe this standard presents severe problems.

The fundamental difficulty is its vagueness and exactly what it would include. What of beliefs connected to an ultimate concern, but not themselves regarded as very important? What of people with multiple things that concern them deeply and with no clear ordering? What of those whose reflective convictions do not take the highest priority in how they live?

An illustration of the first example would be a Protestant, or a collective group of Protestants, whose belief is that communion is a very important aspect of worshipping God, that the drinking of wine is essentially symbolic, and that grape juice is an acceptable substitute but that wine is slightly preferable. Would they have a "religious" claim to use wine? That in itself would hardly be an "ultimate concern," but it would definitely be religious in an ordinary sense and would be tied to other beliefs that could be seen as resting on an ultimate concern. If we say this does not count as ultimate concern, we can see that a claim could be "religious" in any ordinary sense but not count under that standard. If this use of wine does come within that category, we can see that the test does not really require that claims be based on extremely powerful reasons that it would be wrong to act in a certain way.

My second example is this. Many people live their lives with no clearly organized hierarchy of values. They care about success in life, preserving love with their spouse, helping their children, contributing in various ways to the welfare of others, and participating in religious services. If you asked which objective is most important to them, they would really not have an answer; and when conflicts arise between two of their values, their choice depends on how great a sacrifice would be made in respect to one if the other were followed. Do people like this really have *no* ultimate concern, or for them would that consist of some complicated combination of factors? Would they be disqualified from all claims to be able to follow religious conscience or would they in theory have such a right, but one for which the practical application of "ultimate concern" would often be impossible?

A somewhat similar problem can arise with almost any categorization of religion. A person may have certain nonreligious reasons to think an act is wrong, and, though uncertain about what God would want him to do, may think that it is likely that refraining from the act will be in accord with God's will.[27] Whether that weak sense of probability is sufficient to make his conviction "religious" is hard to say.

The third example is a bit simpler. Someone believes a certain ordering is proper, but lives his life completely differently. Imagine a drug addict who believes people should not use such drugs and should help others according to God's will, but whose dominant objective in actual life is to acquire and ingest heroin. What counts as his "ultimate concern"? There is no easy answer. Of course, virtually no one carries out his life completely consistently with what he takes as the actual priorities of a perfect life, so for many the relation of what they believe is right and what they really care about is less than simple. For all those reasons, as well as others, the concept of "ultimate concern" seems very hard to apply in practice; it is not a viable general approach to what counts as "religious" even in the free exercise domain.

The most plausible single-factor approach to "religious" is "higher reality," belief in something beyond the observable world. Although the edges of what counts as higher reality may not always be clear, this approach does include the vast majority of religious groups and beliefs, but would exclude groups like the Ethical Culture Society that engage in practices like those of standard religions but do not assert a realm of meaning that is inaccessible to ordinary understanding.

Given the complexities in what should count as "religion" for constitutional and other legal purposes, can that inquiry be essentially avoided? As we have seen, if the law's approach is to treat religious and nonreligious claims neutrally, officials and judges do not have to decide what counts as religious, but I have urged that sometimes drawing the line at religion is definitely proper. Moreover, when it comes to what schools can teach and what activities the government can support, neutrality is not a feasible general option.

A different approach to claims for particular treatment could be for officials to leave it up to individuals or organizations to determine if they are relying on a religious conviction. This self-determination is obviously not workable for many Establishment Clause concerns, since these largely rest upon what *others* take as the assistance or promotion of religion. The approach is also not really workable for free exercise claims. The simplest problem here is that this would encourage people to lie or stretch their convictions into claims that they are relying on religion. A more subtle problem involves two honest people who have exactly the same views about why performing an act is deeply wrong. The first of these grew up with and has maintained a narrow view of religion; the second studied the *Welsh* case in law school and has a very broad view of religion. These are individual views about the coverage of a concept, not about the basis for what it is wrong to do. To grant an exemption to one person but not the other would not be defensible.

This leaves us with multifactor approaches. We can identify some variations in possibilities here. Perhaps certain factors would necessarily be present, or the existence of some could make up for the absence of others. One might seek a single approach for all religion cases. However, the same differences in values that underlie various kinds of cases may well support slightly different approaches to what counts as religious. What I believe makes the most sense is an analogical approach, one that identifies the central factors of dominant religions and religious convictions and asks how far those are present in debatable borderline instances. Under this approach, no single factor is essential, strengths in some can make up for weaknesses in others, and what finally counts as religion can vary with different legal issues.

Among the aspects of many undoubted religions are beliefs in God or gods, a sense of a spiritual domain, communication with God or gods through worship and prayer, a sense of morality tied to a divine nature, and the use of sacred texts and organizations to facilitate beliefs and practices. In discerning the boundaries of religion, courts and others should see how closely disputed beliefs and practices resemble those. According to this approach, no simple feature is indispensable for religion, and two organizations *could* both be religious without sharing any single common feature.

Although I have at different points suggested that what matters for Establishment Clause purposes can differ from what should count for free exercise exemptions, I do not agree with what Laurence Tribe once suggested, namely that sharp differences can be drawn between "religious" for the two constitutional clauses. He proposed that everything "arguably religious" should count as "religious" for free exercise purposes and that everything "arguably nonreligious" should count as nonreligious for establishment purposes.[28] "Arguably" is highly vague; not everything "arguably" religious should count as such for free exercise purposes; and the government should not be able to teach everything that is "arguably" nonreligious without ever violating the Establishment Clause. Were this approach faithfully followed, an organization that is arguably religious and arguably nonreligious might be best off. It could engage in school sponsored activities that would not be possible for clearly religious organizations, but would have a free exercise right to get tax benefits available to religious bodies. Although no simple division like this works, the particular issue involved can on balance affect just what should count as religious.

Three general points are important about the approach proposed here. The first is that it is not inconsistent with what the Supreme Court has decided in modern times. Although, as we have seen, Judge Adams of the Third Circuit did refer to an analogical approach, the Supreme Court has not used that language in its opinions. In reality, it has not provided any clear guidance about how in general what counts as religion should be determined. Two other points concern the workability of the analogy approach. It can rightly be challenged as vague and possibly unmanageable. It definitely does lack precision, but, as I have claimed, a single standard such as "ultimate concern" is also very uncertain in its application. In brief, I believe this an area in which no simple, easily applicable standard is appropriate, largely because the religion clause values are themselves highly complex in their relation to each other. Another very important reality is one that I previously noted. Even if the borders are hard to identify here, most instances do fall clearly on one side or the other. Officials will typically be able to identify what is religious or not, and only in unusual cases will judicial determination of that border be needed to determine an outcome. Many legal standards are vague at the edges without undermining legal clarity in most circumstances. That is definitely true here.

This discussion of the edges of religion bears on the main focus of this chapter in two ways. The difficulty of determining what counts as religion can itself constitute one argument for not drawing a line between religious claims and otherwise similar nonreligious claims. More generally, whether providing different treatment to what is "religious" and what is "nonreligious" makes sense does depend partly on what counts as religious. Thus, present approaches or wise resolutions about the legal edges of "religion" can bear on when exactly making legal outcomes depend on that boundary is appropriate.

# PART FIVE

# Religious Convictions, Public Reasons, and Political Choices

T HIS LAST PART OF THE BOOK addresses a particularly significant, debatable, and highly complex problem: exactly how far, if at
all, should religious convictions play a role in political and legal choices?[1]
This question is closely interrelated to disagreements over when, if ever, it
is appropriate for citizens, legislators, executive officials, and judges to reach
beyond "public reasons," those that have force for all citizens and officials in
a liberal democracy, when they make decisions about what the law should be
or resolve issues about debatable contents of the existing law.

A major issue in political philosophy continues to be to what extent political decisions must be based on public reasons within liberal democracies. In
one respect, this issue substantially concerns the place of religious convictions. Since most religious convictions do not qualify as public reasons, one
can see faithful reliance on the public reasons as both a form of nonestablishment and a constraint on free exercise. That constraint is particularly strong
insofar as one sees "public reasons" as reaching private citizens as well as
officials. A "public reasons" theory is not just about religious bases that do
not qualify, because it reaches all personal convictions that do not fit. That,
however, does not reduce its significance for the competing values of free
exercise and nonestablishment.

This special relevance rests partly on the reality that many religious individuals can find it easier to distinguish their special religious premises from
what they see as "public reasons" than most people will be able to separate

those reasons from nonreligious personal convictions. The second ground of importance for religion clause themes is that, despite its broader scope, the "public reasons" approach does have the effect of both serving the values of nonestablishment and curbing free exercise. It represents a fairness claim about nonimposition on others that effectively becomes a self-disciplined restriction on one's liberty.

The crucial subjects addressed in Chapters 9 and 10 concern the reliance in political decision-making on religious convictions that do not represent an effort to actually advance the status of one's religion. If a person's over-arching aim is to assure that her religion has a dominant or favored place, we have seen in previous parts of the book why that violates the Establishment Clause with respect to requirements for officials' actions and contravenes the values of the clause with respect to private citizens. But religious convictions are often not focused on that objective. They can bear on more general political issues, such as required treatment of nonhuman animals, the appropriate range of protected abortions and exemptions from performing those, levels of taxation and benefits to aid the poor, and the status of same-sex marriage. These are the sorts of issues addressed in what follows.

The focus of "public reasons" and the following discussion are *not* upon whether religious convictions should ever matter in people's lives, but whether officials and citizens should rely on them in respect to making the law and whether they should ever count for the law's interpretation by judges and other officials. Also relevant is whether they should ever play a role in decisions about actions the government should take, such as whether to engage in military conflict.

As Chapter 4 indicates, "public reason" can support the idea that if many citizens have strong religious convictions that an act is deeply wrong, they should not be legally required to violate their consciences. The force of this claim for exemption does not itself directly rest on a religious conviction, but it may commonly seem more persuasive to believers than to skeptics.

Earlier parts of the book have distinguished actual constitutional viola-tions, only some of which are discernible by courts, from behavior at odds with constitutional values. Whether one focuses on the religious clauses or on broader aspects of a "public reasons" approach that one may see as embraced by the constitution as a whole, virtually no law will amount to a discernible constitutional violation because of subjective bases for support by legislators and private citizens, so long as the law itself is not designed to promote the status of particular religions or religious ideas. For private citizens, behavior may be at odds with constitutional values but will not itself be in direct violation of the document. For legislators and other officials, one might conclude that some deviations from "public reasons" do actually violate the Constitution, and one may also believe that the actual constraints on how officials should behave are greater in respect to reliance upon religious views than other nonpublic opinions. However, so long as the laws themselves do not promote or put down religion, deviations from public reasons will rarely be discernible and correctable by judges. One, unlikely, exception I can imagine is if a lower court judge makes clear that the way he is resolving a particular issue is precisely because his religious convictions direct that. An appellate court could overturn on that basis. This part of the book will focus on behavior that is arguably at odds with the values of the religious clauses and perhaps other constitutional provisions, and may even violate them, but not in a way that is correctible by judicial decision.

It is important to acknowledge two aspects of a "public reasons" theory that do not apply to some other subjects in this book. Someone might think that either the theory should work as a constraint in any liberal democracy or only in some liberal democracies, including ours. However broadly she sees the plausible reach of its coverage, a person might defend the public reasons theory as one that has present application, or as a kind of ideal toward which liberal democracies should move, or as some combination of these.

As I shall develop further, a critical complexity about the theory is what one can really expect of fellow citizens. Insofar as the theory is widely accepted as a guide for political behavior, people should be able to expect most others to adhere to its restraints. This would certainly now be true for judges. But what is a religious citizen to do if she is fully aware that the vast majority of people in her locality are supporting or opposing proposed legislation on the basis of their religious convictions, which differ from hers? It would seem a bit unfair for someone to insist that she should limit herself to public reasons. In a liberal democracy, one aspect of justice would be that citizens adhere to similar standards of how they should reach political decisions. As long as most people are not guided by that restraint, one might see a "public reasons" approach as an ideal, whose actual limiting force should depend on its cultural acceptance. As we shall see, some features of that approach are now embraced in our society, but the status of other aspects is highly dubious.

With these preliminary observations, I shall turn in Chapter 9 to basic approaches with respect to "public reasons"[2] and its limiting of the appropriate use of religious convictions in developing the law. Chapter 10 suggests some of the difficulties in the workability of such an approach for citizens, which includes how natural law ideas fit with public reason and may operate for some religious believers.

# Basic Approaches and Intrinsic Limits

THIS CHAPTER FIRST SKETCHES basic approaches to the concept of "public reasons," which will be opposed to self-conscious reliance on religious convictions in political and legal decisions. It then considers various specific suggestions for what public reasons actually exclude. The final section explores the intrinsic limits and costs of a "public reasons" approach, asking how far these might indicate that the basic idea is misguided or may, instead, support an intermediate approach that acknowledges that "public reasons" has genuine force in many contexts but is often not a wise basis to insist on total exclusion of religious convictions. Many skeptical generalizations offered here are explored in more detail in Chapter 10. That addresses various specific practical issues, distinguishes how a "public reasons" approach may apply differently depending on the positions people occupy in society, and examines the difference between all the bases upon which one relies in reaching decisions and what one offers as a public support of her conclusions.

## The Assumption of Various Theorists

I begin with a variety of formulations of the basic idea of public reasons. Writing about prohibitions of obscenity in 1963, Louis Henkin, who was himself a sincere practitioner of the Jewish religion, urged that in the "domain of government" social problems should be "resolved by rational social processes, in which men can reason together, can examine problems and propose solutions capable of objective proof or persuasion, subject to objective scrutiny by courts and electors."[1] According to Bruce Ackerman in 1980, "nobody has the right to vindicate political authority by asserting a privileged insight into the moral universe. ... No reason is a good reason if" it rests on the power holder's notion that "his conception of the good is better than that asserted by any of his fellow citizens."[2] Thomas Nagel suggested that higher order impartiality depends on beliefs that "can be shown to be justifiable from a more impersonal standpoint."[3] Charles Larmore claimed that the state should be neutral about "disputed and controversial ideas of the good life."[4] And Lawrence Solum indicated that within pluralist societies in which persons should be free and equal, "[p]ublic reasons exclude particular comprehensive conceptions of the good."[5]

The best-known theory of "public reasons" has been that of John Rawls, which he developed over time in various respects. I shall sketch some of its core features but not here explore them in detail, in part because the viability of a theory of public reasons, and its preclusion of distinctive religious convictions, does not stand or fall with the details of his account. In his *A Theory of Justice*,[6] Rawls urged that, at least within a liberal democracy, ideas of justice should be based on what people would choose if they were in an "original position," not knowing their personal characteristics, social status, or conceptions of the good. For issues about what is just for the government to do, this perspective would lead to reliance on forms of reasoning that would be generally recognized by all people.

In his later writing, Rawls made clear that he was not asserting what are necessarily the most rational principles of justice, but setting out principles for liberal democracies that best capture the idea of a "system of fair social cooperation between free and equal persons."[7] He did not claim that citizens should not rely on their own individual perspectives concerning the making of all varieties of laws; instead, he wrote, "there is no reason ... why any citizen, or association of citizens, should have the right to use the state's police power to decide constitutional essentials or basic questions of justice as that person's, or that association's, comprehensive doctrine directs."[8] Rawls contended that, in contrast to a claim about reliance on a rational conception of the good, political liberalism supposes there are many conflicting reasonable comprehensive doctrines. People should rely on what is commonly shared as an "overlapping consensus of those comprehensive doctrines."[9]

In more recent years, various defenses of public reasons have been offered. Jonathan Quong has written that "reasons that we can all share" are needed for discourse "in a large and diverse liberal society."[10] Lawrence Solum has relatedly referred to the "shared capacity of citizens to engage in political deliberation."[11] Andrew Lister claims that in a pluralistic democracy, we need people to try to rely for the making of laws and public institutions on "reasons everyone can reasonably be expected to accept."[12] Micah Schwartzman urges that a "duty of civility" requires that people refrain from relying on nonpublic reasons, despite the claim that public reasons do not settle many controversial matters.[13] Gerald Gaus has developed an account of epistemology that shows how people reach personal convictions in various ways; this leads him to support an account of reliance on public reasons for decisions about coercive laws.[14]

The various formulations of public reasons are not exactly the same, and I have not delved into the precise support each author offers for his proposal, but they do give us a sense of the fundamental assumption of mutual understanding and fairness that underlie the core of "public reasons" claims.

What we can gather from this brief summary of various claims about the role of public reason is that differences of opinion exist about exactly when that limit should apply and how one determines what is excluded. But clearly a core concept is that on many important political and legal issues, neither officials nor citizens should be relying on their religious convictions. This is seen as an aspect of justice and fairness within a liberal democracy, based on values closely related to certain principles underlying nonestablishment and actually serving the nonestablishment values themselves.

I should make clear that in suggesting a number of qualifications about the place of "public reasons" in our liberal democracy, I do not directly address views that are much more skeptical, that argue that at least ordinary citizens should typically feel completely free to rely on their religious convictions about what is correct behavior when they take political positions.[15] Even if one finds this position as having some force for citizens, I do not believe that is so for judges and public officials. They should clearly be constrained to some extent by public reasons.

A crucial aspect of all the accounts of public reasons is that they raise questions about the feasibility of the lines they draw. These questions, which concern both what is conceptually possible and what human beings are actually capable of doing at this stage of history, bear significantly on what is workable and fair. A person's place in society, whether she is a judge, another official, or a private citizen, can be very important for what we can reasonably expect in regard to these claims about proper bases for decisions.

### Bases of Exclusion

This section examines various ideas of what a notion of public reasons actually excludes, after first noting at least one kind of rule-making to which the basic idea may not apply. Sometimes people support binding decisions on the basis of self-interest or personal preference, and everyone understands that this is both the way most vote, or line up, and is fully appropriate in the particular context.

At the beginning of a semester, I ask seminar students if they would like to meet at the law school or in my apartment, and later ask if they would like to reschedule the session on Tuesday of Thanksgiving week. I expect each individual to take the position that fits his or her own interests. These decisions, of course, are not laws, but we can imagine similar public circumstances, for example, a locality considering the construction of a ski area. The welfare of others could count here somewhat, but it might be generally assumed that people mainly will *properly* vote based on whether the ski area would be good for them personally. If it is expected that people will properly vote on the basis of simple personal preference, could they not also rely on religious convictions, so long as their outcome will not disfavor other religions or involve some other unfair violation of equal treatment? Having raised this possibility, I will assume in what follows that the relevant political issues are not ones in which it is assumed that the proper way for people and legislators to develop positions is pure self-interest.

Four possible bases for distinguishing "public reasons" from other bases for public decisions are: (1) nonreliance on ideas of the good life; (2) nonreliance on comprehensive views; (3) having rational bases for one's decision; and (4) relying on grounds that are generally accepted. One might, of course, see these bases as operating in combination, and many "public reasons" do satisfy all four standards. However, each of them presents genuine problems about whether any precise line can be drawn and how workable any theoretical distinction may be in practical life.

## Ideas of the Good

One suggestion is that the liberal state should be neutral about ideas of the good life.[16] "Good life" here is not meant as wealthy and comfortable but how we can best live our lives. Although this idea is sometimes mischaracterized as urging that people not take a public position based on their sense of morality, we need to be clear that "good life" and "morality" are not congruent. Many religious and nonreligious aspects of morality do not depend on ideas of the good life. A person's belief that it is wrong to kill innocent people or to treat classes of people with contempt need not rely on any particular position about what is a good life. Of course, if one believes an act is morally wrong, he can conclude that committing it is at odds with a good life, but the belief about wrongness itself need not depend on any distinctive view about a good life. Similar to this general point about morality, not all religious convictions about human behavior focus on what is a good life. If a religion teaches that we should respect one another and provide equal opportunity, that could strongly support helping those who are poor and severely disadvantaged without resting on a view about how individuals could best lead their lives.

Even if it is offered as only one basis among others to declare reasons for political decisions as unacceptable because they are nonpublic, a principle advocating neutrality about a good life faces major obstacles. As Chapter 5 emphasizes, one aspect of public activity is that we expect public schools to teach students how to lead healthy, productive, and "fulfilling" lives, such as trying to preserve physical and mental health, to avoid becoming an addict or alcoholic, and to appreciate aspects of culture. Even for adults, the government provides support for art and literature and promotes access to our natural environment by funding public parks and zoos. When decisions are made about what literature and arts to support, they rest on judgments of quality that are not neutral. These illustrations raise fundamental doubts about any general exclusion of ideas of the good life. Even when it comes to government coercion of adults, should respect and equality absolutely preclude decision-makers from relying on judgments about what constitutes an unfortunate departure from a good life? The outlawing of drugs that will often produce damaging addiction is one notable example. Whatever other reasons may be present, people may think that the drugs' hurting of the lives of users is a legitimate basis for a prohibition.

A rather different problem about urging nonreliance on a good life is that most people, including legislators, will often find it difficult to determine what they believe because of "public reasons" and what they believe because of perceptions about a good life. Should education for the poor be financed because of the need for equal opportunity, a "public reason," or because education assists developing of perceptions of what genuinely contributes to a good life? Many would see both objectives as relevant here and would find it hard to distinguish in their minds the weight they give to each. To be clear, as I will subsequently develop further, I am not asserting that generally people will lack the capacity to distinguish what they see as "public reasons" from other bases for positions. What I do suggest is that, for this and other proposed limits on what are "public reasons," people will often not be able to discern how far various reasons interconnect in some subtle way, or how much each affects their overall conclusion about what is right, or both.[17]

## Comprehensive Views

Perhaps the most plausible candidate for what should be excluded from public reason is "comprehensive views," including religious outlooks. Although it may be hard to say exactly what counts as a "comprehensive view" that would be relevant here,[18] the basic argument is that the divergent philosophies people have within a liberal democracy do not belong in the political realm. Of course, an actual person will not accept the constraint of "public reasons" unless it fits with her overall perspective on how she should live, but her sense of life in a pluralist society could lead her to conclude that citizens should not rely directly on their comprehensive views when they address political subjects. A more troubling connection between comprehensive views and public reasons is that, when people address debatable issues about which both sides can present genuine "public reasons," they may find it hard, perhaps impossible, to disregard their religious convictions or other comprehensive view in deciding which side is more persuasive.[19] We can see this in regard to proposed statutory exemptions to treating same-sex marriage couples equally. As Chapter 4 indicates, significant public reasons present themselves on each side, but can we expect someone who is weighing these to totally put aside her personal convictions about the propriety of such marriages and participation in them?

An interesting, somewhat related, point is that the effect of not relying on comprehensive views would be much greater for some people then for others. Suppose a man is persuaded by the utilitarian Jeremy Bentham that the ultimate moral standard is the greatest happiness for the greatest number. That is not a widely accepted comprehensive view, but since everyone agrees that happiness is valuable, they will see its promotion as one relevant consideration. Taking the example of how far education for the poor might be supported by equality concerns or what contributes to a good life, a Benthamite would find it very hard to discern *how far* promoting happiness, in comparison with other possible values, fits with "public reasons" and how far it extends beyond those.

For many religious perceptions, such as what God has entrusted us to do, the theoretical exclusion would be total. Of course, what a believer sees as God's instruction may actually coalesce with public reasons, but unlike the utilitarian who can rely on "happiness" consequences, she must attempt to put her sense of God's will totally aside. Thus, the effect of trying to disregard one's comprehensive view will have much more effect on some of us than others. That is not itself necessarily an objection to the basic principle, which rests on notions of fairness to fellow citizens, but it does mean that the restraint of "public reasons" will be much less on many other citizens than on those who see part of their religious exercise as trying to carry out special convictions about what God has intended about how we should live our lives.

A final difficulty concerns exactly what counts as a comprehensive view. Rawls distinguished partial and complete comprehensive views.[20] He also wrote that "Catholic views of the common good and solidarity when they are expressed in terms of political values"[21] can be an appropriate political conception of justice, but that negative perceptions about homosexual relations or polygamy do not provide public reasons.[22] One might, of course, sensibly believe reasons must be greater for prohibiting behavior than encouraging it, but various nonreligious grounds do suggest that in general monogamy can be a richer, more equal, marriage than polygamy. Why should Catholic views be precluded about that but not other aspects of what they perceive as the common good? I shall not explore this problem in depth, but it does suggest that drawing any exact line may be difficult and that telling actual individuals that they should be guided by that line may be asking them to do more than we can reasonably expect of anyone.

Acceptance

One possible position about what should be an appropriate basis for political decision-making in a liberal democracy is that the kinds of reasons presented must be broadly accepted as appropriate. A notable articulation of this approach was given by the late governor Mario Cuomo, a devout Roman Catholic who agreed with the church's teaching that abortion was wrong but nonetheless supported its legalization in New York. At a 1989 lecture given at Notre Dame, he noted that "we are … a people of many religions … who hold different beliefs on many matters. Our public morality, then, the moral standards we maintain for everyone, not just the ones we insist on in our private lives, depends on a consensus view of right and wrong. The values derived from religious belief will not, and should not, be accepted as part of the public morality unless they are shared by the pluralistic community at large, by consensus."[23]

There are a number of nuances about the basic idea of "acceptance" or "consensus," but I shall first note a crucial distinction. One might see consensus as by itself a sufficient basis to guide everyone or, instead, as constituting only a constraining limit on how far people should arrive at positions that would restrict the behavior of others.

If what is involved in an "acceptance" constraint is that people should simply go along with dominant views, whether or not they fit other possible grounds for "public reasons," this would clearly constitute an unfair restriction on dissenters. Should they not be able to reject broad assumptions that strike them as contrary to the fundamental ideas of justice and equality? To take a historical example, what of a dissenter in a state in which almost all actual "citizens" thought slavery for Negroes was completely appropriate? The truth of the matter is that many premises that are now widely accepted, including gender equality and same-sex marriage, began with advocacy by a minority at odds with assumptions widely accepted. General acceptance alone is not sufficient to preclude someone relying on a contrary basis for a political position. A notable example of why this is true is that the religious convictions of a substantial majority should not be sufficient to tell others they cannot rely on their contrary convictions.

Another way "general acceptance" might work is to bear on how far people should feel constrained to put aside their convictions that are not based on public reasons. That could relate to specific issues or to the place of public reasons or both. If a conviction about how to treat particular animals was widespread, a person might properly rely on that even if not supported by public reasons.

On the more general point, suppose that most people in a liberal democracy believe it is perfectly all right to rely on their personal ideas of the good and their comprehensive views in arriving at their political positions. A thoughtful woman concludes that liberal democracy would be most fair if those views were put aside in favor of public reasons. At least if she is an ordinary citizen, telling her that she should not now rely on her concept of a good life and her comprehensive view would be unfair if virtually no other citizens regard themselves as so restricted. In other words, a genuine constraint of "public reasons" may depend on widespread acceptance of its force. Matters are more debatable here for conscientious legislators. But the main point is that a sweeping notion that genuine public reasons should control our political life is not alone a sufficient basis to insist that individuals adhere to that principle, if we all know that almost no one else is doing so.[24] A person who is fully aware that the great majority of her fellow citizens are relying directly on their religious convictions in political life will rightly conclude it would not be unjust for her to rely on her contrary religious convictions. To be clear, my focus at this point is on actual reliance, not public advocacy, which I address in Chapter 10.

Three more subtle points concern how broad the "acceptance" must be under a theory that makes that central, at what level the acceptance should be taken, and what should be done in its absence. Whether one is asking about a particular issue or forms of reasoning, saying just when there is general acceptance or a consensus is harder. An acceptance rate of 52 percent is not enough, 98 percent is sufficient, but what if apparently about 75 percent accept an approach, 10 percent do not, and 15 percent are ignorant or uncertain? When told they should stick with what is generally accepted, citizens aware of the third breakdown may disagree over whether that is sufficient to constrain them in some way.

The level of generality could also be very important. Let us return to Governor Cuomo's example. We could say that a basic premise of liberal democracy, and perhaps virtually all forms of government, is that innocent lives should be protected. A supporter of laws that restrict abortions might say the following. "I believe in protecting human lives. Life begins with conception, and I conclude this based on a simple, rational understanding of existence.

Many people do not understand this, but I am beginning with a generally shared premise of morality and drawing the correct specific conclusion based on a widely accepted form of reasoning."[25] On this account, if "acceptance" is taken at a general level, it can lead to a conclusion about a particular practice that is not broadly accepted.[26] If the "acceptance" theory somehow made clear the relevant level of generality, it would remain difficult for ordinary people to adhere to that line and to discern exactly how it applied to their own convictions.

To take a less controversial example than abortion, suppose a person concluded that all higher animals deserve some respect from human beings. Although most human laws generally protect animals only in limited respects, for example against torture and vindictive, painful treatment, this person, who has become a vegetarian, believes that given the sensibilities and intelligence of many higher animals, their legal protections should be much more extensive.[27] Would it be appropriate for her to urge legal reforms in this direction? And would it matter if her basis rested on what she took as generally accepted broad premises about life and powerful rational grounds to protect animals, as contrasted with personal feelings or religious convictions?

Another issue is what should be done if general acceptance is definitely missing. If a consensus in either direction is absent, should people be left personally at liberty to act as they wish, or should citizens and legislators regard themselves as free to adopt restrictive laws despite the lack of a present consensus? For example, should individuals be left free to kill members of endangered species until consensus at some level supports a restriction? Although, in the abortion context, this conclusion in favor of liberty is sound because of the basic rights of women involved, it would not be appropriate as a general principle. Such a principle would give too great a protection to individual liberty in relation to other values, precluding, for example, laws barring racial or gender discrimination until a consensus existed. Many such legal reforms actually, among other things, can help lead to changes in broadly accepted values.

## Rational Grounds and Natural Law

The basic idea that "public reason" fits with views based on rational grounds has an intuitive appeal, and a degree of actual force, but raises complexities about what count as rational grounds, how much they can be differentiated from other bases for judgment, and what level and bases should count.

Among the varieties of what we consider "rational" grounds are (1) logical realities such as exist in math and can be relevant for discerning the effect of a raised or reduced tax rate, (2) scientific conclusions, (3) direct perceptions, and (4) broader appraisals based on experience. Among the scientific conclusions now relevant are the likelihood that the world is undergoing climate change. As with most scientific conclusions, we nonscientists mainly rely on experts. We assume a rational basis exists based on extensive data collection and experimentation, even if we do not quite grasp all that counts as relevant for the experts. If the vast majority of experts reach a certain conclusion, which may or may not be mildly supported by something in our own experience, such as the rising temperatures where we live, we can rationally believe what they assert about climate change.

Reliance on our own perception can be more straightforward. If I look outside and it appears to be raining, I can rationally conclude that it is raining. If I witness someone being knocked down by a car, appearing unable to move and crying out in pain, reason tells me that he probably needs some help.

A somewhat more complex reliance on experience is that, if I know a friend has been deeply troubled by a particular kind of circumstance, I rationally conclude that if the same thing happens again, he will likely be upset. We can sometimes generalize this kind of insight; we may conclude that we have witnessed enough to believe that certain kinds of events are upsetting for most people. Unless we have convincing contrary information based on the perspectives of others, this can provide a basis to support laws that try to reduce the occurrence of such events.

The experience examples illustrate two kinds of line-drawing difficulties. The first is obvious. If various people have had different experiences in life, their "rational" conclusions about what is likely to happen in the future, and what are the effects on people generally, may differ. Although we may grasp that the experiences of those who are more closely related to what may happen are more reliable, often we lack a solid basis to make that kind of judgment about comparative reliability.

Another line-drawing difficulty is more subtle. When we rely on our own experience about what are probable consequences, we are often affected by our own feelings about things. If a man senses that he will be disadvantaged by a restriction on coal mining or oil production, he may honestly be more skeptical about the judgments of those who assert climate change and its harms.

A rational-basis approach might seem initially to exclude religious convictions, since these are often based on faith and vary greatly. But we can identify at least three matters that complicate this apparent exclusion. These relate in various ways to what someone might perceive as a right to exercise religious convictions.

The first matter perhaps has the most general relevance. Suppose a woman is completely able to distinguish rational bases from her religious convictions. She concludes that both support a position that she understands serves certain values at the cost of others. She perceives that some people relying on rational grounds might reach a different conclusion about what the law should do, but she is absolutely certain based on faith about God's instructions that it should do A rather than B. It would be very hard for her to limit her support and acknowledge what degree of doubt she might have *if* she relied on the rational outlook alone. Indeed, she would almost certainly find it nearly impossible to discern exactly how she would see the issue if she relied solely on her sense of rational bases.

The second complexity concerns what rationality can, and does, establish. When in high school, one of my sons asked me to read a book that claimed to show by rational demonstration that the Bible was the infallible word of God and that Jesus Christ was God's son. Whatever one may think of this particular claim, if we ourselves witnessed a fantastic number of miraculous cures made by someone, saw his undeniable death, and also saw him become alive again, we might well conclude that what he said about our lives had some relation to the will of a higher being. And the same could be true if many others we trusted said they had witnessed these very events. In brief, however hard it may be for us to draw rationalist conclusions about the literal truth of particular parts of the Bible, seeing rational bases grounded in life's experiences as supporting certain religious beliefs is clearly not inconceivable.

In a highly detailed and sophisticated account, Robert Audi has explained numerous connections between rational analysis and religious convictions.[28] If one grasps these complexities, one can see how hard it is to expect a religious believer to rely solely on rational, nonreligious bases for political judgments.

A serious problem for "rational ground" limits is how the sincere assertion by the author who claimed a rational demonstration of the Bible's infal-libility could work in his life and those of others. For him, and individuals convinced by him, any reliance on the Biblical text for political issues would become actually based on rational grounds. Other religious people with simi-lar, or different, basic convictions they see as grounded in faith would need to put those aside as not "public reasons." It would naturally seem unfair to the latter group if they must restrain themselves in this way, while they see others as relying on a misguided rational argument for similar religious premises.

The third complexity concerns the extent to which one believes that the force of a rational argument that itself does not depend on religious truth is in reality supported by belief in that truth. Here is a place where the rela-tion of natural law and public reason comes into play. Although historically natural law was not untied from religious convictions, modern natural law scholars typically claim that the positions they defend are demonstrably true independent of religious convictions.[29]

Whether natural law, primarily connected to the Roman Catholic Church, actually counts as one variation of public reason is itself far from simple. It does claim to be based on rational thought, but can be seen to rest partly on a comprehensive view including concepts of the good life. By certain criteria that disqualifies it, or at least some of its conclusions, from public reasons. But clearly natural law does rest on claimed rationality.

Rather than exploring just how far these complications affect how natural law should be seen in relation to "public reasons" and whether that com-parison helps reveal the difficult line of what should count or not as public reasons, let me turn to an obvious concern about natural law and religious believers. What would a "rational grounds" approach do for the perspectives of other religious believers? Imagine a Protestant who, on the basis of faith, the Bible, and church teachings, has strong views very similar to those of natural lawyers on many moral questions. Will he feel it is fair if he should restrain himself from relying on those reasons, while believers in natural law are free to do so? That problem may well be much more troublesome if he sees the natural law arguments as totally unconvincing on some sub-jects and at odds with his religious beliefs. Suppose he thinks reason itself does not really tell us when life begins; according to his faith it is not until a fetus could survive outside the womb. He is likely to regard it as unfair if he is instructed he should put that judgment aside, while natural lawyers are claiming that, grounded in basic shared reason, life needing protection begins much earlier. Not too surprisingly, some natural law arguments, such as contraceptives should not be used and sexual intercourse should not occur except within marriage, will seem unpersuasive to a great many outside the Catholic tradition. A simple rational-grounds approach to relying on such positions for possible laws and regulations will hardly seem fair to many religious believers who find the "rational" bases of certain natural law positions sharply unconvincing.

A less crucial but even more complicated position concerns devoted Roman Catholics who are aware of what leading natural lawyers have claimed. Suppose these Catholics accept a basic moral position as a matter of faith. They are aware that the position is supported by a natural law argument. They do not quite understand the argument itself but believe that the theorists almost certainly see things correctly. Is that itself a rational ground? Since they believe a rational ground exists, that could be seen as a kind of reliance on experts, but their sense of who are experts is largely dependent on their religious convictions and church doctrine.

All this suggests that drawing the line between rational grounds and other bases is far from simple. Making "public reasons" depend totally on whether one believes one has a rational basis creates definite problems of unfairness and is incredibly hard to implement in human practice.

In what follows, I shall refer to "public reasons" as connected to what are taken generally to be rational arguments not dependent on particular religious convictions or comprehensive views. Virtually all the values and problems we shall see do not depend on any precise delineation of what count as public reasons.

### Nonreliance on Inspiration

I want finally to briefly address a special basis for decision that may well be excluded by all theories of public reason but is not often addressed explicitly. This can be understood in terms of what has been written about George W. Bush, our president from 2001 to 2009. After contact with Billy Graham in 1985, Bush became an evangelical Christian.[30] As one author has written, "the feature that most deeply characterizes [evangelicals] is that the God they seek is more personally intimate and more intimately experienced, than the God most Americans grew up with."[31] When a Christian with this belief prays, he may well feel that sometimes God has answered his prayer and has inspired him to recognize that answer. In terms of personal feelings about what one should do, this may not be completely different from other people first having doubts and seeing arguments on both sides and later moving to a strong conviction that one answer is right, without being blind to the strength of competing arguments. What differs with the prayer response is that someone sees herself as guided by God's will in a way that is not available to those who do not accept the evangelical premises. Such a person may then see herself as inspired by God to act in a certain way, although without perceiving specific religious bases other than "I am responding to God."

However accurate the account may be, some have urged that just this kind of belief did affect some central decisions of President Bush,[32] including his decisions both to invade Iraq after the 9/11 catastrophe and to continue in that war after it became highly controversial. Bush himself once described God as the *primary* force behind his political judgment.[33]

Whether the perception that President Bush sometimes acted on this basis is sound, it does strongly indicate what can go beyond a reliance on other kinds of nonpublic reasons. Even if a man sees the balance of explicable reasons in nonreligious terms, if he takes his overall position because he sees himself as responding to God's direct inspiration of his feelings about what choice is right, he is relying on a nonpublic reason.

## Possible Overriding

Whatever one sees as the best method of defining public reasons, and whether one thinks reliance on them is a basic premise of every or some liberal democracies, one cannot expect all good citizens to always adhere to them. Suppose a person believes that public reasons genuinely point in one direction but also believes that God has clearly revealed that what that conclusion would permit is absolutely forbidden and would be highly damaging to the prospects of human beings. In that event, she is likely to conclude that an extremely powerful reason leads her to override the constraints of "public reason." One could see this as a form of religious exercise overriding the nonestablishment value of public reasons.

Given this reality and the various complexities and doubts about what constitute public reasons, should this basic concept be genuinely important in our society's political life? As I shall urge in what follows, despite all the complications, the answer is definitely "yes." Although I have sometimes been seen as a basic opponent of a public-reasons approach, my position actually is that they play an important role and should be seen as a constraint in various contexts. This is true even if public reasons theory often does not provide a simple line between justified reliance on certain kinds of considerations and unjustified departures from a core premise of liberal democracy. As Chapter 10 explores, the constraints of public reason are especially important for officials, and they bear greatly, though more arguably, on how private citizens should advocate political positions.

# Relevance of a Person's Position, Bases versus Articulation, and Specific Issues

THIS CHAPTER DELVES INTO crucial aspects of a serious inquiry into when and how people should either try to put aside their religious convictions and make public reasons their exclusive bases for political positions or at least afford these public reasons a kind of priority. I first look at various positions individuals occupy in society and how those matter hugely. Connected to this, I suggest a significant difference between what are one's complete bases for taking a position and what it is desirable to articulate in public. I then turn to specific concrete issues, asking how well the notion that people should put aside religious convictions and personal sentiments will work if they actually try to do that. Part of the endeavor here is to evaluate the costs and benefits of seeking reliance on public reasons and how those relate to the particular values of free exercise and nonestablishment, the major theme of this book.

## Positions in Society

If we ask whether political and legal positions should matter for the importance of public reasons, we can recognize fairly quickly that what is right for officials may not be the same for ordinary citizens, and that even among officials, variations between judges, executive officials, and legislators are significant. These variations can include not only the force of public reasons, but what count as those and what is their respective weight. On reflection, certain differences between judges and others is obvious; variations also exist in what should be relied upon by judges at different levels.

Judges apply the law; legislators make laws. It is true that judges must sometimes decide legal cases and resolve legal issues to which the law as it exists provides no clear answer. To take the notable example covered in Chapter 4, the Supreme Court in 2015 determined by a 5–4 margin that same-sex couples had a constitutional right to marriage under both the Due Process and Equal Protection Clauses.[1] But in the vast majority of cases, judges are applying statutory and common law as it already exists. They do have authority to revise a rule of the common law that they now see as badly misguided, and they sometimes stretch statutory language and legislative intentions in terms of what they perceive as basic values. But, for the most part, the public reasons that are critical for judges in the United States are aspects of existing law. Given our Establishment Clause, these reasons do not include specific references to religious convictions and values. Even when judges must resolve issues for which the existing law provides no clear answer and when they need to determine whether to overturn a rule of law created by precedents, they rely substantially on the entire body of law, asking what will fit well together.

Especially when it comes to precedents, the public reasons that count vary in weight for lower court judges and for the highest court judges in a jurisdiction. If the highest court has created a clear rule of law, it is widely assumed (although not everyone agrees) that judges below should apply that rule even if they believe it is misguided; it is up to the highest court to decide whether that rule should be abandoned or at least reformulated.

When it comes to resolving legal issues that existing law does not actually settle, judges at all levels are supposed to decide according to standards that they believe should lead other judges to the same conclusion. Individually or in small groups of three, lower court judges are determining what the law is for the cases they are resolving. Of course, the Supreme Court, with its nine justices, mainly takes cases for which resolution is most debatable, and this leads to fairly frequent divisions among the Justices, a reality to which much attention has been given after the death of Justice Scalia. In those instances, for an individual Justice to ask what he or she believes to be desirable law may be more frequently appropriate. But the main focus of the reasons that should guide all judges is not what they would view as a better or worse law but what individual aspects, and the whole body of the law, already provide.

That analysis is decidedly a form of "public reason," but not the only one, and not the one that is normally referred to in theoretical discussions about the importance and place of those reasons in a liberal democracy.

Legislators have a very different role. They make laws. Of course, because it is good for the whole law to fit together fairly well and be consistent over time, legislators should not wholly disregard authoritative judicial precedents and aspects of law related to what they are considering. But their very job is to decide when the law should be changed. An exception to this is established constitutional law. Unless they are proposing an actual constitutional amendment, legislators should see themselves as largely constrained by well-established constitutional doctrine.

Two other differences between individual legislators and individual judges are that legislators do not act on their own or with one or two colleagues, and they are almost always determining how future practices will be controlled, not how actions in the past may be punished or subjected to civil recovery. These realities provide further reasons why existing law is less weighty for their choices than for those of judges. It follows from all this that the public reasons on which legislators rely are mainly those that will underlie desirable laws; and much more often than with judges, they will not aim to arrive at a conclusion that will necessarily be embraced by most other legislators. Whether legislators should refrain from any reliance on religious conviction is a much more difficult question than the similar question with respect to judges.

When it comes to executive officials, we can see elements of what should guide judges and elements similar to those for legislators. Insofar as the duty of officials is simply to apply the law to individual circumstances, the relevant public reasons are essentially those that should guide lower court judges. But legislation often leaves significant gaps to be filled by administrative regulations. In that context, those forming the regulations are going beyond existing law and deciding what will work well and produce desirable results. This in a sense makes them quasi-legislators, but they are subject to a particular constraint. The reasons they consider should be consistent with the overall objectives of the particular legislation that gives them this authority. Thus, the scope of relevant reasons is typically limited in a way that is greater than for legislators themselves. For some political choices, such as presidential decisions whether to engage in military conflict, executive officials may be less constrained by legislative guidance than when they apply ordinary statutes.

Turning to ordinary citizens, we can quickly see that with respect to any role in law-making they are much further from judges than are legislators. They do not have the power to make laws, only to support or oppose possible legislation. And an individual citizen is one among millions, not one among a few hundred. Perhaps even more important, citizens themselves are not part of the government; they have not taken an oath to represent the population generally. Related to this is the reality that for most citizens, thinking about what public policies should be embraced and what laws should be enacted is a very small part of their lives. I have urged that determining what genuinely count as "public reasons" is far from simple and that many people have a hard time deciding how far what they believe depends on "public reasons," as contrasted with religious convictions that do not rest on those reasons. Given these difficulties, it is a bit much to ask ordinary citizens to rely exclusively on public reasons when it comes to political positions.[2] To be clear, I am not suggesting that people should never give attention to whether reasons are public; indeed, I claim that this matters considerably for advocacy. All I am asserting here is that if the line between these and other reasons is very hard to draw, asking people to totally disregard any "nonpublic" reasons that give them a strong conviction that something is wise or unwise is highly demanding.

A related concern is that someone who would be willing to attempt this exercise *if* she believed others were doing the same with at least moderate success may say to herself, "This is so hard and debatable, I bet a lot of people will reject the idea altogether, or perform the exercise very poorly. If all of them end up relying on convictions not supported by public reasons, it would be unfair for me to restrain myself in what is my religious exercise based on nonestablishment values that others are not following." The overall appropriateness of imposing self-restraint here depends largely on the prospect of reciprocal self-restraint by other citizens.[3]

A somewhat special category of nonofficial citizens is religious leaders and organizations. I shall focus briefly on them at the end of the following section.

## Underlying Bases versus Articulations of One's Positions

When people defend their positions on political and legal issues, how far should they explain all the bases for their support or, instead, emphasize what they see as public reasons? This question has relevance when people see clearly that their stance is defensible in terms of both public reasons and distinguishable religious convictions. It also has a bearing when they themselves find it hard in their own minds to discern exactly where the line is to be drawn between the two kinds of reasons or to sort out the force of each insofar as they can identify the difference. As I have suggested, this aspect of line-drawing and appropriate weight can be illustrated by a Roman Catholic who believes in natural law but does not quite understand the specific reasoned argument urged by natural law theorists.

One possible objection to my position, which follows, is that, because people should always be honest, they should explain exactly what motivates them and how powerful they find the reasons that move them.[4] My own belief is that honesty is highly relevant, that people should not lie or explicitly deny what affects them. But when they urge and publicly defend political positions, it is generally desirable for them to do so in terms that make sense to the general citizenry. Here, as with the actual bases for their support, exactly what people should do is somewhat different depending on the positions they occupy.

Judges are expected to put forward reasons that have power for all in the system. Realistically, judicial opinions are rarely completely honest about the bases for decisions and their weight. The main reason for this is that typically judges put forward their grounds in a way that will seem persuasive to others. They do not tell the rest of us how close they perceived the balance of considerations and whether the opposing position seemed almost as strong as their own. Of course, another factor of majority opinions is that they represent multiple voices. This often results in obscuring the weight that various individual judges may give to particular considerations, and not infrequently it leads to omitting reference to one or more of these. Within the United States and other liberal democracies, judges do not advance arguments that rest explicitly and directly on religious convictions. Of course, as I have already explained, religious convictions should rarely figure in decisions. But suppose existing law is inconclusive *and* the judge finds the balance of relevant public reasons that could bear on her "making" law one way or the other to be even. If she perhaps lets her deep religious beliefs then play a direct role in her decision, or if she at least recognizes that her religious beliefs probably tip the balance of how she weighs public reasons, those bases for her resolution will not appear in her opinion, even if it is an individual concurring or dissenting opinion.

No such restraint is so definite and complete on legislators, but given that legislators represent the general public and their particular constituents, it makes sense for them within the United States to defend what they do on the basis of generally accessible reasons. If they put forward explicit religious arguments, those of different faiths are not likely to be persuaded and may well feel they are being implicitly denied a form of equality. (As earlier chapters have indicated, if religious bases clearly underlie the overall legislative purpose, that may violate the Establishment Clause.)

Matters are less simple for private citizens. Here I think an important difference exists between public advocacy and private conversations and discussions that occur within religious and other collective groups. I believe that for advocacy in public settings, it is usually desirable for even ordinary private citizens to rely on public reasons. Even if somewhat uncertain about their comparative force in the conclusions they have reached, people can usually distinguish relevant public reasons from their religious convictions. To be clear, I am not suggesting that people should deny that they were influenced by religious or other nonpublic reasons, and they may appropriately say that they think those other bases do play a legitimate role in citizen support of particular political positions. Further, in some situations more direct religious advocacy may have no negative effects. However, in most circumstances, people directly urging in detail how their religious beliefs have led them to their correct positions will make political discourse more contentious than it would be if they talked mainly in terms of public reasons, reasons not rejected by members of other faiths and nonbelievers.[5]

In terms of greater candor about all grounds, we have not only the "honesty" argument[6] but also a free speech, and free exercise, consideration that people have the right to try to persuade others of the truth of their religious outlooks and that this actually constitutes a form of religious exercise. Further, a claim may be made that it is helpful for others to grasp exactly why individuals are lining up in one way or another. Both considerations have some force. But advocating a controversial political position in religious terms is not usually a promising way to get others to seriously consider the truth of your basic religious outlook, and full knowledge of why people take their positions can be disquieting and produce feelings of unfairness for these in minorities. Overall, the better approach in this country for broad advocacy, even by private citizens, is generally to rely on public reasons.

The conclusion may well be different when it comes to religious organizations and leaders, especially when clerics and others are communicating to their members, as in sermons. If they believe religious convictions should matter in how their members reach various political positions, conveying that is appropriate. This kind of message is particularly poignant when such leading religious figures as Pope Francis are communicating to a broader audience. In one respect that raises the question of what counts as a relevant faith. Much of what the Pope urges rests on what he takes as Christian assumptions, held by Protestants and the Eastern Orthodox religions as well as Roman Catholicism. In respect to how we should treat the poor and disadvantaged and whether a wall should block the entry of aliens, his positions can often be understood as backed not only by religious premises but also general public reasons. When we consider all this, we may well see religious leaders as distinguishable from ordinary citizens in what they should communicate, even to an audience broader than members of their own faith.

An important caution needs to be made about what I have said about the articulation of bases for decisions. Desirable assumptions about self-imposed limitations may differ among liberal democracies. Apparently in Australia, so many people are nonreligious that virtually everyone thinks it is practically unwise to make religious arguments for political positions. In such a culture, the idea that people would be better citizens if they observed a constraint on their advocacy would be unnecessary, since the impracticality of asserting religious political claims will be sufficient to limit them, and people with opposing views will not see such claims, when made, as carrying the kind of force that could produce a sense of unfairness. In the Union of South Africa, religious advocacy was a major factor in overcoming and changing the extremely harsh discrimination against black citizens, who were and are a substantial majority of the population. In that setting, it is certainly possible that continuing to offer religious arguments about what fairness requires can be, on balance, beneficial, even when those arguments are offered by nonclerical citizens and legislators in public settings. If we understand that desirable limits on the formulation and articulation of political positions can vary depending on cultural settings, it is obvious that within one country, the appropriate limits could shift over time. As I have emphasized, this book focuses primarily on American culture at this stage of history.

## Specific Issues

What follows focuses on some specific, debatable issues about what the law should provide. I employ a bit more detail than in the preceding analysis but without exploring any of the subjects in great depth. What is revealing is that public reasons should certainly play a role in reaching conclusions on any political issue, but just how much those reasons can resolve on their own varies greatly.

Before engaging specific subjects, I want to make clear what I am claiming about the incompleteness of public reasons for some issues. Total reliance on public reasons, and the irrelevance of other bases for decision, will not necessarily produce agreement about what it is actually right to do.[7] This is true because people can reasonably disagree about the precise weight of the reasons relevant in a particular conflict. They have different views about either likely facts or the comparative importance of two undoubted public reasons. What I explore is not about such a balance but how far public reasons are really incomplete on some crucial questions. I want to acknowledge at the outset that in some contexts we may be unable to draw a clear line between uncertainty caused mainly by the incompleteness of public reasons and disagreement over their comparative force.

### Animal Rights and Environmental Policy

I shall begin with two related subjects now much less controversial than abortions, but ones in which public reasons are able to take us only so far. First, what do human beings owe to animals and how far should impairments be barred by law? Aspects of this inquiry are the status of cruelty toward animals; when, if ever, their lives should be protected; and whether they should be used for experimentation of various sorts.

A central concern here is how human beings should value animals' lives in comparison with their own. Certain restrictions on the treatment of animals could be justified in terms of what is desirable for human beings themselves. Thus, one could defend a ban on outright cruelty as a way of discouraging people from giving effect to unhealthy emotions that might, if widely allowed, lead people to treat each other badly. And one might believe that some killing of animals could also harm other people in various ways.

The key question for our purposes, however, is what the animals themselves deserve. Should all kinds of animals be treated equally? The answer here is clearly "no," at least according to rational thought. Whether that thought actually supports the idea that all human beings, regardless of their actual capabilities, should count equally, is itself an interesting question. One may believe, instead, that that view really depends on religious premises.[8] In any event, for nonhuman entities, what they experience and are capable of doing matters for nearly everyone. Nobody has asserted that flies should get significant protections even if apes, dolphins, and dogs do or should. For those animals whose capabilities are much closer to those of people, how far should the law protect them?

Apart from a religious argument, supported by early passages within Genesis,[9] that other creatures were made for the benefit of human beings, are there plausible arguments that all relevant decisions should rest on what is really good for people? So long as it does not impair our lives now or what human lives will be like in the future, is virtually any treatment of animals all right?

I shall mention one possible basis for this position that I believe is in severe conflict with rational thought. It could be contended that since we are human beings, we should simply concentrate on our welfare and disregard that of other species, except when their welfare ties to ours. However, suppose that as time goes by and human beings reach other parts of the universe, we meet species that are physically formed entirely differently, but definitely have all the capacities that we possess. To conclude that it would be fine to simply exterminate all of them if that would give human beings a somewhat more convenient location to live would be indefensible.

A second problem with the notion that all we should care about is human welfare, no matter what animals are like, is that this approach bears some resemblance to the idea that all that should concern us are members of our own nationality, or even some narrower category. A general premise of liberal democracy is that whatever weight one gives to one's own country in comparison with others, human welfare overall is of some importance. A recent illustration of this concern is the notion that in a war against ISIS, it should matter whether airstrikes within Iraq and Syria will kill many innocent civilians.

An effective concentration entirely on human welfare might be defended on the basis that human capacities are so much greater than those of other animals on this earth that limiting fundamental protections of life to them is appropriate. In opposition to this conclusion is the view that some other animals have enough capacity to warrant genuine protections, with how much depending considerably on how they are constituted. A subquestion in respect to the lives of higher animals is this: Apart from benefits to humans, should each individual life deserve protection, or is what counts the number of lives and their quality? With human beings, the definite answer, outside of warfare, is that the taking of an innocent life is not an ordinary justification for an action even if it will preserve other lives. A doctor should not have a patient killed on the basis that doing so will allow the taking of various organs that, transplanted, will probably save the lives of three others. But a nonvegetarian might say that if human beings did not eat meat, fewer cattle and some other animals would ever exist. (That, of course, does not itself justify raising certain animals for eating under extremely harsh conditions, which is now not infrequent.)

My basic thesis here is that, although shared reasons can contribute to possible alternatives, they cannot really tell us just how much higher animals should count in relation to human beings. They also cannot tell us how far protection should reach the not-taking of individual lives. How then are individual citizens and legislators to decide whether various laws that could provide greater animal protection are warranted? Of course, personal experience can play a role. Almost anyone who has had a dog for a pet has developed a sense of affection for it, which might well produce a feeling that dogs deserve some protection, at the very least that people should not be able to torture their similar pets or kill them without good reason. That could lead to a further conclusion that if dogs warrant protection, then some should also be given to animals with capacities for feelings and perceptions that are at least as great, even if they are not suitable pets. Apart from pets, a person might develop a feeling about animals based on visiting zoos or watching television. Religious convictions could obviously matter here; within our culture, given Genesis, those may mostly tend to reduce the sense of any needed protections that reach beyond human welfare. The personal experience of having a pet and the broader witnessing of animals and reading about them can give rise to judgments that are partly based on reason, but "public reasons" can take us only so far here. They do not provide an answer to how far the values of higher animals should count in relation to those of human beings or exactly what kinds of protections those values should produce. For two fundamental reasons, we cannot expect citizens to try to rely exclusively on public reasons to reach their own conclusions about this. One of these is that, as already explored, carving out public reasons from one's other bases for conviction is often very hard. The second is that, although public reason can tell us that apes warrant more protection than mosquitoes, it cannot answer just how much we should value the life of an ape.

In fact, the protection of higher animals has increased over the past half century. The Animal Welfare Act of 1966[10] mainly addresses the handling and transportation of animals and was expanded in 1970 to provide safeguards for "warm-blooded animals" used "for experimentation or exhibition."[11] It is interesting in this connection that the National Institutes of Health issued a 2013 report that recommended reducing the number of chimpanzees used in medical testing and all of these were retired and moved to sanctuaries in 2015[12] and that in 2016 elephants were dropped out of Ringling Brothers circus performances.[13] We also have a Humane Methods of Slaughter Act of 1958 that seeks to preclude needless suffering of farm animals in their slaughtering.[14] Nevertheless, the legal protection of the lives and welfare of even the highest animals still falls far short of that afforded to human beings, including those with severe deficiencies.

When it comes to legislators considering the question of animal protections, can we expect them to put aside their own personal views? Legislators should, of course, be guided substantially by general, shared views, which can be seen as a form of public reason. One may even believe that is, in fact, legislators' overwhelming responsibility.

Although dominant opinion can also affect decisions of ordinary citizens, that definitely does not preclude their advocacy that public opinion in some respect is unjust or misguided and needs to change. Without such an assumption, we could never have witnessed crucial developments in notions of equality in terms of race, gender, and sexual orientation. Conceivably, one might argue that citizens should move against prevailing opinion only if their total reliance is on fundamental public reasons; but what should that entail for a believer in animal rights who understands that to a large extent his sense of public reasons is intertwined with other assessments? Such a combination may be present, whether recognized or not, for many people who have an opinion about animal rights. This would include legislators considering a possible law. Although more restrained by public reasons, including public opinion, than ordinary citizens, they may find it both hard to see this issue totally resolvable by public reasons and to separate those reasons clearly from their other convictions.

This reality sharply raises the question whether religious convictions on this issue should be special in their exclusion. If it is inevitable that people will rely partly on personal experience and intuitions that are not grounded in general rationality, should someone not be able to take her religious convictions into account? A possible argument for excluding religious convictions is that Establishment Clause values bar them. The answer is that unless particular animals are singled out on bases that are at odds with a reasonable appraisal of objective qualities,[15] the protection or failure to do so does not seem to really establish one or more religions, except perhaps in the most remote and indirect way. Moreover, to treat religious convictions worse than nonreligious personal intuitions might itself seem at odds with both free exercise and nonestablishment values.

I shall say relatively little about environmental protections. Obviously many concerns about the environment relate to human beings now and in the future. Even if one focuses on human life, how far should people weigh the quality of life for those now alive in comparison with those likely to exist in the future? Given the increase in uncertainties as estimates of what is likely to occur reach further and further into the future,[16] affording special weight to what consequences will occur now and in the following decades makes sense. But when the question arises how much basic value should be afforded to lives that do not yet exist, I do not believe we can find a convincing rational answer.

A different issue is whether we somehow have a responsibility to protect the environment itself, apart from how that may affect the lives of future humans and perhaps other animals. I don't think reason itself can tell us that we do, but based on intuitions or religious convictions, some people believe in such a responsibility. I think it is hard to say that this is contrary to reason even if it is not really supported by reason. Given that, if various environmental regulations would not significantly support or interfere with human or animal life, should people feel free to favor those as intrinsically desirable, and if so, should reliance only on intuitive convictions but not religious beliefs be appropriate? Without some of the nuances, this presents issues similar to those about animal rights.

## Human Lives and Acts That Do Not Harm Others

When we turn to the lives of human beings, a fairly straightforward question concerning liberal democracies and public reasons is what kinds of actions people should be legally allowed to perform. Any behavior that harms others or is likely to have that effect in the future is, of course, a concern of the state. Just how far tort recovery and criminal penalties should reach is often debatable. Public reasons should be the main guide here, although we still have the question whether other forms of evaluation can also appropriately play a role, at least for private citizens taking a position about what should be done.

I shall focus on a different kind of question: What about behavior that does not cause or risk harm to others? Should people have the liberty to do what they wish? Such liberty generally is a basic value for liberal democracies: People can choose their occupations, locations, companions, and major aspects of their personal lives. Can the government nonetheless sometimes appropriately forbid behavior that does not directly hurt others because it is plainly not sensible for the very people who engage in it or is viewed as fundamentally wrong from some moral perspective?

Two examples of the former are rules that those in cars are not supposed to drive or sit without seatbelts and that people are not allowed to ingest dangerous drugs. In those instances, one can see competing values of liberty versus a social assessment of what is intrinsically too potentially damaging for a person (and indirectly harmful to others who may be dependent on him). Reasonable arguments often exist on both sides,[17] although, because seatbelts are such a mild inconvenience (and it is easy to disobey), that requirement is not now controversial.

Starker examples are ones in which others are not harmed and what people are doing is not dangerous for themselves. This is fundamentally the case with homosexual relations. Whatever may once have been perceived, for people whose strong attraction is to others of the same gender, a bar on such involvement can hardly be seen as protecting them, unless one perceives all such acts as fundamentally wrong, which is the religious conviction of some. When we think about such behavior, public reason points very strongly in favor of allowing it, and people should not regard it as appropriate to rely on religious convictions or personal intuitions to forbid it legally. When we put this in terms of religious clause values, people (so long as they do not harm others) should be able to do what is consistent with their own convictions and not have the criminal law effectively establish the religious perspectives of others by enforcement.[18] Whether the clauses themselves should be seen as providing this protection may be debated, but since the Supreme Court has established a constitutional right based on liberty more broadly,[19] that question lacks practical significance at present (a;though, of course, as Chapter 4 discusses, the issue of exemptions from equal treatment is now very important).

A minor but much more uncertain question concerns human sex with animals, which is broadly forbidden. It is sometimes suggested that this protects the animals, but given that most people can kill animals they own for no reason, it is hard to see animal protection as the underlying reason. Such relations might be seen as harming the humans who engage in them, but I am not aware of much evidence on this front.[20] What is primarily involved is the view that such behavior is basically "unnatural,"[21] that it is not how human beings should behave. This sexual involvement is unusual enough that most people would have to reflect on whether their view that it is misguided is grounded in genuine public reasons, religious convictions, or basic intuitions, but in fact most major religions do preclude such behavior. Many people who see this behavior as wrongful regard it as departing from a fundamental human standard. Given the value of personal liberty and the limits on what public reason can support here, such behavior should likely not be made generally criminal, absent convincing evidence of physical risks. (Individuals coercing such acts or performing them in front of children are separate questions.)

A much more troublesome question which may potentially reach many more people is the current prohibition in all states on assisting suicide. If people are generally free to decide how to live their lives, why should they not be free to decide to end their lives? As far as individuals who attempt this are concerned, the law's present absence of any right to do so makes sense. Many people who try to commit suicide do it on the basis of temporary feelings of psychological distress. That the suicide rate in the United States has risen to a thirty-year high in 2014[22] is genuinely troubling. Among people who do not succeed in attempted suicides, many of them will not try again. This is actually a highly relevant consideration for gun regulation. The majority of gun deaths in this country are suicides. Shooting oneself can be a quick and effective way to take one's life. Although a person really determined over time to commit suicide can almost certainly manage it in one way or another, were this effective means less available, fewer people would commit suicide. States with stricter gun controls have lower rates of suicide by guns. Overall, the legal approach that people have no right to commit suicide and will be prevented when possible but not punished for trying[23] is wise. (At some point in history, those who *did* commit suicide received a kind of punishment in terms of what happened with their assets.)[24]

The hard questions here concern situations in which a wish to die may be both explicable and rational and whether, at least when these conditions are met, others should be allowed to assist. At present, assisting suicide in any circumstance is typically a serious crime, at least formally. The most obvious examples of possibly justified suicides are when people are terminally ill and suffering great pain; does it make sense to insist that they stay alive as long as possible and endure great pain if they know they will never really function again? From a rational point of view, allowing someone who chooses to die in this situation makes sense.[25] In fact, doctors not infrequently agree to withdraw certain forms of treatment, which does not quite count as suicide.[26] And if a person genuinely needs some help to end his life, why should a willing friend or relative not be allowed to provide it? In Canada, the question of whether a right to assist suicide should exist was controversial after a decision by the country's Supreme Court in 1993 that there was no such legal right.[27] In 2015 the Canadian Supreme Court struck down a provision of the federal criminal code that precluded physician-assisted suicide for those with "'grievous and irremediable' medical conditions."[28]

We can conceive some rational, public reasons arguments for a sweeping prohibition. Deciding when someone reaches this special stage is too difficult; allowing suicides then may work to encourage them at other times; if people are free to make this choice and get assistance, family members who do not wish to pay for continuing treatment or who want to inherit more quickly may push those who are ill and suffering to opt for death. These grounds are far from trivial, but I believe a more central explanation for the law as it exists is that suicide is simply seen as fundamentally wrong, a view strongly connected to many religious convictions. As I have noted about much treatment regarding some sexual behavior, it seems to me unwarranted, and at odds with nonestablishment values, for the law to restrict the liberty of how people live their lives simply because of convictions, not supportable by public reasons, that such acts are against God's will. Were people indisputably in these kinds of special circumstances allowed to have a right to decide for themselves whether to live longer, then others should not be punishable for assisting, *unless* it is discerned that too often the "assisters" will have pushed those they assist to decide to die.

A much more important and controversial issue of our time is when human life is perceived to begin and deserve protection and how far competing views about this should be accommodated. For the beginning of life, one can suppose that purely rational analysis or settled cultural traditions can guide us at least part of the way. If a child has developed some of the basic capabilities of people generally, it would be irrational not to count her as a "person," even though she now needs the support of adults to continue living. But what of a newborn baby? Apart from the basic physical capacity and some minimal perception, such a baby has not yet developed human capacities. Would it be irrational to say that at that point parents should have the right to decide about survival? Although we can imagine such a perspective about protecting life, it is extremely distant from that which is well established in our culture. Here the genuine issues concern the time from conception to birth. As I have already indicated, in Chapters 4 and 9, I do not think rationality gives us an answer to when life deserving protection begins, or to whether the best understanding of life's beginning involves a sharp line between no life and one that deserves great protection, or a progression in which the degree of life and warranted protection increases with the development of a single cell to a fetus to a child at birth. As mentioned earlier, this conclusion receives some indirect support from changing perceptions throughout human history.[29]

A crucial value question about abortion is, of course, the rights of the potential mother. A central practical issue is how far a law forbidding abortion is likely to be followed. On the first point, even if one thinks that early fetuses intrinsically count for something and deserve protection, should a woman have to commit her own body to saving the fetus? (The concern about having to care for a born child can be largely answered by putting it up for adoption, although this itself may often cause psychological trauma.) Would a bar on abortion not constitute an infringement on a woman's liberty? One possible answer is that she has chosen to do what has produced the fetus, but that is a harsh oversimplification. It does not, of course, have any application for a woman who has been raped, or for females who, through no fault of their own, have never been educated about how to avoid pregnancy. And when a woman, married or not, who engages in sex takes precautions needed to prevent pregnancy, but these fail, that is quite different from a self-conscious voluntary choice either to become pregnant or to avoid measures likely to prevent that.

Obviously people can disagree not only about when relevant life begins, but also about when it may deserve legal protection. Given the basic rights of women to liberty concerning their own lives, someone may perceive a restriction on abortion as justified only if it is supported by public reasons. As we have seen, that stance led Governor Mario Cuomo, a Roman Catholic who believed abortion was morally wrong, to support the legal right to obtain one. Connected to all this was the practical reality that many women faced increased danger because they chose to have abortions when they were illegal. Given that the law was not effectively enforceable and the risks for women were greater when they had to seek illegal medical help, legalizing abortions made much more sense. Relying mainly on a woman's basic liberty, the Supreme Court established such a right constitutionally in *Roe v. Wade*.[30]

A somewhat different issue arises about stem cells, one that could in the not-too-distant future be important for abortions. Although Robert George has urged that natural reason, quite aside from religious convictions, establishes the intrinsic value of stem cells and should bar any government aid for their use in experiments,[31] I have suggested that few of those who do not subscribe to Roman Catholic natural law will actually be persuaded by the rational argument.[32] That problem sharply presents an illustration of the issue of whether it should be acceptable for those religious believers who accept an extensive natural law to take political positions that those who reach similar conclusions on faith-based religious convictions should not.

A problem that may at some point arise about abortions, and may become highly controversial, is how to address a medical breakthrough that would allow young fetuses that are created outside a woman's body, or removed at an early stage, to be preserved outside until the time of independent living arises.[33] One view is that the fetuses should then be protected since this can be done without imposing on the women's bodies and the babies could be adopted, leaving the genetic mother no responsibility for their upbringing. A competing position is that the women, and perhaps the men who are the genetic fathers, should have the choice whether the fetuses should survive. Here is yet another question to which I believe there is really no rational answer. When citizens and legislators are determining what the law should provide, it would be mistaken to suppose that they must put their religious convictions and personal intuitions to one side and stick to public reasons. My own sense is that a decision either way should be constitutionally acceptable; that is, aborted fetuses could be seen as not yet possessing enough "life" to require protection over the convictions and desires of one or both of their conceiving parents or, alternatively, that their choice to end their responsibility should not extend to a constitutional right to terminate the existence of the fetus if others can preserve and care for it.

### Illustrations of Liberty versus Help and Fairness to Fellow Citizens

Among the crucial premises of liberal democracy are that individuals should have substantial liberty and that the state should see that it provides at least minimum help to those in need and assures fairness for its citizens. Although broader, these ideas are related to religion clause values. Carrying out one's religious conviction is one form of exercise, but others who are disadvantaged can see that as a form of establishment. We have explored this conflict in depth in the part of the book on exemptions. Here my focus is on how people should arrive at judgments about what our government should do. I shall start with three examples in which religious action itself is not directly involved.

How much welfare and other assistance should the government provide to citizens who are disadvantaged in some way? The greater the degree of help, the higher the tax burden on others. Those who believe most strongly in liberty, in the sense that people should be free to succeed or fail on their own and that help to others should come from private choices, will oppose extensive government help for medical expenses, living conditions, and higher education. Those who believe that aiding those who are not so fortunate is important and who doubt that leaving everything to private charity will work sufficiently will accept higher taxes and favor more aid. The recent and continuing conflict between Republicans and Democrats over the Affordable Care Act guaranteeing health insurance to most Americans is a striking example of this disagreement.

About such existing laws and proposed laws, one can certainly see public reasons on each side. In favor of aid are arguments that the assistance will help those who benefit to perform better in the long run in a way that helps the rest of us and will also lead to a more harmonious culture. It can also be contended that part of the consensus of liberal democracy is that the government should not allow others to suffer too much. At this stage of history, for example, very few think the government should simply stand aside if people are starving to death. Against arguments in favor of significant assistance are contentions that the government generally is an ineffective and sometimes corrupt institution, that providing aid encourages those who benefit from not working hard on their own, and that increased taxes are unfair toward those who are performing best and will encourage them to reduce their efforts.

Although rational public reasons arguments do line up on each side, and no doubt many people honestly believe those on one side or the other are decisive, lying in the background are personal convictions about what we genuinely owe to others, not only those close to us but strangers within our society. For many people, the basic question about a society's fundamental responsibilities for those worse off is important. In response, public reasons may tell us that owing nothing and owing all we have are both unworkable principles, but they cannot settle the precise degree of responsibility. People have varying convictions about the range of responsibility. Many of these convictions are related to religious views, as we see in the urging of Pope Francis to pay greater attention to those who suffer disadvantages.[34] To be clear, a religious view that we owe a great deal to others does not necessarily entail that the government, as contrasted with private organizations and individuals, should do this. Religious views can differ on how much support should come from public or private sources.

The overarching lesson of this illustration is that, for almost all of us, it would really be impossible to carve out exactly what we think is the balance of rational grounds here from our perception about what is fundamentally right from a moral point of view. Telling people that they must attempt such a carve-out is not really appropriate, especially since someone who tries hard may well doubt that others are doing so with a fair degree of success. If one cannot expect others to attempt to disregard altogether their personal convictions about what we fundamentally owe to those who are worse off, one cannot expect such exclusion by those whose relevant personal convictions are based at least partly on religious perspectives.

When it comes to when punishment is warranted and what it should entail, public reasons are almost certainly more decisive. But we still have fundamental disagreements about the relevance of bases for punishments, notably to what extent utilitarian considerations and retribution should be crucial. Shared reasons may also provide an incomplete answer to how far various forms of punishment or lenient treatment may lead to better behavior in the future. Again, when people are deciding where to stand on all this, it is hard for them to disregard what they think is fundamentally fair, and this can depend partly on their religious convictions.

One interesting illustration is whether a specific or general justification defense should ever treat as warranted the intentional killing of an innocent person. A subquestion here is whether intentional killing is radically different from an "unintentional" killing that is absolutely certain. For example, when a bomb is dropped on a city in a location with some enemy fighters, the objective can be to kill them, but the likelihood may be virtually 100 percent that some innocent civilians will die. And suppose a terrorist has placed a destructive bomb on a small child who is walking toward a large group of people. Can the child be shot to death in order to save many other lives? As I have indicated in the medical example, it is uncontested that a totally innocent person should not be killed in order to remove organs that could save the lives of three or four others. But it is far from simple exactly what counts as "intentional" killing here and whether that can be justified at least if the innocent person is directly posing a threat to others. My own sense is that public reasons can be more decisive here than with some of the other examples we have reviewed, but fundamental convictions about when deadly force is morally justified may rest partly on a sense about what human beings owe to each other, and to God, that is not totally reducible to rational argument.

When we think about foreign policy and the use of military force, these need to be guided mainly by reasons that carry weight for all of us. But for some people, fundamental views about human nature and also the status of other religions can play a role. Plainly nonestablishment values bar the attacking of other countries simply because they adhere to a "misguided religion," but whether those adhering to that religion can be trusted to genuinely aim for peace and for good relations with others may be relevant. Although one's own religious beliefs could bear on that, I do believe in this respect people should try as hard as they can to make evaluations that do not depend on their particular religious view of the competing religion. That is warranted both by nonestablishment values that are opposed to the quashing of other religions *and* the long history of regrettable conflicts between members of different faiths.

I turn now to exemptions from ordinary legal duties for those whose convictions tell them something is deeply wrong. Exemptions can obviously be seen as a form of free exercise, but granting the concession can also be regarded as a form of establishment, especially if religious objections are privileged over nonreligious ones. More broadly, if others suffer harm when an exemption is allowed from a legal duty, that can be perceived as violating principles of fairness and equal treatment that lie close to the values of nonestablishment.

As I have noted, one need not rest on religious convictions to believe that within a liberal democracy it makes sense to recognize the liberty of citizens to act on their basic convictions, religious or not, unless their doing so causes serious harm to others. Thus, the contentions about exemptions can be framed in terms of public reasons, and my own view, developed in Chapter 4, is that these can, across a wide range, actually give us answers to appropriate exemptions and their limits.[35] But when we think about such questions, it seems both unrealistic and unfair to urge that all citizens must somewhat develop their positions with total disregard of their own religious convictions or their beliefs about the religious convictions of others.

## Costs and Benefits

What does this survey of various issues tell us about the costs and benefits of a "public reasons" approach as a norm for political positions? I want initially to be explicit about three premises of this part of the book. The first is that the argument is much stronger that judges, executive officials, and legislators should try to rely completely on public reasons than that ordinary citizens should do so. The second is that even when it may not be right to expect total reliance on public reasons, they do almost always play an important role and can actually be decisive about many issues. All of us, officials and citizens, do have a responsibility to take them into account. Third, the argument for limiting oneself to public reasons is more powerful when it comes to advocacy in public than as a complete restraint on how people arrive at their positions. In what follows, I shall focus mainly on the cost and benefits of reliance on public reasons by individual citizens.

The basic benefit of genuine reliance on public reasons is that it does not favor the views of some citizens over others and creates decisions and discourse shared by all citizens. This serves the value of nonestablishment with respect to religious views and a broader value of equality with respect to wider sources of personal convictions.

On the opposing side lie the values of free exercise and liberty. Four different aspects are relevant here. The most important in principle is that people with religious convictions see their moral behavior as partly guided by those convictions. That is a form of religious exercise. To tell them that they can carry out those convictions in personal behavior, including joining institutions and contributing to charities, but must disregard them when it comes to deciding what positions to support about government aid to the poor seems a bit artificial. The second aspect is how, in a great many instances, it is hard for us to separate what we think is persuasive based on public reasons and what our personal convictions lead us to believe. To ask ordinary people, contrasted with judges, to undertake this effort in all respects is to ask a great deal. How far does it make good sense to insist that people should aim to do what is often impossible or very difficult? Such an insistence is dubious.[36] Both aspects I have mentioned so far contribute to a third. Any reasonable appraisal of reality is likely to raise substantial doubt about whether most people will be able to put aside their religious and other convictions. A person who is aware of this may see it as unfair to expect her to forego this aspect of what she sees as part of her religious experience.

In all these three respects, a limit on public advocacy is much less of a restraint than one that covers all grounds for reaching decisions. So long as people are free to rely partly on individual convictions, can explain their religious grounds to friends and within religious groups, and need not deny them more broadly, a restraint on public advocacy is a much weaker constraint on free exercise. Of course, as I have mentioned, one form of exercise of religion is trying to persuade others, but advocacy of controversial political positions in religious terms is not typically a good way to persuade others about religious truth, and it is much more likely to be a source of religious conflict. Another respect in which public advocacy works more effectively as a constraint is that people can discern what others are doing here and do not need to guess about motivations. They can know whether others are expressing religious grounds or other personal convictions. If others are not, that allows them to recognize that, if they restrain their own advocacy in that way, they will not be making a kind of free exercise sacrifice that is unfair in relation to what others are doing. This ability to discern what other people say is sharply in contrast with trying to figure out all that leads them to their positions.

When it comes to legislators, their job is not to promote a particular religion but to represent their constituents and the entire population in their work, and their discourse is more widely accessible. For them not to advocate in religious terms is substantially more important for nonestablishment values and is only a minimal restraint on free exercise.

## Political Candidates and Religious Affiliations

Especially given both the impossibility for almost everyone to entirely discount their religious convictions in forming political positions and uncertainties about whether, when, and how hard they should try to do so, it could matter for a voter what are the religious ties of a candidate for political office, most notably for the Presidency. While one can see this as a relevant consideration, we can understand that a deep investigation into every religious assumption of a candidate or her denomination could be deeply unsettling and divisive and could reinforce prejudices that many people have about religions other than their own. Given those conflicting considerations, a sensible resolution, now reached at least to a degree in our national political order, calls for some kind of intermediate compromise between no understanding and complete revelation.

If a candidate claims that her particular religion is a major reason to vote for her, that is unhealthy and contravenes the values of nonestablishment and public reasons within a liberal democracy. However, a candidate's religious convictions and connections can be relevant in at least three ways. They may indicate a person's views about herself and her responsibilities. For example, does she see herself as devoted to a larger cause and the welfare of others? With some religious connections, one may infer likely political conclusions unless an individual indicates otherwise. A voter might assume that a serious Roman Catholic will look less favorably on legal protections of abortions, unless she makes clear, as did Governor Mario Cuomo, that her political position is separate from her pure moral appraisal. If a candidate belongs to a fundamentalist group that asserts that the Old Testament is literally true and that evolution as a theory is totally misguided, a voter might wonder what the effect could be on education, unless the candidate has indicated that he rejects that aspect of his denomination's beliefs or regards them as disqualified for his official position by public reasons. This concern could affect not only worries about particular issues, but about how a candidate reasons. If he belongs to a group that places great weight on established doctrines and the truth of the Biblical text, even when these are in tension with scientific evidence, a voter may worry about what weight he would give to scientific evidence about global warming and climate change.

One conceivable conclusion about all this is that candidates would best reveal everything about their religious convictions and how those might bear on their reaching of political decisions. If that were true, it should also be true for atheists and agnostics. In our culture, however, such complete explanations would encourage religious divisiveness and lead voters to put too much weight on what they believe about a candidate's particular religion.[37] Had that happened, it could certainly have imperiled John F. Kennedy's election and Mitt Romney's campaign for the presidency. Each said something about his religious affiliation but without exploring his religion in real depth. Kennedy did say that no ecclesiastical authority should tell a President what to do, that the President should regard his "views on religion [as] his own private affair," and that voters should not regard affiliation as a test for office.[38] Mitt Romney acknowledged that religion does guide moral sentiments, claiming that churches in America share a common moral code. Noting his belief in the divinity of Jesus Christ, he also objected to any idea that a candidate "describe and explain his church's distinctive doctrines."[39] In a speech made after he was in the Senate but before he ran for the Presidency, Barack Obama urged that officials do not have to leave their religion at the door but do need to translate their convictions into universal, not religion-specific, values, offering proposals that are amenable to reason.[40] He did not make clear just how rigorous his "translation" was intended to be.

All of these proposals will leave voters with a bit less than full information about how candidates may be affected by their convictions. Both Romney's and Kennedy's language sought to preclude any negative effects based on judgments about their particular religions, and Romney sought to benefit from what he perceived as shared with most religious believers in the country. Given all the difficulties of separating religious convictions and concerns about religious prejudice and divisiveness, these partial explorations may be best for our society as it now exists. However, if a candidate chooses to go into considerable detail about his religion, he must expect others to indicate their objections to that religion.

What I have concluded here is about what candidates may best say in our present setting. That does not mean that others should not consider the likely relation of a candidate's religion to his political positions and whether that desirably should be more open and explicit. It also does not address the genuine concern that right now it may still be hard for a non-Christian of some kind to be elected President,[41] as it once was for a Roman Catholic. Without believing that existing outlooks are ideal, I have focused on how candidates may best act given their presence.

This part of the book reveals many conflicts between free exercise and nonestablishment values when it comes to what extent officials and citizens should attempt to disregard their religions and other personal convictions while arriving at political judgments. Among the central difficulties with urging exclusive reliance on public reasons or rational arguments are the near impossibility for most people of drawing a sharp line that promotes exclusion of nonpublic reasons and the doubts that almost anyone will develop about how far other people are trying to do this and are reaching a fair degree of success. Given these difficulties, an absolute position on either side—i.e., no reliance on religious convictions or no special status for public reasons—is unwarranted. Critics may well disagree with various intermediate positions I have offered, but I believe realities do compel us to be less than absolute here. Given the extent to which complexities are partly tied to cultural factors that may well change over time, we should not suppose that what may presently be the wisest approach for the United States is necessarily so for other liberal democracies or will be the best approach generations from now in this country.

# Conclusion

THIS BOOK HAS EXPLORED a variety of circumstances in which the values of free exercise of religion and nonestablishment lie in tension. This conclusion will repeat the major themes and briefly explore what I hope and expect about how readers will respond to various general and special recommendations made in various chapters.

The first point I want to emphasize is that, despite the tensions in many circumstances, at their core the clauses fit together. A government that genuinely establishes a particular religion in some form is curbing the free exercise of others and possibly even that of the dominant faith if public officials are dictating what it should do. Broadly, nonestablishment serves the clear value that people should be able to choose freely what religion to practice and whether to engage themselves in any religion.

Among the circumstances in which the conflicting values of the two clauses come into play are government practices and symbols of religion. These can promote the exercise of religion of those within government and indirectly support religious outlooks of other citizens but do amount to a kind of establishment. Concessions to religious practices assist free exercise but can be regarded as helping establish religion in a way and, in some situations, interfere with the equality rights of those directly affected by things such as refusals of service. When aid is provided for various services, such as hospitals and education, one can see the assistance being given to religious groups along with others as effectively "establishing" the religions by helping them promote their religious outlook, but a denial of equal treatment can be seen as inhibiting free exercise. Within public schools, teaching religious truth and carrying out religious ceremonies are definitely forms of establishment, but declining to teach about religion and barring individual comments about that may "establish" nonreligion and indirectly impair free exercise. Connections are a bit less direct when one considers the place of "public reasons." For many citizens, reliance for political positions on what they perceive as religious truth about such issues as aid to the poor and the morality of abortion seems an aspect of their religious exercise; on the other hand, the notion that in politics people should rely on "public reasons" can be seen as supported by the basic value of nonestablishment of religious views and personal intuitions. As Chapters 9 and 10 indicate, a fair appraisal here may well be very different for public officials and ordinary citizens. In regard to many topics in the book, whether religion should be distinguished from nonreligious claims is very important.

In respect to all the subjects of the book, three distinctions are very important. The conflicts in free exercise and nonestablishment values often come into play when courts are deciding what is constitutionally required or, at least, permissible. On some occasions, judges, for various reasons, are not going to resolve those issues. Other officials need to understand that both the federal and state constitutions may set limits on what they should do that are beyond likely judicial enforcement. And even within the range of what the Constitution permits, according to dominant standards or ideal interpretation, the conflicting values can play a role in what choices are just and wise. This last effect can bear on what private citizens as well as officials choose to do.

When one turns to what various chapters in the book suggest, it helps to distinguish a basic general approach from specific recommendations. The general approach is that we have no simple, straightforward categorical standards that resolve many of these issues. To take a controversial example, in respect to same-sex marriage exemptions we cannot say that there should never be a free exercise right if it causes even a minimal negative effect for others. But the degree of harm to others clearly matters for what rights of free exercise should be accommodated. On distinguishing religious from somewhat analogous nonreligious claims, it does not make sense in terms of constitutional standards or wisdom to conclude that a line may always, or never, be drawn that treats the two differently. Of course, having relatively clear lines is generally healthy for judges and other officials, but often these do not work, given all that is at stake. This is reflected, without great clarity, by the range of Supreme Court decisions in religious cases.

Readers who agree with these general approaches may nonetheless disagree with some or many of my specific suggestions. When the free exercise and nonestablishment values are in conflict, they may see one or both as more weighty than I indicate. For example, with same-sex marriage, one reader may find nonestablishment and equality values as strong enough to preclude any exemption from nondiscrimination requirements; another reader may believe all sincere religious claims should be accommodated regardless of how direct is the involvement in the marriage. Both readers will disagree with my intermediate position as well as with each other. What I want to stress here is that disagreement with some of my specific views is fully understandable with a diverse readership; but those disagreements should neither undercut the truth and value of the book's general themes nor the fundamental importance in our society of people tolerating the conflicting views of other sincere fellow citizens.

# Notes

Introduction

1. For an account of the idea of separation and how in some respects that has varied over time, see Alan M. Hurst, "The Very Old New Separationism," 2015 *B.Y.U. L.* Rev. 1 (2015).
2. In two volumes on *Religion and the Constitution, Free Exercise and Fairness* (vol. 1) and *Establishment and Fairness* (vol. 2) (Princeton, NJ: Princeton University Press, 2006 and 2008), I give an account of that law.
3. *Hosanna-Tabor Evangelical Lutheran Church & Sch. v. E. E. O. C.* 132 S. Ct. 694, 702 (2012) (quoting Cutter v. Wilkinson, 544 U.S. 709, 719 (2005)).
4. Andrew Koppelman, "Corruption of Religion and the Establishment Clause," 50 *Wm. & Mary L. Rev.* 1831 (2009). This thoughtful account includes a review of major theorists who have supported free exercise and nonestablishment in somewhat different ways. More broadly, as Jack M. Balkin has explained, nonestablishment can be seen as protecting both civil liberty and civil equality. *Living Originalism* 203–204 (Cambridge, Mass., Belknap Pr. of Harvard Univ. Pr. 2011).
5. A comprehensive account of approaches in other countries, especially English-speaking ones, is in Rex Ahdar & Ian Leigh, *Religious Freedom in the Liberal State* (2d ed. 2013) (Oxford, Oxford Univ. Pr.).
6. See generally John M. Marrin, "Religion and Politics in America from the First Settlements to the Civil War," in *Religion & American Politics: From the Colonial Period to the 1980s 19–43* (Mark A. Noll, ed., New York, Oxford Univ. Pr. 1990).
7. See, e.g., Lawrence H. Winer & Nina J. Crimm, *God, Schools, and Government Funding: First Amendment Conundrums 87–88* (Burlington, Vt., Ashgate Pub. 2015), for an account of the relevant Northwest Ordinance, reenacted by Congress shortly before the Bill of Rights.

8. However, Justice Clarence Thomas in urging a limitation on Establishment Clause restrictions has written that he would allow states "greater latitude in dealing with matters of religion and education." *Zelman v. Simmons-Harris,* 536 U.S. 639, 680 (2002) (Thomas, J., concurring).

9. This position is explained by Kurt Lash, "The Second Adoption of the Establishment Clause: The Rise of the Nonestablishment Principle," 27 *Ariz. St. L.J.* 1085 (1995). See also Balkin, supra note 4, on nonestablishment as protecting civil liberty and equality.

10. These are explored in much more detail in Kent Greenawalt, *Interpreting the Constitution* (New York, Oxford Univ. Pr. 2015).

11. *Arizona Christian Sch. Tuition Org. v. Winn,* 563 U.S. 125 (2011). This and other related cases are explored extensively in Winer & Crimm, supra note 7, at 149–225. The coauthors are strongly critical of the Court's limitation on when taxpayers can sue concerning tax benefits.

12. Green v. Bock Laundry Mach. Co., 490 U.S. 504 (1989).

13. See an addition to the "Sedition Act" entitled "An Act for the Punishment of Certain Crimes against the United States," ch. 74 § 2, 1 Stat. 596 (1798).

14. In contrast to modern times, Supreme Court Justices with frequency sat on circuit courts of appeals.

15. Chapters in *Interpreting the Constitution,* supra note 10, cover many of these topics.

16. Steven D. Smith, *The Rise and Decline of American Religious Freedom* (Cambridge, Mass., Harvard Univ. Pr. 2014).

17. For one broad, inclusive account of religious exercise, given the outlook of Christians who live by faith, see Ahdar & Leigh, supra note 5, at 157.

Part One: Government Use of Religious Practices, Communications, and Symbols

1. For one thorough account of the more limited original sense and the claim that this actually assisted free exercise, see Steven D. Smith, *The Rise and Decline of American Religious Freedom* (Cambridge, Mass., Harvard Univ. Pr. 2014).

1: Government Engagement in Religious Practices and Messages

1. Barack Obama, "Remarks of President Barack Obama—State of the Union Address as Delivered" (Jan. 13, 2016), https://www.whitehouse.gov/the-press-office/2016/01/12/remarks-president-barack-obama-%E2%80%93-prepared-delivery-state-union-address.

2. 463 U.S. 783 (1983).

3. 675 F. 2d 228 (8th Cir. 1982).

4. 403 U.S. 602, 612–13 (1971).

5. 463 U.S. at 790.

6. Id. at 790–791.

7. Id. at 792.
8. Id. at 797–798 (Brennan, J., dissenting).
9. Id. at 799.
10. Id. at 802–805.
11. Id. at 823–824 (Stevens, J., dissenting).
12. Id. at 818 (Brennan, J., dissenting).
13. Christopher Lund, "Legislative Prayer and the Secret Costs of Religious Endorsements," 94 *Minnesota L. Rev.* 972 (2010).
14. 134 S. Ct. 1811 (2014).
15. Id. at 1817.
16. Id. at 1819.
17. Id. at 1842 (Kagan, J., dissenting).
18. Id. at 1847.
19. Id. at 1853.
20. 370 U.S. 421 (1962).
21. Id. at 422.
22. For one account of Justice Black's role and his positions, see Andrew Koppelman, "Corruption of Religion and the Establishment Clause," 50 *William & Mary Law Review* 1831, 1888–1893 (2009).
23. 370 U.S. at 431.
24. Id. at 432–433.
25. Id. at 436.
26. Id. at 593. at 445–446 (Stewart, J., dissenting).
27. Id. at 450.
28. 374 U.S. 203 (1963).
29. 506 U.S. 577 (1992).
30. Id. at 581.
31. Id. at 593.
32. Id. at 616–617 (Souter, J., concurring).
33. Id. at 631 (Scalia, J., dissenting). On Justice Scalia's general approach to limiting Establishment Clause coverage, see Koppelman, supra note 22, at 1898–1905.
34. 472 U.S. 38 (1985).
35. Id. at 73 (O'Connor, J., concurring in judgment).
36. Braunfeld v. Brown, 366 U.S. 599 (1961). One secular argument against creating this sort of exception is that if the vast majority of stores are closed on Sunday, it may generate a competitive economic advantage for a store allowed to stay open that day.
37. 472 U.S. 38 (1983).
38. To be clear, officials of various sorts can be fired or punished for saying things that private citizens are free to say.
39. In this respect a school teacher would not count as an ordinary official. Given the inability of young children to distinguish personal views from official communications, a teacher's quoting the Bible and telling an individual student he is going to Hell for being gay—which was communicated to one of my

research assistants when he was a student in Texas—could well be declared unconstitutional by a court.

40. I am putting aside here situations in which officials make clear they are merely indicating their own personal views. Of course, the line between those and a form of official endorsement will not always be clear.

41. See Newdow v. Rio Linda Union Sch. Dist., 597 F.3d 1007, 1032 (9th Cir. 2010).

42. U.S. Citizenship & Immigration Servs., *USCIS Policy Manual* (2016) ("To standardize the naturalization ceremony experience, unless exempted, USCIS offices will implement these steps in all administrative ceremonies: Recite the Pledge of Allegiance."). Those being naturalized must also take an Oath of Allegiance that includes "so help me God"; but applicants who object need not recite this.

43. 542 U.S. 1 (2004).

44. Id. at 52–54 (Thomas, J., dissenting).

45. Id. at 30, 32 (Rehnquist, J., concurring in judgment).

46. Id. at 36–37 (O'Connor, J., concurring in judgment).

47. Lambeth v. Bd. Of Comm'rs of Davidson Cty., NC, 407 F.3d 266 (4th Cir. 2005).

48. A somewhat interesting analogue is "born of the Virgin Mary" in the Apostle's Creed, said by many religious believers who doubt that Mary really had not had sexual intercourse.

49. For a claim that the notion of "ceremonial deism" more broadly is "silly," see Koppelman, note 22 supra, at p. 1930.

50. See T. Jeremy Gunn, "A Preliminary Response to Criticism of the International Religious Freedom Act of 1998," 2000 *B.Y.U. L. Rev.* 841; Kristin W. Wuerfiel, "Discrimination among Rights? A Nation's Legislating a Hierarchy of Human Rights in the Context of International Human Rights Customary Law," 33 *Valparaiso L. Rev.* 369 (1998).

51. https://en.wikipedia.org/wiki/list of meetings between the Pope and the President of the United States. See Rachel Wellford, "A history of papal visits by U.S. presidents," *PBS Newshour,* Mar. 27, 2014, http://www.pbs.org/newshour/rundown/history-presidential-visits-pope/.

52. See Peter Baker & Jim Yardley, "Pope Francis, in Congress, Pleads for Unity on World's Woes," *N.Y. Times,* Sept. 24, 2015, http://www.nytimes.com/2015/09/25/us/pope-francis-congress-speech.html.

53. See, e.g., Daniel K. Williams, *God's Own Party: The Making of the Christian Right* (Oxford, Oxford Univ. Pr. 2010).

54. A majority of citizens see the United States as a Christian country. See David A. Butz and Jayson D. Carvalho, "Examining the Psychological Separation of Church and State: The American-Christian Effect," 7 *Psychol. of Religion and Spirituality* 109 (2015). Of course, that identification may, for some individuals, mean only that Christianity is the country's dominant religion. Others may see the basic life of the social order as connected to the Christian religion.

55. 449 U.S. 39 (1980) (per curiam).

56. Id. at 41.

57. 545 U.S. 844 (2005).
58. Van Orden v. Perry, 545 U.S. 677 (2005).
59. *McCreary Cty.*, 545 U.S. at 903–912 (Scalia, J., dissenting).
60. *Van Orden*, 545 U.S. at 688–671.
61. Id. at 692 (Scalia, J., concurring).
62. Id. at 721–722 (Stevens, J., dissenting); id. at 737 (O'Connor, J., dissenting); id. at 742–743 (Souter, J., dissenting).
63. Id. at 700–701 (Breyer, J., concurring in judgment).
64. Id. at 701–702.
65. Id. at 704.
66. 465 U.S. 668 (1984).
67. Id. at 683.
68. Id. at 699–701.
69. Id. at 719.
70. Id. at 691.
71. 492 U.S. 573 (1989).
72. Id. at 616.
73. 465 U.S. 668, 687 (1989) (O'Connor, J., concurring). To be clear, it may fit the "purpose" and "effect" aspects of *Lemon*. It does not cover all aspects of entanglement.
74. Id. at 688.
75. 472 U.S. 38, 76, 83 (1985) (O'Connor, J., concurring).
76. 492 U.S. at 634.
77. Capitol Square Review & Advisory Bd. v. Pinette, 515 U.S. 753, 779–780 (1995) (O'Connor, J., concurring in part and concurring in judgment).
78. At that time, Edgemont School ended in tenth grade, and we were sent with tuition paid to Scarsdale High School for our last two years.
79. In response to a lawsuit, the officials have indicated they will not allow the stickers. See Jon Herskovitz, "Texas county agrees to remove crosses from police cars," Reuters, June 6, 2016, http://www.reuters.com/article/us-texas-cross-idUSKCN0YS2EU.
80. *Capital Square Review and Advisory Bd. v. Pinette*, 515 U.S. 753 (1995).
81. Id. at 760–763 (plurality opinion).
82. Id. at 776 (O'Connor, J., concurring in part and concurring in judgment).

2: Religion and Clerics in Constraining Government Institutions: The Military and Prisons

1. See, e.g., Ira C. Lupu & Robert W. Tuttle, "Instruments of Accommodation: The Military Chaplaincy and the Constitution," 110 *W. Va. L. Rev.* 89 (2007); Steven K. Green, "Reconciling the Irreconcilable: Military Chaplains and the First Amendment," 110 *W. Va. L. Rev.* 167 (2007).
2. See Pew Research Ctr., *U.S. Public Becoming Less Religious* 44 (2015) ("Three-quarters of U.S. adults say religion is at least "somewhat" important in their lives, with more than half (53%) saying it is "very" important."); Pew Research

Ctr., *Religion in Everyday Life* 31 (2016) ("[In the United States, v]irtually all highly religious people regularly express gratitude to God and ask for help, as do majorities of less religious people.")

3. See Pew Research Ctr., *U.S. Public Becoming Less Religious,* supra note 2, at 69, 73.
4. See, e.g., Katcoff v. Marsh, 755 F. 2d 223 (2nd Cir. 1985).
5. See, e.g., ibid.
6. Id. at 238.
7. Captain Malcolm H. Wilkerson, "Picking up Where Katcoff Left off: Developing a Framework for a Constitutional Military Chaplaincy," 66 *Okla. L. Rev.* 245 (2014), argued that military chaplains for nondeployable units in the urban United States "cannot" be constitutional.
8. Katcoff, note 4 supra, 755 F.2d at 236.
9. See, e.g., Larsen v. U.S. Navy, 525 F.3d 1, 4 (D.C. Cir. 2008) (finding a case against the Navy's alleged policy of hiring chaplains based on fixed proportions of faiths moot since both parties agreed that that policy "ended in 2001 and that the Navy now maintains no religious quotas").
10. See U.S. Army, *Army Chaplain Core,* accessed June 10, 2016, http://www.goarmy.com/chaplain/about/requirements.html; Julie B. Kaplan, "Military Mirrors on the Wall: Nonestablishment and the Military Chaplaincy," 95 *Yale L.J.* 1210 (1986).
11. For some concerns about this, see http://militaryatheist.org/advocacy/.
12. Katcoff, note 4 supra, at 755 F.2d at 226.
13. Kaplan, note 10 supra, at 1212, n. 16.
14. 324 F. 3d 880 (7th Cir. 2003).
15. For one account of these two questions, see Daniel W. Sack, "The Establishment Clause and Parole" (unpublished term paper, Columbia Law School, Jan. 8, 2016) (on file with the author).
16. See Harold G. Koenig et al., *Handbook of Religion and Health* (2nd ed.) 247–48. (New York: Oxford Univ. Pr., 2012) (aggregating studies).
17. See, e.g., Editorial, "Racial discrimination in stop-and-frisk," *NY Times,* Aug. 12, 2013, http://www.nytimes.com/2013/08/13/opinion/racial-discrimination-in-stop-and-frisk.html. My views on this have appeared in Kent Greenawalt, "Probabilities, Perceptions, Consequences, and 'Discrimination': One Puzzle about Controversial 'Stop and Frisk,'" 12 *Ohio St. J. Crim. L.* 181 (2014).
18. No. 204-CV-260 TC, 2006 WL 3672901, at 2 (D. Utah, Dec. 8, 2006).
19. The Church of Jesus Christ of Latter-Day Saints, "Do Mormons Practice Polygamy?" accessed June 10, 2016, https://www.mormon.org/faq/topic/polygamy; CNN Library, "Fundamentalist Church of Jesus Christ of Latter-Day Saints Fast Facts," accessed June 13, 2016, http://www.cnn.com/2013/10/31/us/fundamentalist-church-of-jesus-christ-of-latter-day-saints-fast-facts/.

Part Two: Forms of Government Aid to Religious Institutions and Individuals: Financial Support and Exemptions

1. As explained in detail by Laurence H. Winer and Nina J. Crimm, *God Schools, and Government Funding: First Amendment Conundrums* (Burlington, VT: Ashgate, 2015), the forms of benefits, being increasingly used within states, include exemptions from general tax requirements, deductions from income of donations, credits for contributions made, and exclusion from tax income of money parents have spent for educational expenses.

3: Financial Support

1. In their book *God, Schools, and Government Funding: First Amendment Conundrums* (Burlington, VT: Ashgate, 2015), cited in note 1 of the introduction to this part, Laurence H. Winer and Nina J. Crimm provide an extensive account of relevant cases, including their critique of how the Supreme Court has moved toward acceptance of forms of aid.
2. 330 US 1 (1947).
3. See Kent Greenawalt, *Does God Belong in Public Schools?* 13–17 (2005); Kent Greenawalt, 2 *Religion and the Constitution: Establishment and Fairness* 386–388 (2008) [hereinafter Greenawalt, *Establishment and Fairness*].
4. See Jill Goldenziel, "Blaine's Name in Vain?: State Constitutions, School Choice, and Charitable Choice," 83 *Denv. U. L. Rev.* 57 (2005).
5. Id. (locating approximately thirty-eight states with such provisions).
6. Everson, 330 U.S. at 31–32 (Rutledge, J., dissenting).
7. Id. at 22–23 (Jackson, J. dissenting).
8. Id. at 17 (majority opinion).
9. Id. at 16.
10. Id. at 15–16.
11. 392 U.S. 236 (1968).
12. Id. at 243–48.
13. 403 U.S. 602 (1971).
14. Id. at 612.
15. Id. at 612–613.
16. Id. at 622.
17. Tilton v. Richardson, 403 U.S. 672 (1971).
18. Id. at 686.
19. Wolman v. Walter, 433 U.S. 229 (1977).
20. Committee for Public Education and Religious Liberty v. Regan, 444 U.S. 646 (1980).
21. Wolman v. Walter, note 19 supra.
22. Hunt v. Mc.Nair, 413 U.S. 734, 741 (1973).
23. 463 U.S. 398 (1983).
24. See, e.g., Case Comment, "Tax Deductions for Private School Tuition," 97 *Harv. L. Rev.* 148 (1983). ("[I]n *Mueller v. Allen*, a deeply divided Court

signaled its acceptance of a more sympathetic view of government aid to parochial schools.") (internal citation omitted); Juan C. Enjamio, "A Breach in the Impenetrable Wall: An Analysis of Tuition Tax Credits and the Establishment Clause," 38 *U. Miami L. Rev.* 903, 920 (1984) ("[*Mueller*] portends a Court less probing in its review of challenged programs and more limited in its examination of state statutes that grant aid to sectarian institutions. *Mueller* also evidences a Court less demanding in the area of church and state relations and more tolerant of breaches in the once impregnable wall."); J. Edward Goff, "Constitutional Law—First Amendment—A State Statute That Permits a Tax Deduction for Public as well as Nonpublic School Tuition and Related Expenses Does Not Violate the Establishment Clause of the First Amendment *Mueller v. Allen*," 29 *Vill. L. Rev.* 505, 534 (1984) ("The practical impact of *Mueller* will … encourage state legislatures that want to assist nonpublic schools to adopt measures similar or identical to the Minnesota statute. This decision gives state legislatures the guidance that will enable them to provide the aid to nonpublic schools that they have attempted to provide so many times before."); cf. Mark Strasser, "Repudiating Everson: On Buses, Books, and Teaching Articles of Faith," 78 *Miss. L.J.* 567, 609 (2009) ("*Mueller* had the potential to effect an important change in sectarian aid jurisprudence.").

25. School District of Grand Rapids v. Ball, 473 U.S. 373 (1988).
26. Aguilar v. Felton, 473 U.S. 402 (1985). The ruling was overturned in 1997 in Agostini v. Felton, 521 U.S. 203.
27. 536 U.S. 639 (2002).
28. 175 U.S. 291, 298 (1899).
29. David Saperstein, "Public Accountability and Faith-Based Organizations: A Problem Best Avoided," 116 *Harv. L. Rev.* 1353, 1359 (2003).
30. 487 U.S. 589 (1988).
31. *Id.* at 594 (quoting Adolescent Family Life Act, Pub. L. No. 97–35, 95 Stat. 578, 42 U.S.C. § 300z-1(a)(4) (1982 ed. and Supp. IV)).
32. Id. at 625 (Blackmun, J., dissenting).
33. Id. at 605 (majority opinion).
34. Id. at 623 (O'Connor, J., concurring).
35. 42 U.S.C. §604(a) (Supp. V 1999).
36. Freedom from Religion Foundation, Inc. v. McCallum, 179 F. Supp. 2d 950 (W.D. Wis.); on reconsideration in part, 214 F. Supp. 2d 905 (W.D. Wis. 2002), aff'd, 324 F.3d 880 (7th Cir. 2003).
37. 179 F. Supp. at 983.
38. Id. at 955, 957.
39. See, e.g., Carl N. Esbeck, "A Constitutional Case for Government Cooperation with Faith-Based Social Service Providers," 46 *Emory L. J. 1 (1997)*.
40. Mitchell v. Helms, 530 U.S. 793 (2000) (plurality opinion). This position is criticized by Winer and Crimm, note 1 supra at p. 11, on the basis that it "blinks reality, ignoring the real-world consequences."
41. See, e.g., Saperstein, supra note 29.
42. Nelson Tebbe, "Excluding Religion," 156 *Penn. L. Rev.* 1263 (2008).

43. Ira C. Lupu and Robert Tuttle, "Sites of Redemption: A Wide-Angle Look at Government Vouchers and Sectarian Service Providers," 18 *Journal of Law and Politics* 539 (2002).

44. See id. at 575–584.

45. Mitchell v. Helms, 530 U.S. 793, 829 (2000).

46. James A. Davids, "Pounding a Final Stake in the Heart of the Invidiously Discriminatory 'Pervasively Sectarian' Test,' 7 *Ave Maria L. Rev.* 59, 93–103 (2008) (discussing different circuits' approaches to the test after Mitchell).

47. Working Group on Human Needs and Faith-Based and Community Initiatives, *Finding Common Ground: 29 Recommendations of the Working Group on Human Needs and Faith-Based and Community Initiatives* 32. Washington DC: Convergence Center for Policy Resolution, 2002.

48. For an illustration of two sharply different hypothetical private schools, one of which has strict religious requirements, see Winer and Crimm, note 1 supra, at 5–6.

49. In 1965, there were 180,000 nuns and 59,000 priests; in 2014, 50,000 nuns and 38,000 priests. See Michael Lipka, "U.S. nuns face shrinking numbers and tensions with the Vatican," Pew Research Ctr., Aug. 8, 2014, http://www.pewresearch.org/fact-tank/2014/08/08/u-s-nuns-face-shrinking-numbers-and-tensions-with-the-vatican/.

50. Connected to the reduction of priests and nuns has been the closing of a significant number of Catholic schools. See David Gonzales, "A lifetime for minorities, Catholic school retrench," *N.Y. Times,* June 21, 2013, A. 16, on New York schools.

51. These are frequently viewed as mainly less effective in general than in other liberal democracies with similar economic status. Of course, in the United States, since localities largely determine the quality of public schools, those in well-to-do suburbs are likely to be much better than those in poor cities.

52. 330 U.S. 1 (1947).

53. 463 U.S. 388 (1983).

54. School District of Court Rapids v. Ball, 473 U.S. 373, 388 (1985).

55. Aguilar v. Felton, 473 U.S. 402, 412–413 (1985). This decision was overturned twelve years later in Agostini v. Felton, 521 U.S. 203 (1997).

56. 530 U.S. 793 (2000).

57. Id. at 809–810, 821–825.

58. Id. at 837–838 (concurring opinion of O'Connor, J.).

59. Id. at 828.

60. Id. at 829.

61. Roman Catholics within the United States, including bishops and priests, were more accepting of our form of government than the Vatican authority.

62. See Greenawalt, *Establishment and Fairness,* supra note 2, at 386–388.

63. 536 U.S. 639 (2002).

64. Id. at 658.

65. Id. at 704–706 (Souter, J., dissenting).

66. Id. at 704.

67. Id. at 724 (Breyer, J., dissenting).
68. Id. at 726.
69. Id. at 728.
70. Nat'l Ctr. For Educ. Statistics, *Characteristics of Private Schools in the United States: Results from the 2007–08 Private School Universe Survey* 2 (2009) ("Sixty-eight percent (67.9) of private schools, enrolling 80.6 percent of private school students and employing 72.3 percent of private school [full-time equivalent] teachers, in 2007–08 had a religious orientation or purpose."); Nat'l Ctr. for Educ. Statistics, *Digest of Education Statistics* 2014, at 441 (2016) (recording 3,091 private degree-granting postsecondary institutions in 2013, of which 884 [roughly 29 percent] self-reported a religious affiliation).
71. Zelman, 536 U.S. at 644.
72. See the position developed by Nelson Tebbe, note 41 supra.
73. For an account of this history, see Winer and Crimm, note 1 supra, at 45–48.
74. 540 U.S. 712 (2004).
75. Id. at 716.
76. Id. at 718.
77. See, e.g., Bush v. Holmes, 886 So. 2d 340 (Fla. Dist. Ct. App., 2004). The en banc court was divided over the outcome. The basic decision was affirmed by the Florida Supreme Court on the ground that high-quality public schools were required. 919 So. 2d 392 (Fla. 2006).
78. Jackson v. Benson, 578 N.W. 2d 602 (Wis. 1998).
79. 788 F.3d 779 (8th Cir. 2015). A different claim of discrimination in favor of other religions was not addressed because it was raised too late. A clear example of that would be unconstitutional.
80. 788 F.3d at 792.
81. 650 F.3d 30 (2nd Cir. 2011).
82. Stormans, Inc. v. John Weisman, cert. denied, June 26, 2016, 519 U.S. (2016).
83. See Winer and Crimm, note 1 supra, at 185–225.
84. 131 S. Ct. 1436 (2011).
85. Possibilities are explored by Winer and Crimm, note 1 supra, at 227–71, who believe permitted financial assistance to religious schools should be much less than has been accepted in recent decades.

## 4: Exemptions and Other Favored Treatment

1. Kent Greenawalt, *Exemptions: Necessary, Justified, or Misguided?* (Cambridge, Mass., Harvard Univ. Pr. 2016).
2. Hosanna-Tabor Evangelical Lutheran Church and School v. Equal Employment Opportunity Commission, 132 S. Ct. 694 (2012).
3. 494 U.S. 872 (1990).
4. 42 U.S.C.A. §2000 bb-1.
5. Nat'l Conference of State Legislatures, "State Religious Freedom Restoration Acts," Oct. 15, 2015, accessed June 13, 2016, http://www.ncsl.org/research/

civil-and-criminal-justice/state-rfra-statutes.aspx (identifying twenty-one states with RFRAs).

6. 42 U.S.C.A. § 300a-7.
7. See Erik Eckholm, "Next fight for gay rights: bias in jobs and housing," *N.Y. Times,* June 27, 2015, http://www.nytimes.com/2015/06/28/us/gay-rights-leaders-push-for-federal-civil-rights-protections.html?_r=0; David Masci, *How the Supreme Court's Decision for Gay Marriage Could Affect Religious Institutions,* Pew Research Ctr., June 26, 2015, http://www.pewresearch.org/fact-tank/2015/06/26/how-a-supreme-court-decision-for-gay-marriage-would-affect-religious-institutions/.
8. For an account of two federal law provisions, Title IX of the Education Amendment of 1972 and Title VII of the Civil Rights Act of 1969, and their implementations, see Robin Fretwell Wilson, "Squaring Faith and Sexuality in Religious Institutions and the Unique Challenge of Sports" (essay yet to be published, pp. 8–18).
9. See, e.g., James M. Oleske, Jr., "State Inaction, Equal Protection, and Religious Resistance to LGBT Rights," 87 *Univ. of Colorado Law Review* 1 (2016).
10. Douglas NeJaime and Reva B. Siegel, "Conscience Wars: Complicity-Based Conscience Claims in Religion and Politics," 124 *Yale L. Jour.* 2516 (2015).
11. Douglas Laycock, "Religious Liberty for Politically Active Minority Groups: A Response to NeJaime and Siegel," *Yale L. Jour. Forum* 369 (March 16, 2016). Richard Post, "RFRA and First Amendment Freedom of Expression," *Yale L. Jour. Forum* 387 (March 16, 2016), argues that Laycock goes too far in suggesting that it is wrong for the government to take account of the "transmission of social meaning" when it regulates conduct as well as when it directly regulates speech.
12. U.S. Dep't of Treasury, State and Local Taxes, https://www.treasury.gov/resource-center/faqs/Taxes/Pages/state-local.aspx.
13. See generally Erika King, "Tax Exemptions and the Establishment Clause," 49 *Syracuse L. Rev.* 971 (1999); Vaughn E. James, "Reaping Where They Have Not Sowed: Have American Churches Failed to Satisfy the Requirements for the Religious Tax Exemption?" 43 *Cath. Law.* 29 (2004).
14. See King, supra note 9, at 976–981; James, supra note 9, at 36–42. In states with established religions, dissenting religions typically did not receive the tax benefit. See John Witte, Jr., "Tax Exemption of Church Property: Historical Anomaly or Valid Constitutional Practice?" 64 *Southern Cal. L. Rev.* 363, 367 (1991).
15. See, e.g., John W. Whitehead, "Tax Exemption and Churches: A Historical and Constitutional Analysis," 22 *Cumb. L. Rev.* 521, 539 (1992) ("These nineteenth-century tax exemption theories were premised on notions of 'social benefit.'"; internal citations omitted); Walz v. Tax Comm'n of City of New York, 397 U.S. 664, 673 (1970) ("Grants of exemption historically reflect the concern of authors of constitutions and statutes as to the latent dangers inherent in the imposition of property taxes.").

16. 26 U.S.C.A. § 501(c)(3).
17. Boris I. Bittker, George K. Rahdert, "The Exemption of Nonprofit Organizations from Federal Income Taxation," 85 *Yale L.J.* 299 (1976).
18. See generally Sally Schwartz, "William Penn and Toleration: Foundations of Colonial Pennsylvania," 50 *Pa. Hist.* 284 (1983).
19. Resolution of July 18, 1775, *reprinted in 2 Journals of the Continental Congress* 187, 189 (Library of Congress ed. 1905).
20. See Ellis M. West, "The Right to Religion-Based Exemptions in Early America: The Case of Conscientious Objectors to Conscription," 10 *J.L. & Religion* 367, 381 (1994) ("[T]he [military service] exemptions granted to conscientious objectors [in early America] were seldom, if ever, considered by them to be adequate or satisfactory because they were limited or conditional in nature. To avoid military service, the objectors had to secure a substitute or pay a fine or special tax. It is quite clear, moreover, that the lawmakers who imposed the fines or taxes considered them to be the equivalent to military service, and their amount was set accordingly. As a result, the exemptions were rejected by most Mennonites, Brethren, and Quakers, some of whom suffered imprisonment and loss of property for failure to serve, pay a fine/tax, or secure a substitute. Moreover, the lawmakers in the various states were quite aware that pacifists objected to paying a fine or tax in lieu of military service.) (internal footnotes omitted)."
21. 1 *Annals of Cong.* 434 (1789) [1789–1824].
22. Act of Feb. 24, 1864, ch. XIII, § 17, 13 Stat. 9 (1864). Federal adoption of state provisions preceded this act.
23. 40 Stat. 76, 78 (1917).
24. 54 Stat. 885, 889 (1940).
25. Section 6 (j) of the Selective Service Act of 1948, 62 Stat. 613 (1948).
26. 380 U.S. 163 (1965).
27. Id. at 164–165.
28. Welsh v. United States, 398 U.S. 333 (1970).
29. Id. at 344–354 (Harlan, J., concurring in judgment).
30. 401 U.S. 437 (1971).
31. Military Selective Service Act, 50 U.S.C.A. § 3802. The law currently applies only to men.
32. Zubik v. Burwell, 578 U.S. ___ (2016) (per curiam).
33. 42 U.S.C. § 2000 cc to 2000 cc-5 (2000).
34. City of Boerne v. Flores, 521 U.S. 507 (1997).
35. See, e.g., Guru Nanak Sikh Soc'y of Yuba City v. Cty. of Sutter, 326 F. Supp. 2d 1140, 1161 (E.D. Cal. 2003), *aff'd sub nom.* Guru Nanak Sikh Soc. of Yuba City v. Cty. of Sutter, 456 F.3d 978 (9th Cir. 2006) (explaining that RLUIPA's "legislative history establishes a pattern of constitutional violations occasioned by state land-use laws that is within Congress's power to remedy") (citing 146 Cong. Rec. S7774 (daily ed. July 27, 2000); City of Boerne v. Flores, 521 U.S. 507, 531).

36. Islamic Center of Mississippi, Inc. v. City of Starkville, 840 F. 2nd 293 (5th Cir. 1988).
37. Note, "Religious Land Use in the Federal Courts under RLUIPA," 120 *Harv. L. Rev.* 2178, 2188 (2007) ("Since the advent of RLUIPA, religious land use plaintiffs have been more successful in the federal courts than ever before. Free exercise claimants have won substantial victories on fact patterns no more sympathetic than those presented by losing plaintiffs in the pre-Smith era."); James D. Nelson, Note, "Incarceration, Accommodation, and Strict Scrutiny," 95 *Va. L. Rev.* 2053, 2120 (2009) ("[R]eligious prisoners are encountering more success than ever before [since the passage of RLUIPA]."); see also Derek L. Gaubatz, "RLUIPA at Four: Evaluating the Success and Constitutionality of RLUIPA's Prisoner Provisions," 28 *Harv. J.L. & Pub. Pol'y* 501, 557–572, (2005) (noting greater success for prisoners after RLUIPA than after RFRA).
38. A more restrictive view was taken by the Sixth Circuit in a pre-*Smith* constitutional free exercise case, Lakewood, Ohio Congregation of Jehovah's Witnesses, Inc. v. City of Lakewood, 699 F. 2d 303 (6th Cir. 1983).
39. Civil Liberties for Urban Believers v. City of Chicago, 342 F. 2d 752 (7th Cir. 2007).
40. Id. at 770 (Posner, J., dissenting).
41. See Angela C. Carmella, "Landmark Preservation of Church Property," 34 *Cath. Law.* 41, 44 (1991) ("It should come as no surprise that churches are frequently designated as landmarks. They are often examples of fine architectural styles and artistic excellence; in fact, ecclesiastical architecture may be considered a class of architecture worthy of preservation in and of itself. Even apart from architectural distinction, church buildings have often played central roles in the historical and cultural development of the neighborhoods and communities in which they are located, rendering them eligible for landmark status, individually or as part of a district.") (internal citations omitted).
42. Keeler v. Mayor and City Council of Cumberland, 940 F. Supp. 885–887 (D. Md. 1996). An opposite conclusion was reached in Rector of St. Bartholomew's Church v. City of New York, 914 F.2d 348 (2d Cir. 1990).
43. My view about this may be affected by the fact that my father represented St. Bartholomew at the early stage of the case it lost, n. 41 supra, and I gave some advice at a later stage.
44. But see Christopher Serkin and Nelson Tebbe, "Condemning Religion: RLUIPA and the Politics of Eminent Domain," 85 *Notre Dame L. Rev.* 4–5 (2008).
45. Cutter v. Wilkinson, 544 U.S. 709 (2005).
46. O'Lone v. Estate of Shabazz, 482 U.S. 342, 349 (1987).
47. See S. Rep. No. 103–111, p. 10 (1993).
48. See Ira C. Lupu, "The Failure of RFRA," 20 *Univ. Ark. Little Rock. L. Rev.* 575, 607–17 (1998).
49. 135 S.Ct. 853 (2015).
50. Id. at 866.

51. Id. at 867–868 (Sotomayor, J., concurring).
52. I use the "regular basis" term because it might be much more impractical if anyone could choose whether he would want a particular vegetarian meal over that with meat.
53. Williams v. Secretary Pennsylvania Department of Corrections, 450 F. App'x 191 (3d Cir. 2011).]
54. Vigil v. Jones, No. 09-CV-01676-PAB-KLM, 2011 WL 1480679 (D. Colo. Mar. 15, 2011).
55. Bryant v. Gomez, 46 F.3d 948 (9th Cir. 1995).
56. In Kaufman v. McCaughtry, 419 F. 3d 678, 682 (7th Cir. 2005), a court of appeals granted a prisoner's request to form an atheist study group as an exercise of religious liberty.
57. 42 U.S.C. §§2000 bb-1 (a)–(b) (1993).
58. 2 William W. Bassett, W. Cole Durham, Jr. & Robert T. Smith, *Religious Organizations and the Law* § 10:52 New York, Thomson Reuters/West, 2013) ("[T]he language of the act does not clearly indicate whether RFRA can be used as a claim or a defense in suits involving only private parties. The Supreme Court has not decided this issue. Moreover, the federal courts of appeals that have tried the issue have had differing opinions. On one hand, the Second Circuit, the Eighth Circuit, and the District of Columbia Circuit have all, either explicitly or implicitly, ruled that a party can properly use RFRA in such suits, at least where the government could have been a plaintiff.... On the other hand, the Fifth Circuit (in an unpublished case), the Sixth Circuit, and the Seventh Circuit have all ruled that a party cannot properly use RFRA in such cases.... Additionally, the Ninth Circuit ruled that a private party can use RFRA to state a claim against another private party in only limited circumstances.") (internal citations omitted); see also Sara Lunsford Kohen, "Religious Freedom in Private Lawsuits: Untangling When RFRA Applies to Suits Involving Only Private Parties," 10 *Cardozo Pub. L. Pol'y & Ethics J.* 43 (2011) (discussing when RFRA should apply against private actors).
59. See generally Alan Stephens, Annotation, "Free Exercise of Religion Clause of First Amendment as Defense to Tort Liability," 93 *A.L.R. Fed.* 754 (1989) (citing cases and explaining general themes).
60. Guinn v. Church of Christ of Collinsville, 775 P. 2d 766 (Okla. 1989).
61. Hadnot v. Shaw, 826 P. 2d 978 (Okla. 1992).
62. Edward J. Imwinkelried & Richard D. Friedman, *The New Wigmore: A Treatise on Evidence: Evidentiary Privileges* § 6.2.3 (2d ed., New York, Aspen Publishers 2010).
63. See generally Imwinkelried & Friedman, *The New Wigmore: A Treatise on Evidence: Evidentiary Privileges* § 6.5.1.
64. Contrary to my conclusion, a California court did once decide that parents could recover from a church because a cleric told a son that committing sin was worse than suicide, and the son later did commit suicide. Nally v. Grace Community Church, 240 Cal. Rptr. 215, 219 (Ct. App. 1987), rev'd on other grounds, 763 P. 2d 948 (Cal. 1988), cert. denied, 480 U.S. 1007 (1989).

65. Edward F. Anderson, *Peyote: The Divine Cactus,* 25, 42–48 (2d ed. Tucson, University of Arizona Press, 1996).

66. See, e.g., John H. Halpern et al., "Psychological and Cognitive Effects of Long-Term Peyote Use among Native Americans," 58 *Biological Psychiatry* 624 (2005) (finding "no evidence of psychological or cognitive deficits among Native Americans using peyote regularly in a religious setting," but cautioning that these findings may not generalize to illicit hallucinogen users); cf. Employment Div., Dep't of Human Res. of Oregon v. Smith, 494 U.S. 872, 909–919 (1990) (Blackmun, J., dissenting).

67. People v. Woody, 394 P. 2d 813 (Sup. Ct. Cal. 1964).

68. 494 U.S. 872 (1990).

69. A new report said nearly 50,000. Nat'l Ctr. for Health Statistics, *NCHS Data on Drug-poisoning Deaths* 1 (2016), https://www.cdc.gov/nchs/data/factsheets/factsheet_drug_poisoning.pdf

70. In one factual situation of this sort, a man from Afghanistan had kissed his baby son's penis in accord with a cultural tradition. See State v. Kargar, 679 A.2d 81 (Me. 1996).

71. Kent Greenawalt, "The Cultural Defense: Reflection in Light of the Moral Penal Code and the Religious Freedom Restoration Act," 6 *Ohio State Journ. of Criminal Law* 299, 320–321 (2008–2009).

72. See Washington v. Glucksberg, 521 U.S. 702, 703 (1997) (finding that "the 'liberty' specially protected by the [Due Process] Clause [does not] include[] a right to commit suicide which itself includes a right to assistance in doing so"); Deborah F. Buckman, Annotation, "Validity of Criminalization of Urging or Assisting Suicide under State Statutes and Common Law," 96 *A.L.R.*6th 475 (2014) ("Although no state currently has a law on its books criminalizing suicide or attempted suicide, the act of assisting another to commit suicide is broadly condemned. Except for fewer than a handful, all the states in the United States strongly disapprove of, and the majority outright criminalize, assisted suicide.") (internal citation omitted).

73. See Rebecca Williams, Note, "Faith Healing Exceptions versus Parens Patriae: Something's Gotta Give," 10 *First Amend. L. Rev.* 692, 719–726 (2012).

74. Id. at 695.

75. See Aleksandra Sandstrom, "Most states allow religious exemptions from child abuse and neglect laws," *Pew Res. Ctr.*, Aug. 12, 2016, http://www.pewresearch.org/fact-tank/2016/08/12/most-states-allow-religious-exemptions-from-child-abuse-and-neglect-laws/ (noting that six states have exemptions to manslaughter laws).

76. Luke E. Taylor et al., "Vaccines Are not Associated with Autism: An Evidence-based Meta-analysis of Case-control and Cohort Studies," 34 *Vaccine* 3223 (2014).

77. 406 U.S. 205 (1972).

78. Elizabeth Sepper, "Taking Conscience Seriously," 98 *Virginia L. Rev.* 1501 (2012), offers a substantial argument that convictions about performing acts should be more often recognized. I do think one reason for laws giving more

attention to refusals to perform is that most people feel, at least if a benefit will
be provided by others, much stronger about not performing what they take as
deeply wrong, than performing what is not allowed.

79. 410 U.S. 113 (1973).
80. Carol Sanger, "Abortion in Twenty-First Century America," ch. 4 (to be
    published).
81. A yearly national poll asks, "[d]o you think abortions should be legal under any
    circumstances, legal only under certain circumstances, or illegal in all circum-
    stances?" In May of 2016, the percentage for each answer was 29, 50, and 19
    respectively, with 2 percent expressing no opinion. Lydia Saad, *American's
    Attitudes toward Abortion Unchanged,* Gallup, May 26, 2015.
82. I am putting aside statutes consciously designed to make getting abortions
    more difficult. In late June of 2016, the Supreme Court held invalid Texas law
    with that purpose. Whole Woman's Health et al. v. Hellerstedt, 579 U.S. 136
    S.C. 2292 (2016).
83. 42 U.S.C. § 300a-7(b)(1).
84. For an argument that, at least for doctors and nurses with a conviction of con-
    science, they should be able to perform abortions even within such hospitals,
    see Sepper, note 77 supra.
85. See, e.g., Pew Research Ctr., *Support for Legal Abortion Falls Sharply among
    Conservative Republicans* 1 (2015), http://www.people-press.org/2015/09/28/
    majority-says-any-budget-deal-must-include-planned-parenthood-fund-
    ing/9-28-2015_08/ (finding 40 percent of both men and women in 2014
    believed that abortion should be illegal in all or most cases, and 42 percent of
    men and 43 percent of women in 2015 believed the same); Lydia Saad, *Ameri-
    cans Choose "Pro-Choice" for First Time in Seven Years,* Gallup (May 29, 2015),
    http://www.gallup.com/poll/183434/americans-choose-pro-choice-first-time-
    seven-years.aspx ("Majority of women, 54%, now pro-choice, vs. 46% of men
    ... [This] slight gender gap has emerged over the last three years, with women
    more likely than men to be pro-choice. This contrasts with 2001 through 2011,
    when there was virtually no gender gap.").
86. See, e.g., S. Amdt. 2321, 106th Cong. (1999) (Roll Call Vote). In the course of
    considering a bill entitled the Partial Birth Abortion Ban Act of 2000, there
    was a vote taken in the Senate on a proposal to express the sense of Congress
    in support of the Supreme Court's decision *Roe v. Wade* that was passed,
    51–47.
87. See Sepper, note 77 supra, at 1570.
88. Rachel Benson Gold, "Advocates Work to Preserve Reproductive Health Care
    Access When Hospitals Merge," 3 *Guttmacher Pol'y Rev.* 3 (2000), https://
    www.guttmacher.org/sites/default/files/article_files/gr030203.pdf.
89. *La. Rev. Stat. Ann.* § 40:1299.35.9 (2009).
90. See Germain Grisez, *The Way of the Lord Jesus,* v. 2, *Living a Christian Life,*
    ch. 8, "Life, Health, and Bodily Inviolability, Question E: Why Is Contracep-
    tion Always Wrong?, E-2: Contraception Always Is Contralife" (originally
    published Quincy, Ill., Franciscan Press 1993, copyright reverted to au. 2008),

http://www.twotlj.org/G-2-8-E.html,. See also G. E. M. Anscombe, *Contraception and Chastity* (London, Catholic Truth Society, 1925).

91. Sarah Pulliam Bailey & Michelle Boorstein, "Pope Francis suggests contraception could be permissible in Zika fight," *Wash. Post*, Feb. 18, 2016, https://www.washingtonpost.com/news/acts-of-faith/wp/2016/02/17/mexico-confirms-zika-virus-cases-in-pregnant-women-as-pope-francis-exits-the-country/

92. See Stormans, Inc. v. John Weisman, 579 U.S. (2016). Stormans, Inc. v. Wiesman, 136 S. Ct. 2433, 2433 (2016) (Alito, J., dissenting from the denial of certiorari). Joined by two other Justices, Justice Alito wrote a vigorous dissent. Currently four states explicitly require a pharmacy to fill valid prescriptions for emergency contraception, and one state mandates that the pharmacist himself or herself fill the prescription. Between three and seven states explicitly allow pharmacies to refuse to dispense emergency contraception, and between six and eleven states allow the pharmacist in particular to refuse. Guttmacher Institute, *State Policies in Brief: Emergency Contraception* 2 2016, https://www.guttmacher.org/state-policy/explore/emergency-contraception.

93. See id. See also Camille Fischer & Jaye Kasper, "Access to Contraception," 15 *Geo. J. Gender & L.* 37, 49–51 (2014).

94. Burwell v. Hobby Lobby Stores, 154 S. Ct. 2751 (2014).

95. This critique is more fully described in Kent Greenawalt, "Hobby Lobby: Its Flawed Interpretive Techniques and Standards of Application," in *The Rise of Corporate Liberty* 125 (Micah Schwartzman, Chad Flanders, and Zoe Robinson, eds., New York, Oxford Univ. Pr. 2016). A version also appeared in 115 *Columbia Law Review Sidebar* (October 2015).

96. 42 U.S.C. § 300gg-13(a)(4).

97. This view was arguably mistaken about Plan B. See Robin Fretwell Wilson, "The Erupting Clash between Religion and the State over Contraception, Sterilization, and Abortion," in *Religious Freedom in America: Constitutional Roots and Contemporary Challenges* 149–154 (Allen D. Hertzke, ed., Norman, Oklahoma, University of Oklahoma Press, 2015).

98. 42 U.S.C. § §2000 bb-1–2000 bb-4 (1993).

99. *Burwell*, 154 S. Ct. at 2768–69.

100. 455 U.S. 452 (1982).

101. 406 U.S. 205 (1972).

102. A separate concern not mentioned by the Court is that allowing an exemption for such businesses might provide an incentive to hire only workers with views similar to theirs.

103. Zubik v. Burwell, 578 U.S. (2016), 136 S.C. 1557.

104. 135 S. Ct. 2584 (2015).

105. Kent Greenawalt, *Interpreting the Constitution* (New York, Oxford University Press 2015).

106. Briefly, it is highly doubtful that the clause was intended to provide this sort of substantive protection and the range of such protection is amorphous. Given the controversiality of the topic, Justices may well have wanted a single

majority opinion, and given that Justice Kennedy was the most conservative justice on that side and had written earlier Court opinions on homosexual rights, it was not surprising that he was the author.

107. Masci, supra note 7.
108. 42 U.S.C. § 3603(b)–(c).
109. *Obergefell v. Hodges,* 135 S. Ct. 2584, 2641 (2015) (Alito, J., dissenting).
110. See Douglas NeJaime, "Marriage Inequality: Same-Sex Relationships, Religious Exemptions, and the Production of Sexual Orientation Discrimination," 100 *California L. Rev.* 1168–1169 (2012).
111. See Laurie Goodstein, "Utah passes antidiscrimination bill backed by Mormon leaders," *N.Y. Times,* Mar. 12, 2015, http://www.nytimes.com/2015/03/12/us/politics/utah-passes-antidiscrimination-bill-backed-by-mormon-leaders.html?_r=0.
112. 388 U.S. 1 (1967).
113. Hrishi Karthikeyan & Gabriel J. Chin, "Preserving Racial Identity: Population Patterns and the Application of Anti-Miscegenation Statutes to Asian Americans, 1910–1950," 9 *Asian L.J.* 1 (2002).
114. Major among these was the idea that God had planted different races in different locations and that whites generally had skills superior to blacks. If one seriously considered these as the basis for different treatments, shouldn't someone who was ¾ white count as white rather than black?
115. Elane Photography, L.L.C. v. Willock, 309 P. 2d 53 (N.M. 2013).
116. See Craig v. Masterpiece Cakeshop, Inc., No. 14-CA-1351, 2015 WL 4760453 (Colo. App. 2015), *cert. denied,* No. 15SC738, 2016 WL 1645027 (Colo. 2016). Andrew Koppelman perceives these two situations as much closer, see "A Zombie in the Supreme Court: The Elane Photography Cert. Denial," 7 *Alabama Civil Rights & Civil Liberties Rev.* 77, 79 (2015), and he notes that the bakery shop actually shut down after being sanctioned.
117. The importance of this notice is stressed by Andrew Koppelman, "Gay Rights, Religious Accommodations, and the Purposes of Antidiscrimination Law," 88 *S. Cal. L. Rev.* 619, 649 (2015).
118. See Alan Brownstein, "Gays, Jews, and Other Strangers in a Strange Land: The Case for Reciprocal Accommodation of Religious Liberty and the Rights of Same-Sex Couples to Marry," 45 *U.S. F. L. Rev.* 389, 414–22 (2010); Mary Ann Case, "Why 'Live-and-Let-Live' Is Not a Viable Solution to the Difficult Problems of Religious Accommodation in the Age of Civil Rights," 88 *S. Cal. L. Rev.* 463, 470 (2015).

Part Three: Discourse Regarding Religion within Public Schools

1. In 2007, approximately 88.8 percent of students in grades 1–12 in the United States were enrolled in public school. U.S. Dep't of Educ., Nat'l Ctr. for Educ. Statistics, *Trends in the Use of School Choice: 1993 to 2007, at 7, 2010,* nces.ed.gov/pubs2010/2010004.pdf.

2. See Bernie 2016, "It's Time to Make College Tuition Free and Debt Free," https://berniesanders.com/issues/its-time-to-make-college-tuition-free-and-debt-free/; Hillary for America, "Hillary Clinton's New College Compact," https://www.hillaryclinton.com/briefing/factsheets/2015/08/10/college-compact/.

## 5: Teaching about Religion

1. 403 U.S. 602 (1971).
2. An assertion about Jesus not being the son of God could be so perceived if made before a mostly Jewish student body.
3. Abington Township v. Schempp, 374 U.S. 203, 225 (1963).
4. Id. at 300 (Brennan, J., concurring); id. at 306 (Goldberg, J., concurring).
5. See, e.g., John Corrales, "Donald Trump asks for Evangelicals' support and questions Hillary Clinton's faith," *N.Y. Times*, June 21, 2016, http://www.nytimes.com/2016/06/22/us/politics/donald-trump-asks-for-evangelicals-support-and-questions-hillary-clintons-faith.html?_r=0; Robert Draper, "Ted Cruz's Evangelical gamble," *N.Y. Times Mag.*, Jan. 26, 2016, http://www.nytimes.com/2016/01/31/magazine/ted-cruzs-evangelical-gamble.html.
6. Gallup, "Religion" (2015), http://www.gallup.com/poll/1690/Religion.aspx (showing that between 1948 and 2015, the percentage of individuals who identified as Roman Catholic has hovered fairly consistently at around 25 percent, while the percentage identifying as Protestant has been slowly declining from a high of around 70 percent in the 1950s to 38 percent in 2015).
7. See Tracy Wilkinson & Marisa Gerber, "Pope Francis, visiting a bastion of poverty, envisions Mexico as a land of opportunity," *L.A. Times*, Feb. 14, 2016, http://www.latimes.com/world/mexico-americas/la-fg-pope-mexico-20160214-story.html.
8. B. Douglas Hayes, "Secular Humanism in Public School Textbooks: Thou Shalt Have No Other God (Except Thyself)," 63 *Notre Dame L. Rev.* 358, 372 n.100 (1988).
9. See Sarah Pulliam Bailey & Michelle Boorstein, "Pope Francis suggests contraception could be permissible in Zika fight," *Wash. Post,* Feb. 18, 2016, https://www.washingtonpost.com/news/acts-of-faith/wp/2016/02/17/mexico-confirms-zika-virus-cases-in-pregnant-women-as-pope-francis-exits-the-country/.
10. Gladys M. Martinez & Joyce C. Abma, *Sexual Activity, Contraceptive Use, and Childbearing of Teenagers Aged 15–19 in the United States* 2 (Ctrs. for Disease Control & Prevention, Nat'l Ctr. for Health Statistics, 2015) (noting that almost 70 percent of males and females have had sexual intercourse by age 19).
11. See Sexuality Info. & Educ. Council of the U.S. ("SIECUS"), *A Brief History of Federal Funding for Sex Education and Related Programs,* http://www.siecus.org/document/docWindow.cfm?fuseaction=document.viewDocument&documentid=69&documentFormatId=69.

12. Ibid.
13. Obergefell v. HodgeLemons, 135 S. Ct. 2071 (2015).

6: Teaching or Not Because of Religion

1. In 1650, Archbishop James Ussher of Ireland published *Annales veteris testamenti* ("Annals of the Old Testament"). Ussher calculated the date of the Creation as Saturday night, October 22, 4004 B.C.E., "a date immortalized in the margins of countless Bibles for nearly three centuries." Ronald L. Numbers, "'The Most Important Biblical Discovery of Our Time': William Henry Green and the Demise of Ussher's Chronology," 69 *Church Hist.* 257, 257 (2000).
2. Philip Kitcher, *Abusing Science: The Case against Creationism* (Cambridge, Mass., MIT Pr. 1982).
3. From the 1960s to the 1980s, some "neutralists" believed that much of the DNA of known organisms was the consequence of genetic drift. Massimo Pigliucci & Jonathan Kaplan, *Making Sense of Evolution: The Conceptual Foundations of Evolutionary Biology* 251–254 (Chicago: Univ. of Chicago Pr., 2006).
4. Frank S. Ravitch, "Proof of the Game: Intelligent Design and the Law," 113 *Penn State L. R.* 841, 873 (2009), after explaining why "intelligent design" is not science, suggests correctly that it "need not" be taught in a science course. However, it does not follow that it is misguided or even unconstitutional for teachers to say something about certain limits of what science can explain and indicate that intelligent design is one theory that may be relevant for those.
5. 393 U.S. 97 (1968).
6. 484 U.S. 578 (1987).
7. See, e.g., Freshwater v. Mount Vernon City School District Board of Education, N.E. 2d 338 (Ohio 2013) upholding a school board's termination of a teacher's employment because he continually made efforts to impose his religious views on his eighth-grade classes.
8. See Kitzmiller v. Dover Area School Dist., 400 Supp. 2d 707 (M.D. Pa. 2005).
9. For cases considering the advocacy of intelligent design as essentially about a religious alternative to evolution, see Kitzmiller v. Dover Area School Dist., note 8 supra, at 720–723, and Bishop v. Aronov, 926 F.2d 1066, 1077 (11th Cir. 1991).
10. Kwang Y. Cha, Daniel P. Wirth & Rogerio A. Lobo, "Does Prayer Influence the Success of in Vitro Fertilization-Embryo Transfer: Report of a Masked, Randomized Trial," 46 *J. of Reprod. Med.* 781 (2001). For a discussion of the commentary and criticism on the Cha study and other such studies, see Candy Gunther Brown, *Testing Prayer: Science and Healing* 64–98 (Cambridge, Mass.: Harvard Univ. Pr., 2012).
11. One might see climate change as a consequence of divine intervention but I am assuming that it can be more fully explained on the basis of scientific evidence and undoubted human behavior. See Edward Maibach, Teresa Myers, & Anthony Leiserowitz, "Climate Scientists Need to Set the Record Straight: There is a Scientific Consensus that Human-Caused Climate Change Is

Happening," 2 *Earth's Future* 295, 295 (2014) (noting that both "surveys of experts and reviews of the peer-reviewed literature ... converge on the following conclusion: 97 percent or more of climate scientists are convinced that human-caused climate change is happening") (internal citations omitted); Naomi Oreskes, "The Scientific Consensus on Climate Change," 306 *Sci.* 1686 (2004) (reviewing 928 papers published in refereed scientific journals between 1993 and 2003 and stating that "[w]ithout substantial disagreement, scientists find human activities are heating the Earth's surface").

## 7: Individual Communication by Students and Their Teachers

1. See, e.g., Epperson v. State of Arkansas, 393 U.S. 97, 104 (1968) ("By and large, public education in our Nation is committed to the control of state and local authorities. Courts do not and cannot intervene in the resolution of conflicts which arise in the daily operation of school systems and which do not directly and sharply implicate basic constitutional values.").
2. My criticism of this approach as taken in Employment Division v. Smith is in Chapter 4. To be clear, I am not asserting that a second claim cannot add to the total strength of an argument, only that if religious claims can succeed when joined with others, they should sometimes be sufficient by themselves.
3. 515 U.S. 819 (1995).
4. Id. at 819.
5. Id. at 895–897 (Souter, J., dissenting).
6. 496 U.S. 226 (1990).
7. Widner v. Vincent, 454 U.S. 263 (1981).
8. 533 U.S. 98 (2001).
9. Jim Yardley, "Pope Francis suggests Donald Trump is 'not Christian,'" *N.Y. Times,* Feb. 18, 2016, http://www.nytimes.com/2016/02/19/world/americas/pope-francis-donald-trump-christian.html.
10. Alan Rappeport, "Donald Trump calls Pope's criticism 'disgraceful,'" *N.Y. Times,* Feb. 18, 2016, http://www.nytimes.com/politics/first-draft/2016/02/18/donald-trump-calls-popes-criticism-disgraceful/.
11. Catherine J. Ross, *Lessons in Censorship: How Schools and Courts Subvert Students' First Amendment Rights* (Cambridge, Mass., Harvard Univ. Pr. 2015).
12. 53 F. 3d 152 (6th Cir. 1995), cert. denied, 516 U.S. 989 (1995).
13. Id. at 156.
14. 976 F. Supp. 659 (S.D. Tex. 1997).
15. Tinker v. Des Moines Independent Community School Dist., 393 U.S. 503 (1969).
16. Law No. 2004–228 of Mar. 15, 2004, Journal Officiel de la République Française [J.O.] [Official Gazette of France], Mar. 17, 2004, p. 5190. For a discussion of the legal status of headscarves in the United States, see Aliah Abdo, "The Legal Status of Hijab in the United States: A Look at the Sociopolitical Influences on the Legal Right to Wear the Muslim Headscarf," 5 *Hastings Race & Poverty L. J.* 441 (2008).

17. Muller v. Jefferson Lighthouse Sch., 98 F.3d 1530 (7th Cir. 1996). This position was unchallenged in the court of appeals.
18. 274 F.3d 464 (7th Cir. 2001).
19. Id. at 467.
20. John 3:16.
21. *Fleming v. Jefferson City. Sch. Dist. R-1*, 298 F.3d 918 (10th Cir. 2002).
22. Prior to Employment Division v. Smith, the federal Free Exercise Clause would have been similarly viewed.
23. 827 F.2d 1058 (6th Cir. 1987), cert. denied, 484 U.S. 1066 (1988).
24. Id. at 1069.
25. Id. at 1075–1076 (Boggs, J., concurring).
26. Id. at 1080–1081.
27. Id. at 1071–1072(Kennedy, J., concurring).
28. I am putting aside here special courses such as sex education for which excuses may be granted without undercutting basic school requirements.

8: Religious Beliefs and Endeavors Distinguished from Nonreligious Ones

1. 494 U.S. 872 (1990).
2. Hosanna-Tabor Evangelical Lutheran Church & Sch. v. Equal Employment Opportunities Commission, 132 S. Ct. 694 (2012).
3. See generally Michael W. McConnell, "The Origins and Historical Understanding of Free Exercise of Religion," 103 *Harv. L. Rev.* 1409, 1421–1430 (1990).
4. At present, they are a basis for someone in the military to be free of his contractual obligation to remain in the service for a set period of time.
5. Selective Training and Service Act of 1940, Pub. L. No. 73–783, ch. 720, 54 Stat. 885.
6. United States v. Kanten, 133 F.2d 703, 708 (2d Cir. 1943).
7. Berman v. United States, 156 F.2d 377, 380 (9th Cir, 1946) (en banc).
8. Selective Service Act of 1948, ch. 625, § 6(j), 62 Stat. at 604, 613.
9. 380 U.S. 163 (1965).
10. 398 U.S. 333 (1970).
11. Id. at 339–340.
12. Some readers may be aware that I was once a law clerk to Justice Harlan, but that was six years prior to this decision.
13. I explore this practice in Kent Greenawalt, *Statutory and Common Law Interpretation* (N.Y., Oxford Univ. Pr. 2012).
14. National Prohibition Act of 1919, ch. 85, Title II, § 6, 41 Stat. 308 (1919) (repealed 1935).
15. See Jose A. DelReal, "Trump: 'I think Islam hates us'," *Wash. Post*, Mar. 9, 2016, https://www.washingtonpost.com/news/post-politics/wp/2016/03/09/trump-i-think-islam-hates-us/.
16. The "perhaps" here is meant to convey doubt about whether it would be

acceptable to limit that form of help to churches and other religious institutions and not include donations to charitable institutions.

17. Davis v. Beason, 133 U.S. 333, 342 (1890).
18. United States v. Macintosh, 283 U.S. 605, 633–634 (Hughes, J., dissenting).
19. 367 U.S. 488 (1961).
20. Washington Ethical Soc. v. D.C., 249 F.2d 127 (D.C. Cir. 1957).
21. Fellowship of Humanity v. Alameda Cty., 153 Cal. App. 2d 673, 315 P. 2d 394 (1957).
22. Malnak v. Yogi, 592 F.2d 197 (3d Cir. 1979) (per curiam).
23. Africa v. Com. of Pa., 662 F.2d 1025 (3d Cir. 1981).
24. 592 F.2d at 207 (Adams, J., concurring).
25. Id. at 208–210.
26. Jesse H. Choper, "Defining 'Religion' in the First Amendment," 1982 *U. Ill. L. Rev.* 579 (1982); Jesse H. Choper, *Securing Religious Liberty: Principles for Judicial Interpretation of the Religion Clauses* 77 (Chicago, Univ. of Chicago Pr. 1995).
27. The complexities of how essentially ordinary moral evaluations can connect to religious convictions are explored in depth in Robert Audi, *Rationality and Religious Commitment* (Oxford, Oxford Univ. Pr. 2011).
28. See Laurence Tribe, *American Constitutional Law* §14–6, at 828 (Mineola, N.Y., Foundation Press 1978). He abandoned this proposal in his second edition: *American Constitutional Law*, §14–6, at 1186 n.53 (2d ed. 1988).

Part Five: Religious Convictions, Public Reasons, and Political Choices

1. The questions here are more complicated and harder to explain than those in earlier parts.
2. I have explored many of these matters in greater detail in Kent Greenawalt, *Religious Convictions and Political Choice* (1988), and *Private Consciences and Public Reasons* (1995) (both published in N.Y., Oxford Univ. Pr.).

9: Basic Approaches and Intrinsic Limits

1. Louis Henkin, "Morals and the Constitution: The Sin of Obscenity," 63 *Colum. L. Rev.* 441 (1963).
2. Bruce Ackerman, *Social Justice in the Liberal State* 11–12 (New Haven, Conn., Yale Univ. Pr. 1980).
3. Thomas Nagel, *Equality and Partiality* 230 (N.Y., Oxford Univ. Pr. 1987).
4. Charles Larmore, *Patterns of Moral Complexity*, at x (N.Y., Cambridge Univ. Pr. 1989).
5. Lawrence B. Solum, "Faith and Justice," 39 *DePaul L. Rev.* 1083, 1087, 1091–1092 (1990).
6. John Rawls, *A Theory of Justice* (Cambridge, Mass., Harvard Univ. Pr. 1971).
7. John Rawls, "Justice as Fairness: Political not Metaphysical," 14 *Phil. & Pub. Aff.* 223, 229 (1985).

8. John Rawls, *Political Liberalism 62* (N.Y., Columbia Univ. Pr. 1993).

9. Id. at 134–135.

10. Jonathan Quong, *Liberalism without Perfection 273* (Oxford, Oxford Univ. Pr., 2011).

11. Lawrence B. Solum, "Public Legal Reason," 92 *Va. L. Rev.* 1449, 1465 (2006).

12. Andrew Lister, *Public Reason and Political Community 116* (London, Bloomsbury Academy 2013).

13. Micah Schwartzman, "The Completeness of Public Reason," 3 *Pol., Phil. & Econ,* 191, 191–220 (2004).

14. See Gerald F. Gaus, *Justificatory Liberalism* (N.Y., Oxford Univ. Pr. 1996); Gerald F. Gaus, "The Place of Religious Belief in Public Reason Liberalism," in *Multiculturalism and Moral Conflict* (Maria Dimova-Cookson and Peter M. R. Stirk, eds., New York, Routledge 2010).

15. This view is developed carefully in Christopher J. Eberle, *Religious Conviction in Liberal Politics* (Cambridge, U.K., Cambridge Univ. Pr. 2002). Professor Eberle devotes a few pages to challenging my account of "replicability" as one basis to distinguish "public reasons," Id. at 160–163.

16. Ackerman, supra note 2, at 10–11; Larmore, supra note 4, at 50–53.

17. In a thoughtful discussion of distinguishing public reasons, Gerald F. Gaus rejects the idea that belief systems are "akin to seamless webs," which he attributes to me. Gaus, supra note 14, at 143. My position is that typically it is much easier to distinguish various bases than to identify how much they influence each other and what weight each carries in one's overall judgment.

18. Andrew Koppelman has suggested to me that the idea of "comprehensive views" is incoherent, because most people don't have fully comprehensive views. Even if this is true, one might distinguish fundamental beliefs about human existence from shared assumptions within a society and say the latter are what should count in our political life. For a strong contrary position, see Andrew Koppelman, And I Don't Care What It Is: Neutrality in American Law, 39 *Pepp. L. Rev.* 1115 (2013).

19. Paul Billingham has noted that changes in the perceived balance of public reasons may be partly due to changes in comprehensive doctrine, "which inevitably influences that understanding to some degree." Paul Billingham, "Does Political Community Require Public Reason?: On Lister's Defense of Political Liberalism," 15 *Pol., Phil. & Econ.* 20, 27 (2016).

20. Rawls, supra note 8, at 175.

21. John Rawls, "The Idea of Public Reason Revisited," 64 *U. Chi. L. Rev.* 765, 774–775 (1997).

22. Id. at 779–780.

23. Mario M. Cuomo, "Religious Belief and Public Morality: A Catholic Governor's Perspective," 1 *Notre Dame J. L. Ethics & Pub. Pol'y* 13, 18 (1984).

24. Andrew Lister develops the connection of public reasons to notions of reciprocity in terms of what others are doing and suggests why one may not be constrained by them if most others are not exercising the mutual respect of following them. Lister, supra note 12, at 120–121.

25. Though phrased somewhat differently, this defense fits with how some natural law scholars would understand the moral status of abortions.
26. This conclusion, of course, does not itself answer the argument that laws forbidding abortions are frequently violated and threaten and endanger the lives of women who do not believe they are doing wrong, but this practical argument is not the basis on which Governor Cuomo defended his position.
27. Interestingly, as noted in the next chapter, animal protections have become more extensive in recent decades.
28. Robert Audi, *Rationality and Religious Commitment* (Oxford, Oxford Univ. Pr. 2011).
29. See, e.g., John Finnis, "Religion and Public Life in a Pluralist Society," in 5 John Finnis, *Religion and Public Reasons, Collected Essays,* 42–55 (Oxford, Oxford Univ. Pr., 2011); Christopher Wolfe, *Natural Law Liberalism* 221 (New York, Cambridge Univ. Pr. 2006).
30. George W. Bush, *A Charge to Keep: My Journey to the White House* (N.Y., Morrow 1999).
31. Tanya M. Luhrmann, *When God Talks Back: Understanding the American Evangelical Relationship with God* 16–17 (N.Y., Alfred A. Knopf 2012).
32. Bridgette P. Volochinsky, "The Bush Presidency: Undermining the Separation Between Church and State," 2 *Inquiries J. / Student Pulse* 1 (2010).
33. See Bob Woodward, *Plan of Attack* 372 (N.Y., Simon & Schuster 2004).

10: Relevance of a Person's Position, Bases versus Articulation, and Specific Issues

1. Obergefell v. Hodges, 135 S. Ct. 2584 (2015).
2. For a critique of what he takes as my "impossibility" position conveyed by this sentence, see Micah Schwartzman, "The Sincerity of Public Reason," 19 *J. of Pol. Phil.* 376, 396 (2010).
3. The importance of reciprocal self-restraint has been emphasized by Andrew Lister, *Public Reason and Political Community 116, 121 (London, Bloomsbury Academy 2013).*
4. See, e.g., Schwartzman, supra note 2, at 385–386 n.29.
5. Michael Perry, "Why Political Reliance in Religiously Grounded Morality Is Not Illegitimate in a Liberal Democracy," 36 *Wake Forest L. Rev.* 217, 233 (2001), makes the point that religious discourse is not necessarily more divisive than secular moral discourse.
6. This is emphasized by Michael Perry, id., at 239–240, and Michael Perry, *Religion in Politics: Constitutional and Moral Perspectives* 49–61 (New York, Oxford Univ. Pr., 1999).
7. See, e.g., Daniel A. Dombrowski, *Rawls and Religion: The Case for Political Liberalism* 75 (Albany, State Univ. of N.Y. Pr. 2001).
8. See John Finnis, "Religion and Public Life in a Pluralist Society," in 5 John Finnis, *Religion and Public Reasons, Collected Essays* 51 (Oxford, Oxford Univ. Pr. 2011).

9. Genesis 1:26–28.

10. 7 U.S.C § 2131–2156 (1966).

11. Animal Welfare Act Amendments of 1970, Pub. L. 91–579.

12. Francis S. Collins, "NIH Will No Longer Support Biomedi-
cal Research on Chimpanzees," Nat'l Insts. of Health, Nov. 18, 2015,
https://www.nih.gov/about-nih/who-we-are/nih-director/statements/
nih-will-no-longer-support-biomedical-research-chimpanzees.

13. "Ringling Bros. and Barnum & Bailey Herd of Asian Elephants Will Move to
Their Permanent Home at the Ringling Bros. Center for Elephant Conserva-
tion in Florida in May 2016," https://www.ringlingelephantcenter.com.

14. Humane Methods of Slaughter Act, 7 U.S.C. 1901–1907.

15. I have in mind here particular religious convictions that certain animals are
favored in God's eyes, or that it is sinful to eat them. If restrictive laws are
based on those premises, they could be seen as establishing the relevant religions in a broad sense. One might see reliance on such bases as supported by
free exercise.

16. One would need to distinguish here between what will happen if human
behavior does not change and what may be a consequence of human conduct.

17. In terms of what is defensible and desirable law, matters are much more complicated than the text suggests. It may well be that our present prohibitions of
uses of many drugs result in high enforcement expenditures, counterproductive
prison sentences that also constitute a troubling form of racial discrimination, and unnecessary restrictions on individual freedom. But, even if this calls
for significant reform, state interventions to prevent serious misuses may be
warranted in somewhat different ways. This thesis is forcefully developed in
Andrew Koppelman, "Drug Policy and the Liberal Self," 100 *Nw. U. L. Rev.*
279 (2006).

18. Although generally defending reliance on religious convictions against claims
favoring limits to public reasons, Michael Perry is clear that belief that an act is
morally wrong need not lead to the conclusion that it should be legally barred.
Perry, supra note 5, at 223.

19. Obergefell v. Hodges, 135 S. Ct. 2584 (2015).

20. For one possibility in this respect, see, e.g., Stefan Lovgren, "HIV Originated
with Monkeys, Not Chimps, Study Finds," Nat'l Geographic News, 2003,
http://news.nationalgeographic.com/news/2003/06/0612_030612_hivvirus-
jump.html (describing origin of HIV).

21. Exactly what plausibly counts as "unnatural" is itself a complex question. John
Stuart Mill roughly a century and a half ago urged that this term does not
properly cover inclinations to act in ways that are ill advised or contrary to
fundamental human standards. See John Stuart Mill, "Nature," in *Three Essays
on Religion* 3–65 (Amherst, N.Y., Prometheus Books 1998). According to this
view, the whole notion that rational moral thought can be about "natural law"
would be misguided. What matters for my analysis is not this terminologi-
cal issue but whether there are substantial general reasons why it is obviously
inappropriate for humans ever to have sexual relations with other animals.

22. See Sabrina Tavernise, "Sweeping pain as suicides hit a 30-year high," *N.Y. Times*, April 22, 2016, at A1.

23. Occasionally, an exception has been made for women whose attempted suicide caused the death of a fetus. Ewan MacAskill, "Woman who attempted suicide while pregnant is accused of murder," *The Guardian*, April 15, 2011, https://www.theguardian.com/world/2011/apr/15/woman-attempted-suicide-pregnant-accused (describing case of Bei Bei Shuai, 34, charged with murder and attempted feticide of her unborn child and ultimately pleading guilty to misdemeanor charge of criminal recklessness).

24. It often remains true that an exception is made for life insurance provisions. John Dorfman, "How Life Insurance Policies Deal with Suicide," *Time*, August 15, 2014, http://time.com/money/3117698/how-life-insurance-policies-deal-with-suicide/.

25. California, in June of 2016, actually enacted a law permitting such behavior. End of Life Option Act, Cal. Health & Safety Code §§ 443–443.22. California joined Oregon, Washington, and Vermont as the only states to have passed such legislation. Jennifer Medina, "Who may die? California patients and doctors wrestle with assisted suicide," *N.Y. Times*, June 9, 2016, http://www.nytimes.com/2016/06/10/us/assisted-suicide-california-patients-and-doctors.html.

26. An interesting variation on this is the choice to stop eating, which could involve others behaving in certain ways. In India, the Jain religious group supported such a practice but a state made it criminal. The High Court of the state sustained the law. See Milind Ghatwai, "The Jain religion and the right to die by *santhara*," *The Indian Express*, Sept. 2, 2015, http://indianexpress.com/article/explained/the-jain-religion-and-the-right-to-die-by-santhara/.

27. See Mary Anne Waldron, *Free to Believe: Rethinking Freedom of Conscience and Religion in Canada* 3–5 (Toronto, Univ. of Toronto Pr. 2013). The Canadian Supreme Court recently overturned that decision and now allows for doctor-assisted suicide in certain circumstances.

28. Carter v. Canada (Attorney General), 2015 SCC 5. See Ian Austen, "Canadian court strikes down ban on aiding patient suicide," *N.Y. Times*, Feb. 6, 2015, http://nytimes.com/2015/02/07/world/americas/supreme-court-of-canada-overturns-bans-on-doctor-assisted-suicide.html.

29. See Carol Sanger, "Abortion in Twenty-first Century America," ch. 4 (to be published).

30. 410 U.S. 113 (1979).

31. Robert P. George, "Stem cell research: A debate—Don't destroy human life," *Wall St. J.*, July 30, 2001, at A18.

32. Kent Greenawalt, "Natural Law and Public Reasons," 47 *Vill. L. Rev.* 531 (2002).

33. Jeremy Laurance, "The future of fertility," *The Independent* (London), July 17, 2008. See also Eric Steiger, Note, "Not of Woman Born: How Ectogenesis Will Change the Way We View Viability, Birth, and the Status of the Unborn," 23 *Jour. L. & Health* 143 (2010).

34. Pope Francis, "Pope Francis Address to the United Nations (September 25, 2015)," http://w2.vatican.va/content/francesco/en/speeches/2015/september/documents/papa-francesco_20150925_onu-visita.html.
35. See also Kent Greenawalt, *Exemptions: Necessary, Justified, or Misguided* (Cambridge, Mass., Harvard Univ. Pr. 2016).
36. Its wisdom can depend partly on how crucial that may be for society.
37. It may now be true that negative values about certain religions or views opposing those of religions may make election nearly impossible. An explicit atheist, agnostic, or Muslim could now find it very hard to be elected in most locations in the United States.
38. Paul Horwitz, "Religion and American Politics: Three Views of the Cathedral," 39 *U. Mem. L. Rev.* 973, 983–84 (2009).
39. Mitt Romney, "Transcript: Mitt Romney's Faith Speech," NPR, December 6, 2007, http://npr.org/templates/story/story.php?storyId=16969460.
40. Sen. Barack Obama, "Call to Renewal" Keynote Address, June 28, 2006, http://www.nytimes.com/2006/06/28/us/politics/2006obamaspeech.html. He developed these suggestions in Barack Obama, *The Audacity of Hope* 218 (New York, Crown Publishers 2006).
41. However, one might see the broad attraction of Bernie Sanders in the 2016 primary campaign as indicating that being Jewish would not now be an obstacle to being President.

# Acknowledgments

This book draws heavily from my previous scholarship in these areas and from my teaching about Church and State, using the excellent casebook, *Religion and the Constitution*, whose most recent edition is authored by Michael McConnell, Thomas Berg, and Christopher Lund. Some of the most important help for my previous work on these subjects has been from Lawrence Alexander, Robert Audi, Vince Blasi, Michael Dorf, Harold Edgar, Elizabeth Emens, Paul Horwitz, Andrew Koppelman, Gillian Metzger, Michael Perry, David Pozen, Joseph Raz, Carol Sanger, Stephen Shiffrin, Stephen Smith, Nelson Tebbe, Jeremy Waldron, and John Witte, Jr. This book in particular has benefited greatly from thoughtful comments made by Andrew Koppelman and Nelson Tebbe in review. In respect to the chapters dealing with public schools, Bonnie and Kim Greenawalt, my sister-in-law and brother, both former teachers, did much to give me a sense of reality and show me what made sense.

I benefited greatly from research assistance, whose importance increases as does the import of my electronic ineptitude. The very valuable research assistants included Larry Hong, Gautam Rao, Becky Robbins (who was mainly responsible for helping me to bring my work on public reasons up to date), Daniel Sack (who did a great deal to make possible the whole final version), Peyton Sharp, Thomas White, and Sasha Zheng. I am very grateful to all of them. Katherine Bobbitt and Michael Roig provided absolutely necessary help in discerning and editing my handwritten drafts and comments, allowing revisions to move forward.

I should also mention that I would probably not have written this book were it not for the encouragement of Thomas LeBien. When my book on Exemptions was being edited, he visited New York and met with me. He let me know that my assumption that that was probably my last book would be deeply regrettable. As a consequence, this topic entered my mind as a promising possibility.

# Index

Defamation, 104–106, 168
Desegregation, 71
Discrimination: antidiscrimination laws, 5, 82–86, 133, 190; employment discrimination, 69; nondiscrimination laws, 5, 82–86, 133, 190; viewpoint discrimination, 78–79, 165–167, 172
Diversity, 3–4, 15, 22, 37–38, 151–152
Divisiveness, 40, 74–75, 175, 244
Draft Act, 92–93
Due Process Clause, 9, 127, 222
Durham, W. Cole, Jr., 266n58

Educational institutions: financial support for, 57–62, 70–76; government aid to, 57–62, 70–76, 80; importance of, 135–137; tuition for, 60–61, 71–75, 79–80, 259n24; vouchers for, 61–62, 71–75. *See also* Schools
*Edwards v. Aguillard*, 156
*Elk Grove Unified School Dist. v. Newdow*, 34
Employment discrimination, 69. *See also* Discrimination
*Employment Division v. Smith*, 82, 96–98, 100, 111, 116, 123–124, 163, 171, 174, 180
*Engel v. Vitale*, 27, 28
Environmental policy, 228–232, 278n16
*Epperson v. Arkansas*, 156
Equal Access Act, 166, 172
Equal protection: denial of, 56, 84, 180; laws for, 4, 9
Equal Protection Clause, 13, 127–128, 133, 222
Esbeck, Carl N., 260n39
Establishment Clause: challenging, 34, 64, 67, 79; development of, 27; divisiveness and, 40, 199; explanation of, 14–17; favoring specific religions, 84–85; financial aid and, 55–57; meaning of, 29; religious messages and, 179; school aid and, 72–73; understanding, 8–9, 15, 23–29, 57–59, 63; values of, 83–84; violations of, 17, 24, 64, 66, 69, 97, 133, 140, 175

Ethical Cultural Society, 194–195, 197
*Everson vs. Board of Education*, 57–59, 71
Evolution theory, 5, 135, 153–163
Exemptions: abortion and, 4, 83–86, 116–126; for clerics, 4–5, 103–110; common law and, 103–110; constitutionality of, 4–5, 82–87, 263n15; contraceptives and, 85, 116–126; denying, 82–86; explanation of, 4–5, 81–87; for favored treatment, 81–133; forbidden substances and, 110–113; "harm to others" and, 4, 85, 109–110, 150–151, 175, 232–233, 241, 248–249, 278n17, 278n18; for individuals, 81–133; legal duties and, 4–5, 81–85; medical treatments and, 113–116; military and, 90–96, 181–184, 264n20; nonmedical exemption, 115–116; observations of, 81–87; priest-penitent privileges, 4–5, 107; for prisons, 100–103; property tax exemptions, 88–89, 96, 186–187; for religious institutions, 55–56, 81–133; for religious land use, 96–104; religious practices and, 81–90, 103–110; same-sex marriage and, 85–87, 127–133, 189–190; standards for, 86; statutory duties and, 59, 82–86, 103–110; substance use and, 110–113; tax benefits of, 57, 87–90, 96, 186–187; unconstitutionality of, 83–84, 263n15
"Extratemporal consequences," 195–196

Faith Works program, 66
Favored treatment: abortion and, 116–126; common law and, 103–110; constitutional rights and, 82–87; contraceptives and, 116–126; exemptions for, 81–133; legal privilege and, 106–109; medical treatments and, 113–116; military and, 90–96; for religious institutions, 81–133; religious land use and, 96–104; same-sex marriage and, 127–133; substance use, 110–113; tax codes and, 88–90
Fellowship of Humanity, 194–195
Financial support: for educational